3rd Workshop on Knowledge Augmented Methods for NLP (KnowledgeNLP 2024)

Bangkok, Thailand
16 August 2024

ISBN: 979-8-3313-0166-8

Printed from e-media with permission by:

Curran Associates, Inc.
57 Morehouse Lane
Red Hook, NY 12571

Some format issues inherent in the e-media version may also appear in this print version.

Association for Computational Linguistics
209 N. Eighth Street
Stroudsburg, Pennsylvania 18360

Phone: 1-570-476-8006
Fax: 1-570-476-0860

acl@aclweb.org

Additional copies of this publication are available from:

Curran Associates, Inc.
57 Morehouse Lane
Red Hook, NY 12571 USA
Phone: 845-758-0400
Fax: 845-758-2633
Email: curran@proceedings.com
Web: www.proceedings.com

KnowledgeNLP 2024

The 3rd Workshop on Knowledge Augmented Methods for NLP

Proceedings of the Workshop

August 16, 2024

Association for Computational Linguistics (ACL)
317 Sidney Baker St. S
Suite 400 - 134
Kerrville, TX 78028
USA
Tel: +1-855-225-1962
acl@aclweb.org

Preface by the Organizers

Welcome to the 3rd International Workshop on Knowledge-Augmented Methods for Natural Language Processing (KnowledgeNLP'24), held in conjunction with ACL 2024. KnowledgeNLP will take place on August 16th, 2024, allowing for both virtual and in-person attendance in Thailand.

Recent progress in large-scale models like ChatGPT has significantly advanced NLP capabilities. However, these models face limitations in memorizing rare information, are prone to hallucinations, and cannot access up-to-date information. Additionally, their fixed parameter size prevents them from fully encapsulating the continuously evolving world knowledge.

The field of knowledge-augmented NLP spans a wide array of techniques and applications. Acquiring relevant knowledge is challenging due to its diversity and distribution across numerous sources. Once acquired, effectively representing and utilizing this knowledge to support model predictions presents another major challenge. This workshop seeks to bring researchers together to share their insights and progress in this domain, aiming to highlight the importance of knowledge-augmented NLP.

In response to our call for papers, we received 35 submissions. Each submission was rigorously reviewed by at least two Program Committee members selected for their expertise. Based on the reviewers' feedback, we accepted 30 papers, including 8 oral presentations and 22 poster presentations. We are honored to invite six keynote speakers: Prof. Minlie Huang (Tsinghua University), Dr. Scott Yih (Meta AI), Prof. Yulia Tsvetkov (University of Washington), Prof. Greg Durrett (University of Texas Austin), Prof. Minjoon Seo (KAIST AI), and Prof. Zhuosheng Zhang (Shanghai Jiaotong University).

We hope you find the workshop papers insightful and inspiring. We express our gratitude to the keynote speakers for their engaging talks, the authors for their valuable contributions, and the Program Committee members for their thorough reviews. Special thanks to the emergency reviewers for their expertise and to the ACL 2024 workshop chairs for their support during the organization process.

Wenhao Yu, Tencent AI Seattle Lab
Weijia Shi, University of Washington
Michihiro Yasunaga, Stanford University
Meng Jiang, University of Notre Dame
Chenguang Zhu, Zoom AI
Hannaneh Hajishirzi, University of Washington
Luke Zettlemoyer, University of Washington
KnowledgeNLP-ACL24 Workshop Chairs

Organizing Committee

Program Chairs

Wenhao , Tencent AI Seattle Lab
Weijia Shi, University of Washington
Michihiro Yasunaga, Stanford University
Meng Jiang, University of Notre Dame
Chenguang Zhu, Zoom AI
Hannaneh Hajishirzi, University of Washington
Luke Zettlemoyer, University of Washington

Publication Chairs

Zhihan Zhang, University of Notre Dame

Program Committee

Reviewers

Tong Chen, University of Washington
Zhehui Huang, University of Southern California
Mengzhao Jia, University of Notre Dame
Pengwei Li, Meta
Zheyuan Liu, University of Notre Dame
Xiao Liu, University of California, Davis
Renze Lou, Pennsylvania State University
Bang Nguyen, University of Notre Dame
Siru Ouyang, University of Illinois Urbana-Champaign Champaign
Zhaoxuan Tan, University of Notre Dame
Jiaxiang Tang, University of Minnesota
Qingyun Wang, University of Illinois, Urbana Champaign
Zijie Wang, University of Arizona
Zhepeng Wang, Yahoo and George Mason University
Zhenyu Wu, University of Notre Dame and Xi'an Jiaotong University
Di Wu, University of California, Los Angeles
Zilin Xiao, Rice University
Mengxia Yu, University of Notre Dame
Wenhao Yu, Tencent AI Lab
Zhihan Zhang, University of Notre Dame
Daoan Zhang, University of Rochester
Yuwei Zhang, University of California, San Diego
Yunxiang Zhang, University of Michigan - Ann Arbor
Anni Zou, Shanghai Jiao Tong University

Table of Contents

Program

Friday, August 16, 2024

09:00 - 09:10	*Opening Remarks*
09:10 - 09:45	*Keynote Talk 1 by Minlie Huang (Tsinghua University)*
09:45 - 10:20	*Keynote Talk 2 by Scott Yih (Meta AI)*
10:20 - 11:20	*Poster Session (including break)*
11:20 - 11:55	*Keynote Talk 3 by Yulia Tsvetkov (University of Washington)*
11:55 - 12:30	*Keynote Talk 4 by Greg Durrett (UT Austin)*
12:30 - 14:00	*Lunch Break*
14:00 - 14:40	*Keynote Talk 5 by Minjoon Seo (KAIST AI)*
14:40 - 15:30	*Oral Presentation Session 1*
	How Easily do Irrelevant Inputs Skew the Responses of Large Language Models? Siye Wu, Jian Xie, Jiangjie Chen, Tinghui Zhu, Kai Zhang and Yanghua Xiao
	Editing Conceptual Knowledge for Large Language Models Xiaohan Wang, Shengyu Mao, Shumin Deng, Yunzhi Yao, Yue Shen, Lei Liang, Jinjie GU, Huajun Chen and Ningyu Zhang
	How Well Do Large Language Models Truly Ground? Hyunji Lee, Doyoung Kim, Se June Joo, Chaeeun Kim, Joel Jang, Kyoung-Woon On and Minjoon Seo
	INSTRUCTIR: A Benchmark for Instruction Following of Information Retrieval Models Hanseok Oh, Hyunji Lee, Seonghyeon Ye, Haebin Shin, Hansol Jang, ChangWook Jun and Minjoon Seo
15:30 - 16:00	*Coffee Break*

Friday, August 16, 2024 (continued)

16:00 - 16:40 *Keynote Talk 6 by Zhuosheng Zhang (Shanghai Jiao Tong University)*

16:40 - 17:30 *Oral Presentation Session 2*

Repoformer: Selective Retrieval for Repository-Level Code Completion
Di Wu, Wasi Uddin Ahmad, Dejiao Zhang, Murali Krishna Ramanathan and Xiaofei Ma

KnowAgent: Knowledge-Augmented Planning for LLM-Based Agents
Yuqi Zhu, Shuofei Qiao, Yixin Ou, Shumin Deng, Ningyu Zhang, Shiwei Lyu, Yue Shen, Lei Liang, Jinjie GU and Huajun Chen

Merging Facts, Crafting Fallacies: Evaluating the Contradictory Nature of Aggregated Factual Claims in Long-Form Generations
Cheng-Han Chiang and Hung-yi Lee

Agent Planning with World Knowledge Model
Shuofei Qiao, Runnan Fang, Ningyu Zhang, Yuqi Zhu, Xiang Chen, Shumin Deng, Yong Jiang, Pengjun Xie, Fei Huang and Huajun Chen

17:30 - 17:35 *Closing Remarks*

GADePo: Graph-Assisted Declarative Pooling Transformers for Document-Level Relation Extraction

Andrei C. Coman
Idiap Research Institute, EPFL
andrei.coman@idiap.ch

Christos Theodoropoulos
KU Leuven
christos.theodoropoulos@kuleuven.be

Marie-Francine Moens
KU Leuven
sien.moens@kuleuven.be

James Henderson
Idiap Research Institute
james.henderson@idiap.ch

Abstract

Document-level relation extraction typically relies on text-based encoders and hand-coded pooling heuristics to aggregate information learned by the encoder. In this paper, we leverage the intrinsic graph processing capabilities of the Transformer model and propose replacing hand-coded pooling methods with new tokens in the input, which are designed to aggregate information via explicit graph relations in the computation of attention weights. We introduce a joint text-graph Transformer model and a graph-assisted declarative pooling (GADePo) specification of the input, which provides explicit and high-level instructions for information aggregation. GADePo allows the pooling process to be guided by domain-specific knowledge or desired outcomes but still learned by the Transformer, leading to more flexible and customisable pooling strategies. We evaluate our method across diverse datasets and models and show that our approach yields promising results that are consistently better than those achieved by the hand-coded pooling functions.

1 Introduction

Document-level relation extraction is an important task in natural language processing, which involves identifying and categorising meaningful relationships between entities within a document, as exemplified in Figure 1. This task is foundational to many applications, including knowledge base population and completion (Banko et al., 2007; Ji et al., 2020), information retrieval and extraction (Manning et al., 2008; Theodoropoulos et al., 2021), question answering (Chen et al., 2017; Feng et al., 2022) and sentiment analysis (Pang and Lee, 2008), to name a few.

Standard methods that approach this challenge generally employ pretrained text-based encoders (Devlin et al., 2019; Beltagy et al., 2019; Zhuang et al., 2021; Cui et al., 2021), which are responsible for capturing the nuances of information con-

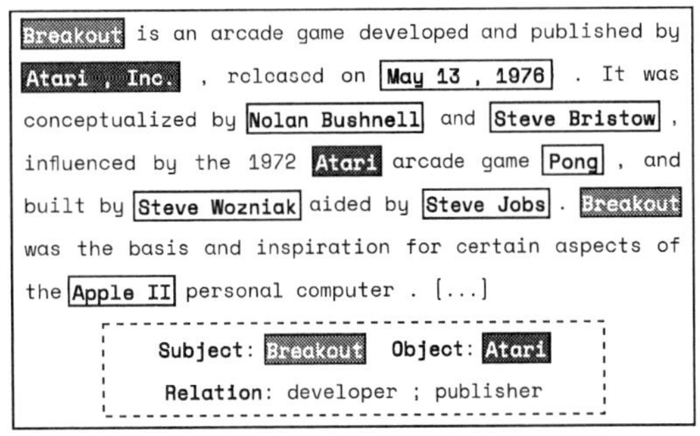

Figure 1: Document from the Re-DocRED (Tan et al., 2022b) dataset involving multiple entities and labels. Subject entity Breakout (red) and object entity Atari (blue) express relations "developer" and "publisher". Other entities are indicated as Mention (white).

tained in the entity mentions and their contextual surroundings. Previous successful methods often then use hand-coded pooling heuristics to aggregate the information learned by the encoder, with some aimed at creating entity representations, while others directly exploiting the pattern of attention weights to capture context aware relations between entity mentions (Zhou et al., 2021; Xiao et al., 2022; Tan et al., 2022a; Ma et al., 2023). These pooling heuristics can be very effective at leveraging the information in a pretrained encoder. However, as shown in Conneau et al. (2017); Jia et al. (2019); Reimers and Gurevych (2019); Choi et al. (2021), the selection of an appropriate pooling function can be model-dependent, task-specific, resource-intensive and time-consuming to determine, thereby limiting flexibility.

In this paper, we address these issues with a new approach where we leverage the intrinsic graph processing capabilities of the Transformer model (Vaswani et al., 2017), leveraging insights from the work of Mohammadshahi and Henderson (2020); Henderson (2020); Mohammadshahi and Henderson (2021); Henderson et al. (2023). They argue that attention weights and graph relations are functionally equivalent and show how to incorporate

Proceedings of the 3rd Workshop on Knowledge Augmented Methods for NLP, pages 1–14
August 16, 2024 ©2024 Association for Computational Linguistics

structural dependencies between input elements by simply adding relation features to the attention functions. Transformers easily learn to integrate these relation features into their pretrained attention functions, resulting in very successful graph-conditioned models (Mohammadshahi and Henderson, 2021; Miculicich and Henderson, 2022; Mohammadshahi and Henderson, 2023). Given this effective method for integrating explicit graphs with pretrained attention functions, we propose to use the attention function itself for aggregation. We replace the rigid pooling methods with new tokens which act as aggregation nodes, plus explicit graph relations which steer the aggregation.

We introduce a joint text-graph Transformer model and a graph-assisted declarative pooling (GADePo) method[1] that leverages these special tokens and graph relations, to provide an explicit high-level declarative specification for the information aggregation process. By integrating these graphs in the attention functions of a pretrained model, GADePo exploits the pretrained embeddings and attention patterns but still has the flexibility of being trained on data. This enables the pooling to be guided by domain-specific knowledge or desired outcomes but still learned by the Transformer, opening up a more customisable but still data-driven relation extraction process.

We evaluate our method across diverse datasets and models commonly employed in document-level relation extraction tasks, and show that our approach yields promising results that are consistently better than those achieved by the hand-coded pooling functions.

Contributions We propose a new method for exploiting pretrained Transformer models which replaces hand-coded aggregation functions with explicit graph relations and aggregation nodes. We introduce a novel form of joint text-graph Transformer model. We evaluate our approach across various datasets and models, showing that it yields promising results that are consistently better than those achieved by hand-coded pooling functions.

2 Related Work

In recent studies, the scope of relation extraction has been expanded to include not only individual sentences but entire documents. This extension, known as document-level relation extraction, presents a more realistic and challenging scenario as it seeks to extract relations both within sentences and across multiple sentences (Yao et al., 2019). Transformer-based (Vaswani et al., 2017) models have shown great potential in addressing this task.

Wang et al. (2019) and Tang et al. (2020) show that the BiLSTM-based (Hochreiter and Schmidhuber, 1997) baselines lack the capacity to model complex interactions between multiple entities. They propose a more robust approach, which consists of using the pretrained BERT (Devlin et al., 2019) model and a two-step prediction process, i.e., first identifying if a link between two entities exists, followed by predicting the specific relation type.

GAIN (Zeng et al., 2020) leverages BERT as a text encoder and GCNs (Kipf and Welling, 2017) to process two types of graphs, one at mention level and another at entity level, showing notable performance in inter-sentence and inferential scenarios.

Mohammadshahi and Henderson (2020, 2021) propose the G2GT model and show how to leverage the intrinsic graph processing capabilities of the Transformer model by incorporating structural dependencies between input elements as features input to the self-attention weight computations.

SSAN (Xu et al., 2021) leverages this idea and considers the structure of entities. It employs a transformation module that creates attentive biases from this structure to regulate the attention flow during the encoding phase.

DocuNet (Zhang et al., 2021) reformulates the task as a semantic segmentation problem. It employs a U-shaped segmentation module and an encoder module to capture global interdependencies and contextual information of entities, respectively.

PL-Marker (Ye et al., 2022) introduces a method that takes into account the interplay between spans via a neighbourhood-oriented and subject-oriented packing approach, highlighting the importance of capturing the interrelation among span pairs in relation extraction tasks.

SAIS (Xiao et al., 2022) explicitly models key information sources such as relevant contexts and entity types. It improves extraction quality and interpretability, while also boosting performance through evidence-based data augmentation and ensemble inference.

KD-DocRE (Tan et al., 2022a) proposes a semi-supervised framework with three key components. Firstly, an axial attention module enhances performance in handling two-hop relations by capturing the interdependence of entity pairs. Secondly,

[1] `https://github.com/idiap/gadepo`

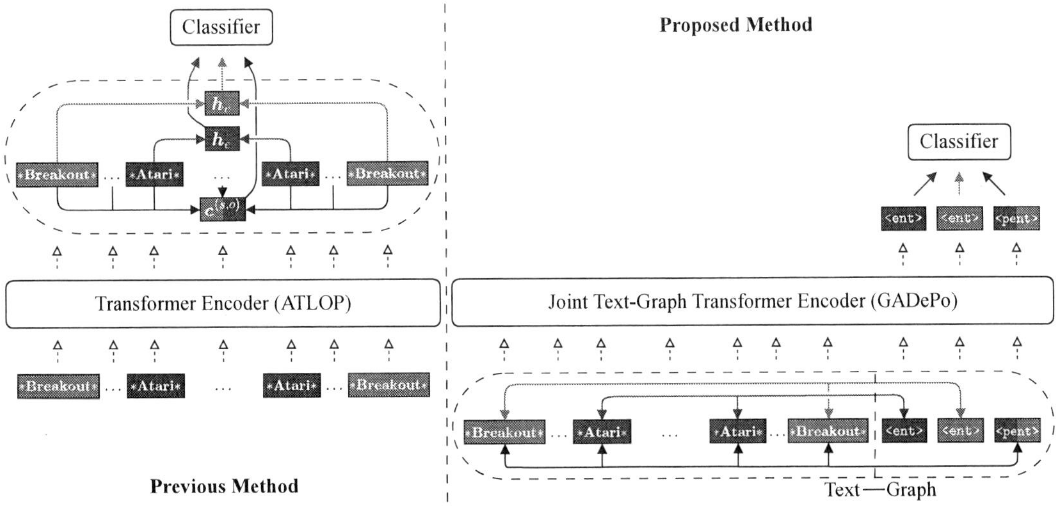

Figure 2: Comparison between the previous method ATLOP (left) and the proposed method GADePo (right), illustrating the document in Figure 1 containing two entities (red and blue), each with two mentions. In ATLOP, the mentions' encoder outputs are aggregated into entity representations $\boldsymbol{h}_e$, and the encoder's attention weights are used to identify which outputs to aggregate for entity-pair representations $\boldsymbol{c}^{(s,o)}$. In GADePo, the textual input is extended to include the graph special tokens <ent> for entity representations and <pent> for entity-pair representations, and explicit directional graph relations specify their associated mentions. A joint text-graph Transformer model is then used to encode this declarative pooling specification graph and compute the relevant aggregations.

an adaptive focal loss solution addresses the class imbalance issue. Lastly, the framework employs knowledge distillation to improve robustness and overall effectiveness by bridging the gap between human-annotated and distantly supervised data.

DREEAM (Ma et al., 2023) is a method designed to enhance document-level relation extraction by addressing memory efficiency and annotation limitations in evidence retrieval. It employs evidence as a supervisory signal to guide attention and introduces a self-training strategy to learn evidence retrieval without requiring evidence annotations.

SAIS (Xiao et al., 2022), KD-DocRE (Tan et al., 2022a), and DREEAM (Ma et al., 2023) have been built upon the foundations of ATLOP (Zhou et al., 2021). ATLOP introduces two innovative techniques, adaptive thresholding, and localised context pooling, to address challenges in multi-label and multi-entity problems. Adaptive thresholding employs a learnable entities-dependent threshold, replacing the global threshold used in previous approaches for multi-label classification (Peng et al., 2017; Christopoulou et al., 2019; Nan et al., 2020; Wang et al., 2020). Localised context pooling leverages the attention patterns of a pretrained language model to identify and extract relevant context crucial for determining the relation between entities, using specific hand-coded pooling functions.

3 Background

The foundational work of ATLOP (Zhou et al., 2021) has been the basis of many State-of-the-Art (SotA) models (Xiao et al., 2022; Tan et al., 2022a; Ma et al., 2023). Given the problems with hand-coded pooling functions, discussed in Section 1, we aim to provide a new baseline that can serve as the foundation for future SotA models. For this reason, we evaluate our proposed models by comparing them to this established baseline. Our goal is to demonstrate that our method not only achieves results comparable to or better than ATLOP, but also offers a novel approach which addresses its limitations. To provide a better understanding of ATLOP and its components, we present a detailed breakdown in the left portion of Figure 2, which we elaborate on in this section.

3.1 Problem Formulation

The document-level relation extraction task involves analysing a document D that contains a set of entities $\mathcal{E}_D=\{e_i\}_{i=1}^{|\mathcal{E}_D|}$. The main objective is to determine the presence or absence of various relation types between all entity pairs $(e_s, e_o)_{s,o\subset\mathcal{E}_D, s\neq o}$, where the subject and object entities are denoted as e_s and e_o, respectively. A key aspect to consider is that an entity can appear multiple times in the document, resulting in a cluster of multiple mentions $\mathcal{M}_e=\{m_i\}_{i=1}^{|\mathcal{M}_e|}$ for each entity e. The set of relations is defined as $\mathcal{R} \cup \emptyset$, where $\emptyset$ represents the absence of a relation, often referred to as "no-relation". Given the clusters of mentions $\mathcal{M}_{e_s}$ and $\mathcal{M}_{e_o}$, the task consists of a multi-label classification problem where there can be multiple relations between entities e_s and e_o.

3.2 Previous Method: ATLOP

Text Encoding A special token $*$ is added at the start and end of every mention. Tokens $\mathcal{T}_D=\{t_i\}_{i=1}^{|\mathcal{T}_D|}$ are encoded via a Pretrained Language Model (PLM) as follows:

$$\boldsymbol{H}, \boldsymbol{A} = PLM(\mathcal{T}_D), \tag{1}$$

where $\boldsymbol{H} \in \mathbb{R}^{|\mathcal{T}_D| \times d}$ and $\boldsymbol{A} \in \mathbb{R}^{|\mathcal{T}_D| \times |\mathcal{T}_D|}$ represent the token embeddings and the average attention weights of all attention heads, respectively, extracted from the last layer of the PLM.

Entity Embedding (EE) For each individual entity e with mentions $\mathcal{M}_e=\{m_i\}_{i=1}^{|\mathcal{M}_e|}$, an entity embedding $\boldsymbol{h}_e \in \mathbb{R}^d$ is computed as follows:

$$\boldsymbol{h}_e = log \sum_{i=1}^{|\mathcal{M}_e|} exp(\boldsymbol{H}_{m_i}), \tag{2}$$

where $\boldsymbol{H}_{m_i} \in \mathbb{R}^d$ is the embedding of the special token $*$ at the starting position of mention m_i. The choice of the $logsumexp$ pooling function is based on the research conducted by Jia et al. (2019). Their study offers empirical evidence that supports the use of this pooling function over others, as it facilitates accumulating weak signals from individual mentions, thanks to its smoother characteristics.

Localised Context Embedding (LCE) ATLOP introduces the concept of localised context embedding to accommodate the variations in relevant mentions and context for different entity pairs (e_s, e_o). Since the attention mechanism in the PLM captures the importance of each token within the context, it can be used to determine the context relevant for both entities. The importance of each token can be computed from the cross-token dependencies matrix $\boldsymbol{A}$ obtained in Equation 1. When evaluating entity e_s, the importance of individual tokens is determined by examining the cross-token dependencies across all mentions associated with e_s, denoted as $\mathcal{M}_{e_s}$. Initially, ATLOP collects and averages the attention $\boldsymbol{A}_{m_i} \in \mathbb{R}^{|\mathcal{T}_D|}$ at the special token $*$ preceding each mention $m_i \in \mathcal{M}_{e_s}$. This process results in $\boldsymbol{a}_s \in \mathbb{R}^{|\mathcal{T}_D|}$, which represents the importance of each token concerning entity e_s (and analogously $\boldsymbol{a}_o$ for e_o). Subsequently, the importance of each token for a given entity pair (e_s, e_o), denoted as $\boldsymbol{q}^{(s,o)} \in \mathbb{R}^{|\mathcal{T}_D|}$, is computed using $\boldsymbol{a}_s$ and $\boldsymbol{a}_o$ as follows:

$$\boldsymbol{q}^{(s,o)} = \frac{\boldsymbol{a}_s \circ \boldsymbol{a}_o}{\boldsymbol{a}_s^\top \boldsymbol{a}_o}, \tag{3}$$

where $\circ$ represents the Hadamard product. Consequently, $\boldsymbol{q}^{(s,o)}$ represents a distribution that indicates the importance of each token for both tokens in (e_s, e_o). Finally, the localised context embedding is computed as follows:

$$\boldsymbol{c}^{(s,o)} = \boldsymbol{H}^\top \boldsymbol{q}^{(s,o)}, \tag{4}$$

So $\boldsymbol{c}^{(s,o)} \in \mathbb{R}^d$ corresponds to a weighted average over all token embeddings that are important for both e_s and e_o.

Relation Classification and Loss Function The representations $\boldsymbol{h}_{e_s}$, $\boldsymbol{h}_{e_o}$ and $\boldsymbol{c}^{(s,o)}$ are input to a relation classifier, and the full model is fine-tuned to predict the relation labels for (e_s, e_o). The relation classifier and its loss function are detailed in Appendix Subsection A.1.

4 Proposed Method: GADePo

We propose to avoid the reliance on the EE (i.e., $\boldsymbol{h}_e$) and LCE (i.e., $\boldsymbol{c}^{(s,o)}$) heuristic aggregation functions by leveraging Transformers' attention functions to do aggregation. Given the observation of Henderson (2020); Mohammadshahi and Henderson (2020, 2021); Henderson et al. (2023) that attention weights and graph relations are functionally equivalent, we introduce the inductive biases of EE and LCE directly into the model's input as graph relations.

Our proposed graph-assisted declarative pooling (GADePo) method replaces the hand-coded aggregation functions EE and LCE with a declarative graph specification. By using the intrinsic graph processing capabilities of the Transformer model, the specified graph serves as an explicit high-level directive for the information aggregation process of the Transformer. By inputting the graph relations to the Transformer's self-attention layers, GADePo enables the aggregation to be steered by domain-specific knowledge or desired outcomes, while still allowing it to be learned by the Transformer, opening up the possibility for a more tailored and customised yet data-driven relation extraction.

Our GADePo model is illustrated in the right portion of Figure 2. We address both EE and LCE with the introduction of two special tokens, <ent> (i.e., entity) and <pent> (i.e., pair entity), and two explicit graph relations of types <ent> $\longleftrightarrow *$ and <pent> $\longleftrightarrow *$ in both directions, where $*$ represents the special token at the starting position of a specific mention. The set of relations is specified as $c_{ij} \in \mathcal{C}$ which each identify the relation label from i to j. Each of these relation labels is associated with an embedding vector of dimension d, as are the special token inputs <ent> and <pent>. These two special tokens are added to the PLM's vocabulary of input tokens, while relation label embeddings are input to the self-attention functions for every pair of related tokens. These new embeddings represent learnable parameters that are trained during the PLM fine-tuning on the downstream tasks. As reported in Appendix Subsection A.2, GADePo adds a negligible number of extra parameters, namely only the special token inputs and the graph directional relation inputs.

Special Token <ent> To tackle the EE pooling function, we add to the input tokens $\mathcal{T}_D$ as many <ent> special tokens as entities in the document. This way each entity e has a corresponding entity token <ent> in the input. We connect each <ent> token with its corresponding cluster of mentions $\mathcal{M}_e = \{m_i\}_{i=1}^{|\mathcal{M}_e|}$, and vice-versa. The two graph relations we use are thus <ent> $\longrightarrow *$ and $* \longrightarrow$ <ent>, where $*$ represents the special token at the starting position of mention m_i. Each <ent> token receives the same <ent> embedding, with no positional encoding, since each one collectively represents a set of mentions from different positions in the input graph. These identical inputs are only disambiguated through the connections to and from mentions expressed as the <ent> $\longrightarrow *$ and $* \longrightarrow$ <ent> graph relations. These relations tell the self-attention mechanism to use the <ent> token to aggregate information from the associated mentions, and thus the <ent> tokens have a direct correspondence to the computed $\boldsymbol{h}_e$ in Equation 2.

Special Token <pent> ATLOP performs information filtering by calculating via Equation 4 a localised context embedding (LCE) $\boldsymbol{c}^{(s,o)}$ that is dependent on the cross-token attention matrix $\boldsymbol{A}$ output by the PLM. The intuition behind it is that the dependencies between different tokens are encoded as attention weights. We propose a straightforward adjustment of the input graph used for the EE pooling to effectively model and capture these dependencies. To address the LCE pooling function, we add to the input tokens $\mathcal{T}_D$ as many <pent> special tokens as the number of all possible pairs of entities. Each special token <pent> thus refers to a pair of entities (e_s, e_o). We connect each <pent> token with each mention in the two clusters of mentions $\mathcal{M}_{e_s} = \{m_i\}_{i=1}^{|\mathcal{M}_{e_s}|}$ and $\mathcal{M}_{e_o} = \{m_i\}_{i=1}^{|\mathcal{M}_{e_o}|}$ and vice-versa. Since the attention weights used in LCE are computed from these mention embeddings, we expect that they are sufficient for the Transformer to learn to find the relevant contexts. The two graph relations we use are thus <pent> $\longrightarrow *$ and $* \longrightarrow$ <pent>. Analogously to the <ent> tokens, the <pent> tokens all receive the same <pent> embedding, with no positional embeddings, and thus are only disambiguated by their different <pent> $\longrightarrow *$ and $* \longrightarrow$ <pent> graph relations. These relations tell the <pent> token to pay attention to its associated mentions, which in turn allows it to find the relevant context shared by these mentions. Thus, each <pent> token can be seen as having a direct correspondence to the computed $\boldsymbol{c}^{(s,o)}$ in Equation 4.

All equations relative to the relation classification and the corresponding loss function reported in Appendix Subsection A.1 remain valid as we merely substitute the hand-coded computations of $\boldsymbol{h}_e$ and $\boldsymbol{c}^{(s,o)}$ with the embeddings of <ent> and <pent>, respectively.

Text-Graph Encoding We follow Mohammadshahi and Henderson (2020, 2021); Henderson et al. (2023) in leveraging the intrinsic graph processing capabilities of the Transformer model by incorporating graph relations as relation embeddings input to the self-attention function. For every pair of input tokens ij, the pre-softmax attention weight $e_{ij} \in \mathbb{R}$ is computed from both the respective token embeddings $\boldsymbol{x}_i, \boldsymbol{x}_j \in \mathbb{R}^d$, and an embeddings of the graph relation $\boldsymbol{c}_{ij}$ between the i-th and j-th tokens. However, we change the attention weight computation to:

$$e_{ij} = \frac{\boldsymbol{x}_i \boldsymbol{W}_Q \ \mathrm{diag}(\mathrm{LN}(\boldsymbol{c}_{ij} \boldsymbol{W}_C)) \ (\boldsymbol{x}_j \boldsymbol{W}_K)^\top}{\sqrt{d}}, \tag{5}$$

where $\boldsymbol{W}_Q, \boldsymbol{W}_K \in \mathbb{R}^{d \times d}$ represent the query and key matrices, respectively. $\boldsymbol{c}_{ij} \in \{0,1\}^{|\mathcal{C}|}$ represents a $0/1$ encoded label of the graph relation between the i-th and j-th input elements, and $\boldsymbol{W}_C \in \mathbb{R}^{|\mathcal{C}| \times d}$ represents the relations' embedding

Model	Aggregation	**Re-DocRED**		**HacRED**		
		Ign F_1	F_1	P	R	F_1
ATLOP*	$\boldsymbol{h}_e$	75.27	75.92	**76.27**	76.83	76.55
GADePo (ours)	<ent>	**75.55**	**76.38**	74.13	**79.46**	**76.70**
ATLOP•,◇	$\boldsymbol{h}_e$; $\boldsymbol{c}^{(s,o)}$	76.82	77.56	77.89	76.55	77.21
ATLOP*	$\boldsymbol{h}_e$; $\boldsymbol{c}^{(s,o)}$	77.62	78.38	76.36	78.86	77.59
GADePo (ours)	<ent> ; <pent>	**77.70**	**78.40**	**78.27**	**79.03**	**78.65**

Table 1: Comparative analysis between the previous method ATLOP and the proposed method GADePo on the test set. ATLOP* indicates our reimplementation of the previous method. For Re-DocRED and HacRED we report in percentage the results obtained by Tan et al. (2022b) (ATLOP•) and Cheng et al. (2021) (ATLOP◇), respectively. The results are reported in terms of F_1 scores, Precision (P), and Recall (R), following the same metrics reported in prior research specific to each dataset. Ign F_1 denotes the F_1 score that excludes relational facts shared between the training and evaluation sets. We also comply with the standard practice where test scores are determined based on the best checkpoint from five training runs with distinct random seeds.

matrix, so $\boldsymbol{c}_{ij}\boldsymbol{W}_C$ is the embedding of the relation between i and j. Finally, LN stands for the $LayerNorm$ operation and diag returns a diagonal matrix.

Compared to the standard attention function, where $e_{ij} = \boldsymbol{x}_i\boldsymbol{W}_Q(\boldsymbol{x}_j\boldsymbol{W}_K)^\top/\sqrt{d}$, the relation embedding determines a weighting of the different dimensions. This is a novel way to condition on the relation embedding compared to the original formulation, which only models query-relation interactions (Mohammadshahi and Henderson, 2020). This change is motivated by our task requiring a more flexible formulation which models query-relation-key interactions via a multiplicative mechanism, without requiring a full $d \times d$ matrix of bilinear parameters. This way, a key will be relevant to a query only when both agree on the relation. In preliminary experiments, we explored various methods for biasing attention and found that the formulation presented in Equation 5 produced the best results.

5 Experiments

5.1 Datasets and Models

Re-DocRED (Tan et al., 2022b) is a revisited version of the DocRED (Yao et al., 2019) dataset. It is built from English Wikipedia and Wikidata and contains both distantly-supervised and human-annotated documents with named entities, coreference data, and intra- and inter-sentence relations, supported by evidence. It requires analysing multiple sentences to identify entities, establish their relationships, and integrate information from the entire document. We comply with the model used by the authors and employ the RoBERTa$_{\text{LARGE}}$ (Zhuang et al., 2021) model in our experiments.

HacRED (Cheng et al., 2021) is a large-scale, high-quality Chinese document-level relation extraction dataset, with a special focus on practical hard cases. As the authors did not provide specific information about the model used in their study, we conducted our experiments using the Chinese BERT$_{\text{BASE}}$ with whole word masking model (Cui et al., 2021).

Datasets statistics Re-DocRED and HacRED exhibit notable distinctions in their statistics, as summarised in Table 2. Re-DocRED comprises a larger number of facts, entities per document, and relations compared to HacRED. This indicates a potentially richer and more extensive dataset in terms of factual information and relationship types. However, HacRED contains more documents and may present a broader range of scenarios for relation extraction, including more challenging cases, as it has been specifically created with a focus on practical hard cases.

Statistic	Re-DocRED	HacRED
Facts	120,664	65,225
Relations	96	26
Documents	4,053	9,231
Average Entities	19.4	10.8

Table 2: Re-DocRED and HacRED human-annotated datasets statistics.

5.2 Results and Discussion

We follow the standard practice from prior research and report the results of our experiments on the Re-DocRED and HacRED datasets in Table 1 and Figure 4. For all datasets and models, we provide our reimplementation of the ATLOP baseline (indicated as ATLOP*), which achieves or surpasses pre-

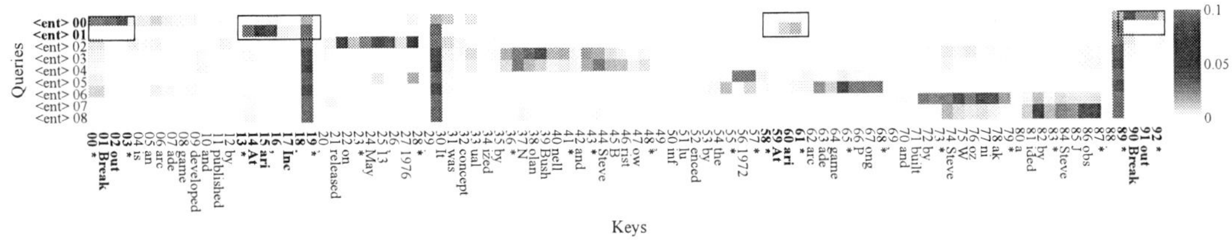

Figure 3: Attention weights $\boldsymbol{A}$ from GADePo via Equation 1 for the document in Figure 1. For clarity, only a subset of <ent> and document tokens are shown on the y-axis (queries) and x-axis (keys), respectively.

viously reported results for ATLOP, and compare the proposed GADePo model against this model. We evaluate all datasets using the F_1 metric. For Re-DocRED, Ign F_1 (or Ignored F_1) is also reported, and refers to the F_1 score that excludes relational facts that are shared between the training and development/test sets. This is done to avoid potential biases in the evaluation metrics due to overlap in content between the sets, which might not reflect the model's ability to generalise to truly unseen data. For HacRED, we adhere to the format introduced by Cheng et al. (2021) and report also the Precision (P) and Recall (R) metrics. We comply with previous research and report the test score achieved by the best checkpoint on the development set. In Appendix Subsection A.4, we additionally present the mean and standard deviation on the development set, calculated from five training runs with distinct random seeds. We also provide in Appendix Subsection A.4, the same set of experiments conducted on the original DocRED dataset. Training details and hyperparameters are outlined in Appendix Subsection A.3.

Re-DocRED Results We evaluate our proposed GADePo method against the previous ATLOP method in two stages, first comparing the use of <ent> tokens against the use of EE pooling ($\boldsymbol{h}_e$), and then comparing our full model against the full ATLOP model, including <pent> tokens and LCE pooling ($\boldsymbol{c}^{(s,o)}$), respectively.

Table 1 highlights the effectiveness of our proposed method. When comparing $\boldsymbol{h}_e$ with <ent>, we observe a noticeable improvement in both Ign F_1 and F_1 scores, achieving 75.55% and 76.38% respectively, compared to 75.27% and 75.92% attained by ATLOP*. This demonstrates the practical utility of employing the special token <ent> for information aggregation. This is illustrated in the attention weights heatmap in Figure 3. Incorporating $\boldsymbol{c}^{(s,o)}$ and <pent> into the comparison, GADePo maintains performance parity with the significantly enhanced ATLOP*, which outperformed ATLOP• from Tan et al. (2022b). The latter improvement suggests that a more refined hyperparameter search can lead to performance gains, as evidenced by the increase in F_1 score from 77.56% to 78.38%. GADePo achieves an F_1 score of 78.40%, affirming its competitive edge and the effectiveness of employing <pent> for aggregation.

Model	Aggregation	Ign F_1	F_1
ATLOP*	$\boldsymbol{h}_e$	76.39	76.97
GADePo (ours)	<ent>	**76.99**	**77.79**
ATLOP*	$\boldsymbol{h}_e$; $\boldsymbol{c}^{(s,o)}$	77.49	78.09
GADePo (ours)	<ent> ; <pent>	**77.50**	**78.15**

Table 3: Re-DocRED results on the test set following prior finetuning on the distantly supervised dataset.

Table 3 illustrates the results obtained with prior finetuning on the distantly supervised dataset, which contains approximately $100K$ documents (Yao et al., 2019). Interestingly, distant supervision appears to have a slightly negative impact on the results of both methods when incorporating $\boldsymbol{c}^{(s,o)}$ or <pent>. However, it proves to be highly beneficial when utilising solely $\boldsymbol{h}_e$ or <ent> for aggregation. This suggests that although distant supervision might introduce noise into the training process, it can also provide valuable information that improves model generalisation, particularly when leveraging simpler feature representations like $\boldsymbol{h}_e$ and <ent>, possibly due to their robustness in capturing essential information amidst noise.

HacRED Results We observe a similar pattern to Re-DocRED, with ATLOP* displaying a slight performance advantage over ATLOP◇ from Cheng et al. (2021) (Table 1). On this dataset, GADePo shows a significantly improved performance, primarily driven by a substantial increase in Recall (R), indicating that the GADePo model is more effective at identifying relevant instances. As already reported for the Re-DocRED dataset, the performance boost after the inclusion of $\boldsymbol{c}^{(s,o)}$ and

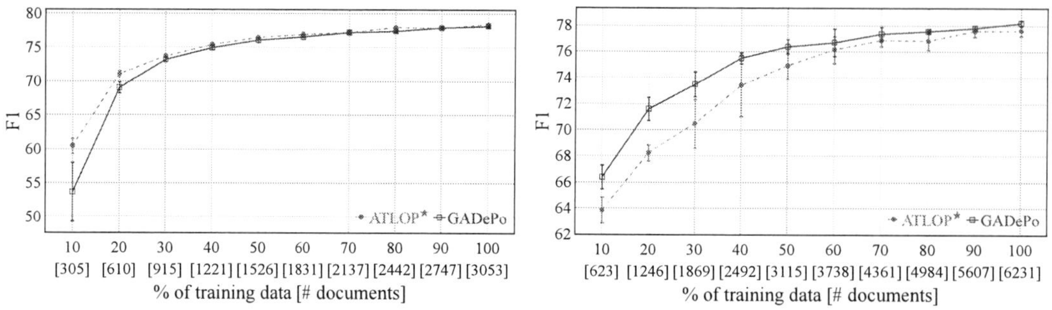

(a) Re-DocRED

(b) HacRED

Figure 4: Performance of ATLOP* ($\boldsymbol{h}_e$; $\boldsymbol{c}^{(s,o)}$) and GADePo (<ent> ; <pent>) on the development set under varying data availability conditions on Re-DocRED (4a) and HacRED (4b). The x-axis represents the percentage and number of documents from the training dataset, while the y-axis displays the F_1 score in percentage. Each point on the graph represents the mean value, while error bars indicate the standard deviation derived from five distinct training runs with separate random seeds.

<pent> into ATLOP* and GADePo, respectively, highlight the significant contributions of these features. GADePo outperforms ATLOP* with an F_1 score of 78.65% compared to 77.59%. This larger improvement on HacRED suggests that GADePo is better at handling challenging cases, which is not surprising given its greater flexibility over the fixed pooling functions of ATLOP.

Data Ablation To evaluate the models' sensitivity to dataset size, the performance evaluation depicted in Figure 4 compares ATLOP* ($\boldsymbol{h}_e$; $\boldsymbol{c}^{(s,o)}$) and GADePo (<ent> ; <pent>) on the development set, considering different levels of training data availability on the Re-DocRED and HacRED datasets. Accuracies generally converge as the dataset sizes increase, but on the challenging cases of HacRED, GADePo maintains a substantial advantage across the full range. On Re-DocRED, GADePo catches up with and slightly outperforms ATLOP* as data size increases. This lower performance on smaller datasets is presumably because GADePo must learn how to exploit the graph relations to the special tokens <ent> and <pent> and pool information through them, whereas for ATLOP this pooling is hand-coded. On the Re-DocRED dataset, ATLOP* appears to have relatively consistent variance, while GADePo exhibits higher variance in the smaller training sets, while on the HacRED dataset, GADePo is significantly more stable for smaller datasets.

The data ablation analysis shows that the performance of hand-coded pooling functions can be dataset-specific, which restricts their adaptability. In contrast, GADePo consistently outperforms its hand-coded counterparts on larger datasets, and matches them on all but some smaller datasets, presumably due to its flexibility. This pattern suggests that GADePo has a greater potential for optimisation, particularly on larger datasets. This is supported by GADePo's better performance on HacRED, which is both larger and designed to be more challenging than Re-DocRED.

6 Conclusion

In this paper we proposed a novel approach to document-level relation extraction, challenging the conventional reliance on hand-coded pooling functions for information aggregation. Our method leverages the power of Transformer models by incorporating explicit graph relations as instructions for information aggregation. By combining graph processing with text-based encoding, we introduced the graph-assisted declarative pooling (GADePo) specification, which allows for more flexible and customisable specification of pooling strategies which are still learned from data.

We conducted evaluations using diverse datasets and models commonly employed in document-level relation extraction tasks. The results of our experiments demonstrated that our approach achieves promising performance that is comparable to or better than that of hand-coded pooling functions. This suggests that our method can serve as a viable basis for other relation extraction methods, providing a more adaptable and tailored approach. In particular, recent methods have improved performance by exploiting information about evidence, which can naturally be incorporated in our graph-based approach.

Limitations

While the proposed GADePo model offers a promising and innovative approach to relation extraction, there are issues which the current study does not address. According to the data in Appendix Table 2, the average number of entities per document across datasets is approximately 15. This means that, on average, there will be an additional 15 `<ent>` tokens and 105 `<pent>` tokens. Given that the maximum allowable input length for the models is 512 tokens, the inclusion of these extra tokens results in roughly a 3% and 20% increase in the overall input length for `<ent>` and `<pent>`, respectively. It's evident that the majority of the increase in input length is due to the quadratic number of `<pent>` special tokens, but we believe that an appropriate pruning strategy could easily reduce this number to linear in the number of entities without degrading accuracy. One such pruning strategy could involve an `<ent>`-only model with a binary classifier which is trained to predict pairs of related entities. This model could then be used to prune the set of candidate entity pairs for the final relation classification, with `<pent>` tokens being instantiated only for these candidate pairs. We have chosen to leave this approach as a potential avenue for future work, opting instead to focus on demonstrating the promise of the current simpler formulation.

Ethics Statement

We do not anticipate any ethical concerns related to our work, as it primarily presents an alternative approach to a previously proposed method. Our main contribution lies in introducing a novel methodology for relation extraction. In our experiments, we use the same datasets and pretrained models as previous research, all of which are publicly available. However, it is important to acknowledge that these datasets and models may still require further examination for potential fairness issues and the knowledge they encapsulate.

Acknowledgements

We extend our special gratitude to the Swiss National Science Foundation (SNSF) and Research Foundation – Flanders (FWO) for funding this work under grants 200021E_189458 and G094020N.

References

Michele Banko, Michael J. Cafarella, Stephen Soderland, Matthew Broadhead, and Oren Etzioni. 2007. Open information extraction from the web. In *CACM*.

Iz Beltagy, Kyle Lo, and Arman Cohan. 2019. SciBERT: A pretrained language model for scientific text. In *Proceedings of the 2019 Conference on Empirical Methods in Natural Language Processing and the 9th International Joint Conference on Natural Language Processing (EMNLP-IJCNLP)*, pages 3615–3620, Hong Kong, China. Association for Computational Linguistics.

Danqi Chen, Adam Fisch, Jason Weston, and Antoine Bordes. 2017. Reading Wikipedia to answer open-domain questions. In *Proceedings of the 55th Annual Meeting of the Association for Computational Linguistics (Volume 1: Long Papers)*, pages 1870–1879, Vancouver, Canada. Association for Computational Linguistics.

Qiao Cheng, Juntao Liu, Xiaoye Qu, Jin Zhao, Jiaqing Liang, Zhefeng Wang, Baoxing Huai, Nicholas Jing Yuan, and Yanghua Xiao. 2021. HacRED: A large-scale relation extraction dataset toward hard cases in practical applications. In *Findings of the Association for Computational Linguistics: ACL-IJCNLP 2021*, pages 2819–2831, Online. Association for Computational Linguistics.

Hyunjin Choi, Judong Kim, Seongho Joe, and Youngjune Gwon. 2021. Evaluation of bert and albert sentence embedding performance on downstream nlp tasks. *2020 25th International Conference on Pattern Recognition (ICPR)*, pages 5482–5487.

Fenia Christopoulou, Makoto Miwa, and Sophia Ananiadou. 2019. Connecting the dots: Document-level neural relation extraction with edge-oriented graphs. In *Proceedings of the 2019 Conference on Empirical Methods in Natural Language Processing and the 9th International Joint Conference on Natural Language Processing (EMNLP-IJCNLP)*, pages 4925–4936, Hong Kong, China. Association for Computational Linguistics.

Alexis Conneau, Douwe Kiela, Holger Schwenk, Loïc Barrault, and Antoine Bordes. 2017. Supervised learning of universal sentence representations from natural language inference data. In *Proceedings of the 2017 Conference on Empirical Methods in Natural Language Processing*, pages 670–680, Copenhagen, Denmark. Association for Computational Linguistics.

Yiming Cui, Wanxiang Che, Ting Liu, Bing Qin, and Ziqing Yang. 2021. Pre-training with whole word masking for chinese bert. *IEEE/ACM Trans. Audio, Speech and Lang. Proc.*, 29:3504–3514.

Jacob Devlin, Ming-Wei Chang, Kenton Lee, and Kristina Toutanova. 2019. BERT: Pre-training of deep bidirectional transformers for language understanding. In *Proceedings of the 2019 Conference of the North American Chapter of the Association for Computational Linguistics: Human Language Technologies, Volume 1 (Long and Short Papers)*, pages 4171–4186, Minneapolis, Minnesota. Association for Computational Linguistics.

William Falcon and The PyTorch Lightning team. 2019. PyTorch Lightning.

Yue Feng, Zhen Han, Mingming Sun, and Ping Li. 2022. Multi-hop open-domain question answering over structured and unstructured knowledge. In *Findings of the Association for Computational Linguistics: NAACL 2022*, pages 151–156, Seattle, United States. Association for Computational Linguistics.

James Henderson. 2020. The unstoppable rise of computational linguistics in deep learning. In *Proceedings of the 58th Annual Meeting of the Association for Computational Linguistics*, pages 6294–6306, Online. Association for Computational Linguistics.

James Henderson, Alireza Mohammadshahi, Andrei Coman, and Lesly Miculicich. 2023. Transformers as graph-to-graph models. In *Proceedings of the Big Picture Workshop*, pages 93–107, Singapore. Association for Computational Linguistics.

Sepp Hochreiter and Jürgen Schmidhuber. 1997. Long short-term memory. *Neural Computation*, 9:1735–1780.

Shaoxiong Ji, Shirui Pan, E. Cambria, Pekka Marttinen, and Philip S. Yu. 2020. A survey on knowledge graphs: Representation, acquisition, and applications. *IEEE Transactions on Neural Networks and Learning Systems*, 33:494–514.

Robin Jia, Cliff Wong, and Hoifung Poon. 2019. Document-level n-ary relation extraction with multiscale representation learning. In *Proceedings of the 2019 Conference of the North American Chapter of the Association for Computational Linguistics: Human Language Technologies, Volume 1 (Long and Short Papers)*, pages 3693–3704, Minneapolis, Minnesota. Association for Computational Linguistics.

Thomas N. Kipf and Max Welling. 2017. Semi-supervised classification with graph convolutional networks. In *International Conference on Learning Representations (ICLR)*.

Liyuan Liu, Haoming Jiang, Pengcheng He, Weizhu Chen, Xiaodong Liu, Jianfeng Gao, and Jiawei Han. 2020. On the variance of the adaptive learning rate and beyond. In *International Conference on Learning Representations*.

Youmi Ma, An Wang, and Naoaki Okazaki. 2023. DREEAM: Guiding attention with evidence for improving document-level relation extraction. In *Proceedings of the 17th Conference of the European Chapter of the Association for Computational Linguistics*, pages 1971–1983, Dubrovnik, Croatia. Association for Computational Linguistics.

Christopher D. Manning, Prabhakar Raghavan, and Hinrich Schütze. 2008. *Introduction to Information Retrieval*. Cambridge University Press.

Lesly Miculicich and James Henderson. 2022. Graph refinement for coreference resolution. In *Findings of the Association for Computational Linguistics: ACL 2022*, pages 2732–2742, Dublin, Ireland. Association for Computational Linguistics.

Alireza Mohammadshahi and James Henderson. 2020. Graph-to-graph transformer for transition-based dependency parsing. In *Findings of the Association for Computational Linguistics: EMNLP 2020*, pages 3278–3289, Online. Association for Computational Linguistics.

Alireza Mohammadshahi and James Henderson. 2021. Recursive non-autoregressive graph-to-graph transformer for dependency parsing with iterative refinement. *Transactions of the Association for Computational Linguistics*, 9:120–138.

Alireza Mohammadshahi and James Henderson. 2023. Syntax-aware graph-to-graph transformer for semantic role labelling. In *Proceedings of the 8th Workshop on Representation Learning for NLP (RepL4NLP 2023)*, pages 174–186, Toronto, Canada. Association for Computational Linguistics.

Guoshun Nan, Zhijiang Guo, Ivan Sekulic, and Wei Lu. 2020. Reasoning with latent structure refinement for document-level relation extraction. In *Proceedings of the 58th Annual Meeting of the Association for Computational Linguistics*, pages 1546–1557, Online. Association for Computational Linguistics.

Bo Pang and Lillian Lee. 2008. Opinion mining and sentiment analysis. *Found. Trends Inf. Retr.*, 2:1–135.

Adam Paszke, Sam Gross, Francisco Massa, Adam Lerer, James Bradbury, Gregory Chanan, Trevor Killeen, Zeming Lin, Natalia Gimelshein, Luca Antiga, Alban Desmaison, Andreas Kopf, Edward Yang, Zachary DeVito, Martin Raison, Alykhan Tejani, Sasank Chilamkurthy, Benoit Steiner, Lu Fang, Junjie Bai, and Soumith Chintala. 2019. PyTorch: An Imperative Style, High-Performance Deep Learning Library. In *Advances in Neural Information Processing Systems 32*, pages 8024–8035. Curran Associates, Inc.

Nanyun Peng, Hoifung Poon, Chris Quirk, Kristina Toutanova, and Wen-tau Yih. 2017. Cross-sentence n-ary relation extraction with graph LSTMs. *Transactions of the Association for Computational Linguistics*, 5:101–115.

Nils Reimers and Iryna Gurevych. 2019. Sentence-BERT: Sentence embeddings using Siamese BERT-networks. In *Proceedings of the 2019 Conference on Empirical Methods in Natural Language Processing and the 9th International Joint Conference on Natural Language Processing (EMNLP-IJCNLP)*, pages 3982–3992, Hong Kong, China. Association for Computational Linguistics.

Qingyu Tan, Ruidan He, Lidong Bing, and Hwee Tou Ng. 2022a. Document-level relation extraction with adaptive focal loss and knowledge distillation. In *Findings of the Association for Computational Linguistics: ACL 2022*, pages 1672–1681, Dublin, Ireland. Association for Computational Linguistics.

Qingyu Tan, Lu Xu, Lidong Bing, Hwee Tou Ng, and Sharifah Mahani Aljunied. 2022b. Revisiting DocRED - addressing the false negative problem in relation extraction. In *Proceedings of the 2022 Conference on Empirical Methods in Natural Language Processing*, pages 8472–8487, Abu Dhabi, United Arab Emirates. Association for Computational Linguistics.

Hengzhu Tang, Yanan Cao, Zhenyu Zhang, Jiangxia Cao, Fang Fang, Shi Wang, and Pengfei Yin. 2020. Hin: Hierarchical inference network for document-level relation extraction. In *Advances in Knowledge Discovery and Data Mining: 24th Pacific-Asia Conference, PAKDD 2020, Singapore, May 11–14, 2020, Proceedings, Part I 24*, pages 197–209. Springer.

Christos Theodoropoulos, James Henderson, Andrei Catalin Coman, and Marie-Francine Moens. 2021. Imposing relation structure in language-model embeddings using contrastive learning. In *Proceedings of the 25th Conference on Computational Natural Language Learning*, pages 337–348, Online. Association for Computational Linguistics.

Ashish Vaswani, Noam M. Shazeer, Niki Parmar, Jakob Uszkoreit, Llion Jones, Aidan N. Gomez, Lukasz Kaiser, and Illia Polosukhin. 2017. Attention is all you need. In *NIPS*.

Difeng Wang, Wei Hu, Ermei Cao, and Weijian Sun. 2020. Global-to-local neural networks for document-level relation extraction. In *Proceedings of the 2020 Conference on Empirical Methods in Natural Language Processing (EMNLP)*, pages 3711–3721, Online. Association for Computational Linguistics.

Hong Wang, Christfried Focke, Rob Sylvester, Nilesh Mishra, and William Yang Wang. 2019. Fine-tune bert for docred with two-step process. *ArXiv*, abs/1909.11898.

Thomas Wolf, Lysandre Debut, Victor Sanh, Julien Chaumond, Clement Delangue, Anthony Moi, Pierric Cistac, Tim Rault, Remi Louf, Morgan Funtowicz, Joe Davison, Sam Shleifer, Patrick von Platen, Clara Ma, Yacine Jernite, Julien Plu, Canwen Xu, Teven Le Scao, Sylvain Gugger, Mariama Drame, Quentin Lhoest, and Alexander Rush. 2020. Transformers: State-of-the-art natural language processing. In *Proceedings of the 2020 Conference on Empirical Methods in Natural Language Processing: System Demonstrations*, pages 38–45, Online. Association for Computational Linguistics.

Yuxin Xiao, Zecheng Zhang, Yuning Mao, Carl Yang, and Jiawei Han. 2022. SAIS: Supervising and augmenting intermediate steps for document-level relation extraction. In *Proceedings of the 2022 Conference of the North American Chapter of the Association for Computational Linguistics: Human Language Technologies*, pages 2395–2409, Seattle, United States. Association for Computational Linguistics.

Benfeng Xu, Quan Wang, Yajuan Lyu, Yong Zhu, and Zhendong Mao. 2021. Entity structure within and throughout: Modeling mention dependencies for document-level relation extraction. *Proceedings of the AAAI Conference on Artificial Intelligence*, 35(16):14149–14157.

Yuan Yao, Deming Ye, Peng Li, Xu Han, Yankai Lin, Zhenghao Liu, Zhiyuan Liu, Lixin Huang, Jie Zhou, and Maosong Sun. 2019. DocRED: A large-scale document-level relation extraction dataset. In *Proceedings of the 57th Annual Meeting of the Association for Computational Linguistics*, pages 764–777, Florence, Italy. Association for Computational Linguistics.

Deming Ye, Yankai Lin, Peng Li, and Maosong Sun. 2022. Packed levitated marker for entity and relation extraction. In *Proceedings of the 60th Annual Meeting of the Association for Computational Linguistics (Volume 1: Long Papers)*, pages 4904–4917, Dublin, Ireland. Association for Computational Linguistics.

Shuang Zeng, Runxin Xu, Baobao Chang, and Lei Li. 2020. Double graph based reasoning for document-level relation extraction. In *Proceedings of the 2020 Conference on Empirical Methods in Natural Language Processing (EMNLP)*, pages 1630–1640, Online. Association for Computational Linguistics.

Ningyu Zhang, Xiang Chen, Xin Xie, Shumin Deng, Chuanqi Tan, Mosha Chen, Fei Huang, Luo Si, and Huajun Chen. 2021. Document-level relation extraction as semantic segmentation. In *International Joint Conference on Artificial Intelligence*.

Wenxuan Zhou, Kevin Huang, Tengyu Ma, and Jing Huang. 2021. Document-level relation extraction with adaptive thresholding and localized context pooling. In *Proceedings of the AAAI Conference on Artificial Intelligence*.

Liu Zhuang, Lin Wayne, Shi Ya, and Zhao Jun. 2021. A robustly optimized BERT pre-training approach with post-training. In *Proceedings of the 20th Chinese National Conference on Computational Linguistics*, pages 1218–1227, Huhhot, China. Chinese Information Processing Society of China.

A Appendix

A.1 ATLOP: Relation Classification and Loss Function

Relation Classification To predict the relation between the subject entity e_s and object entity e_o,

ATLOP first generates context-aware subject and object representations as follows:

$$z_s = tanh(W_s[h_{e_s}; c^{(s,o)}] + b_s) \quad (6)$$

$$z_o = tanh(W_o[h_{e_o}; c^{(s,o)}] + b_o), \quad (7)$$

where $z_s, z_o \in \mathbb{R}^d$, $[\cdot;\cdot]$ represents the concatenation of two vectors, and $W_s, W_o \in \mathbb{R}^{d \times 2d}$ together with $b_s, b_o \in \mathbb{R}^d$ are trainable parameters. Then, the entity pair representation is computed as:

$$x^{(s,o)} = z_s \otimes z_o, \quad (8)$$

where $x^{(s,o)} \in \mathbb{R}^{d^2}$ and $\otimes$ stands for the vectorised Kronecker product. Finally, relation scores are computed as:

$$y^{(s,o)} = W_r x^{(s,o)} + b_r, \quad (9)$$

where $y^{(s,o)} \in \mathbb{R}^{|\mathcal{R}|}$, with $W_r \in \mathbb{R}^{|\mathcal{R}| \times d^2}$ and $b_r \in \mathbb{R}^{|\mathcal{R}|}$ representing learnable parameters. The probability of relation $r \in \mathcal{R}$ between the subject and object entities is computed as follows:

$$P(r|s,o) = \sigma(y^{(s,o)}), \quad (10)$$

where σ is the sigmoid function. To reduce the number of parameters in the classifier, a grouped function is used, which splits the embedding dimensions into k equal-sized groups and applies the function within the groups as follows:

$$z_s = [z_s^1; \ldots; z_s^k] \quad (11)$$

$$z_o = [z_o^1; \ldots; z_o^k] \quad (12)$$

$$x^{(s,o)} = [x^{(s,o)^1}; \ldots; x^{(s,o)^k}] \quad (13)$$

$$y^{(s,o)} = \sum_{i=1}^{k} W_r^i x^{(s,o)^i} + b_r, \quad (14)$$

where $z_s^i, z_o^i \in \mathbb{R}^{d/k}$, $x^{(s,o)^i} \in \mathbb{R}^{d^2/k}$, and $W_r^i \in \mathbb{R}^{|\mathcal{R}| \times d^2/k}$. This way, the number of parameters can be reduced from d^2 to d^2/k.

Loss Function ATLOP introduces the adaptive thresholding loss concept. This approach involves training a model to learn a hypothetical threshold class TH, which dynamically adjusts for each relation class $r \in \mathcal{R}$. During training, for each entity pair (e_s, e_o), the loss enforces the model to generate scores above TH for positive relation classes $\mathcal{R}_P$ and scores below TH for negative relation classes $\mathcal{R}_N$. The loss is computed as follows:

$$\mathcal{L} = -\sum_{s \neq o} \sum_{r \in \mathcal{R}_P} \frac{exp(y_r^{(s,o)})}{\sum_{r' \in \mathcal{R}_P \cup \{TH\}} exp(y_{r'}^{(s,o)})} - \frac{exp(y_{TH}^{(s,o)})}{\sum_{r' \in \mathcal{R}_N \cup \{TH\}} exp(y_{r'}^{(s,o)})} \quad (15)$$

A.2 GADePo's Extra Parameters

GADePo introduces few extra parameters to the PLM. The amount of parameters is reported in Table 4.

Parameter	Model	
	RoBERTa$_{\text{LARGE}}$	BERT$_{\text{BASE}}$
<ent>	1024	768
<pent>	1024	768
<ent> $\longrightarrow *$	24×1024	12×768
$* \longrightarrow$ <ent>	24×1024	12×768
<pent> $\longrightarrow *$	24×1024	12×768
$* \longrightarrow$ <pent>	24×1024	12×768
Total	100,352	38,400

Table 4: GADePo's extra parameters count.

The introduction of these parameters results in only a minimal increase in the overall parameter count of the models. Specifically, GADePo's augmentation amounts to a mere 0.036% increase over the BERT$_{\text{BASE}}$ model. In contrast, even a slight increase of just one unit in BERT$_{\text{BASE}}$'s hidden dimensions would result in a 0.139% parameter increase, which is roughly four times greater than the augmentation introduced by GADePo. Given that such a small change is incompatible with other architectural constraints, such as the number of heads, it is implausible that this minimal augmentation would solely account for the observed performance gains.

This indicates that the performance improvements are largely due to the effective inductive bias introduced by GADePo, rather than the increase in parameter count. The same rationale applies to the results observed with RoBERTa$_{\text{LARGE}}$.

A.3 Training Details

We generally comply with the hyperparameters of ATLOP and set the output dimension in Equation 6 and Equation 7 to 768. We also set the block size in Equation 11 and Equation 12 to 64, i.e., $k = 12$.

In all our experiments we perform early stopping on the development set based on the Ign $F_1 + F_1$

score for DocRED and Re-DocRED, and F_1 score for HacRED. The five different seeds we use are $\{73, 21, 37, 7, 3\}$.

We use RAdam (Liu et al., 2020) as our optimiser. On the RoBERTa$_{\text{LARGE}}$ based models we train for 8 epochs and set the learning rates to $3e^{-5}$ and $1e^{-4}$ for the PLM parameters and the new additional parameters, respectively. On the BERT$_{\text{BASE}}$ based models we train for 10 epochs and set the learning rates to $1e^{-5}$ and $1e^{-4}$ for the PLM parameters and the new additional parameters, respectively. We use a cosine learning rate decay throughout the training process.

In all our experiments the batch size is set to 4 for ATLOP and 2 for GADePo, with gradient accumulation set to 1 and 2, for ATLOP and GADePo, respectively. We clip the gradients to a max norm of 1.0. All models are trained with mixed precision.

We run our experiments on two types of GPUs, namely the NVIDIA V100 32GB for the RoBERTa$_{\text{LARGE}}$ based models and NVIDIA RTX 3090 24GB for the BERT$_{\text{BASE}}$ based models, respectively.

We use PyTorch (Paszke et al., 2019), Lightning (Falcon and The PyTorch Lightning team, 2019), and Hugging Face's Transformers (Wolf et al., 2020) libraries to develop our models.

A.4 Additional Results

Re-DocRED and HacRED Table 5 and Table 6 present additional results for Re-DocRED and HacRED, respectively. In addition to the results outlined in Section 5, these tables include the mean and standard deviation on the development set, calculated from five training runs with distinct random seeds, as reported in Appendix Subsection A.3.

DocRED results The DocRED (Yao et al., 2019) dataset consists of 56,354 facts, 96 relations, 5,053 documents, and 26.2 average number of entities per document. In line with the approach taken for Re-DocRED and HacRED, Table 7 and Figure 5 illustrate the results for DocRED.

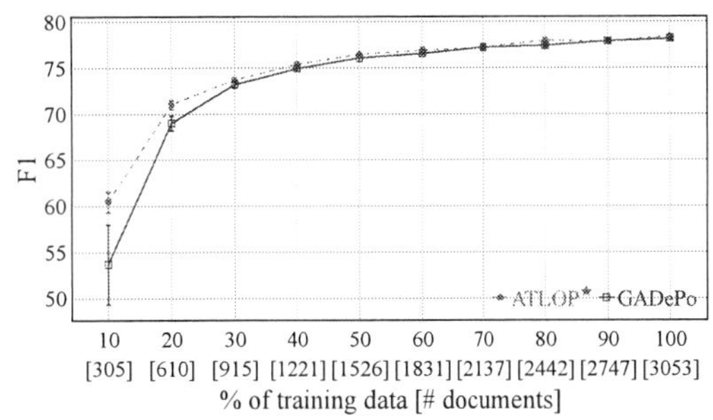

Figure 5: Performance of ATLOP⋆ $(\boldsymbol{h}_e\ ;\ \boldsymbol{c}^{(s,o)})$ and GADePo (<ent> ; <pent>) on the development set under varying data availability conditions on DocRED. The x-axis represents the percentage and number of documents from the training dataset, while the y-axis displays the F_1 score in percentage. Each point on the graph represents the mean value, while error bars indicate the standard deviation derived from five distinct training runs with separate random seeds.

		Dev		Test	
Model	**Aggregation**	Ign F_1	F_1	Ign F_1	F_1
ATLOP*	$\boldsymbol{h}_e$	75.46 ± 0.16	76.16 ± 0.16	75.27	75.92
GADePo (ours)	<ent>	75.46 ± 0.20	76.31 ± 0.24	**75.55**	**76.38**
ATLOP$^\bullet$	$\boldsymbol{h}_e$; $\boldsymbol{c}^{(s,o)}$	76.79	77.46	76.82	77.56
ATLOP*	$\boldsymbol{h}_e$; $\boldsymbol{c}^{(s,o)}$	77.75 ± 0.08	78.41 ± 0.10	77.62	78.38
GADePo (ours)	<ent> ; <pent>	77.48 ± 0.12	78.19 ± 0.14	**77.70**	**78.40**

Table 5: Results in percentage for the development and test sets of Re-DocRED. We report the results obtained by Tan et al. (2022b) (ATLOP$^\bullet$) on Re-DocRED. ATLOP* indicates our reimplementation of the previous method. We report the mean and standard deviation of Ign F_1 and F_1 on the development set, calculated from five training runs with distinct random seeds. We report the test score achieved by the best checkpoint on the development set. Ign F_1 refers to the F_1 score that excludes relational facts shared between the training and development/test sets.

		Dev			Test		
Model	**Aggregation**	P	R	F_1	P	R	F_1
ATLOP*	$\boldsymbol{h}_e$	77.37 ± 0.22	77.40 ± 0.31	77.39 ± 0.13	**76.27**	76.83	76.55
GADePo (ours)	<ent>	72.96 ± 0.96	79.22 ± 1.20	75.96 ± 0.99	74.13	**79.46**	**76.70**
ATLOP$^\diamond$	$\boldsymbol{h}_e$; $\boldsymbol{c}^{(s,o)}$	–	–	–	77.89	76.55	77.21
ATLOP*	$\boldsymbol{h}_e$; $\boldsymbol{c}^{(s,o)}$	77.18 ± 0.14	77.98 ± 0.66	77.58 ± 0.36	76.36	78.86	77.59
GADePo (ours)	<ent> ; <pent>	75.98 ± 0.94	80.54 ± 0.72	78.19 ± 0.19	**78.27**	**79.03**	**78.65**

Table 6: Results in percentage for the development and test sets of HacRED. We report the results obtained by Cheng et al. (2021) (ATLOP$^\diamond$) on HacRED. ATLOP* indicates our reimplementation of the previous method. We report the mean and standard deviation of Precision (P), Recall (R) and F_1 on the development set, calculated from five training runs with distinct random seeds. We report the test score achieved by the best checkpoint on the development set.

		Dev		Test	
Model	**Aggregation**	Ign F_1	F_1	Ign F_1	F_1
ATLOP*	$\boldsymbol{h}_e$	59.66 ± 0.20	61.60 ± 0.21	59.22	61.37
GADePo (ours)	<ent>	59.04 ± 0.52	61.18 ± 0.46	**59.30**	**61.63**
ATLOP$^\circ$	$\boldsymbol{h}_e$; $\boldsymbol{c}^{(s,o)}$	61.32 ± 0.14	63.18 ± 0.19	61.39	63.40
ATLOP*	$\boldsymbol{h}_e$; $\boldsymbol{c}^{(s,o)}$	61.41 ± 0.26	63.38 ± 0.28	**61.62**	63.72
GADePo (ours)	<ent> ; <pent>	61.19 ± 0.55	63.26 ± 0.48	61.52	**63.75**

Table 7: Results in percentage for the development and test sets of DocRED. We report the results obtained by Zhou et al. (2021) (ATLOP$^\circ$) on DocRED. ATLOP* indicates our reimplementation of the previous method. We report the mean and standard deviation of Ign F_1 and F_1 on the development set, calculated from five training runs with distinct random seeds. We report the test score achieved by the best checkpoint on the development set. Ign F_1 refers to the F_1 score that excludes relational facts shared between the training and development/test sets.

KaPQA: Knowledge-Augmented Product Question-Answering

Swetha Eppalapally[1], Daksh Dangi[1], Chaithra Bhat[1], Ankita Gupta[1], Ruiyi Zhang[2], Shubham Agarwal[2], Karishma Bagga[2], Seunghyun Yoon[2], Nedim Lipka[2], Ryan A. Rossi[2], Franck Dernoncourt[2]

[1]University of Massachusetts Amherst, [2]Adobe Research

Abstract

Question-answering for domain-specific applications has recently attracted much interest due to the latest advancements in large language models (LLMs). However, accurately assessing the performance of these applications remains a challenge, mainly due to the lack of suitable benchmarks that effectively simulate real-world scenarios. To address this challenge, we introduce two product question-answering (QA) datasets focused on Adobe Acrobat and Photoshop products to help evaluate the performance of existing models on domain-specific product QA tasks. Additionally, we propose a novel knowledge-driven RAG-QA framework to enhance the performance of the models in the product QA task. Our experiments demonstrated that inducing domain knowledge through query reformulation allowed for increased retrieval and generative performance when compared to standard RAG-QA methods. This improvement, however, is slight, and thus illustrates the challenge posed by the datasets introduced.

1 Introduction

The advancements in large language models (LLMs) led to exponential growth in domain-specific applications. Question Answering has emerged as one of the prominent domain-specific applications. As the demand for accurate and reliable QA systems increases, generic RAG-QA approaches often struggle to deliver satisfactory results within the specialized domains. This challenge has spurred active exploration in this area, with researchers employing various novel methodologies (Nguyen et al., 2024; Setty et al., 2024; Jiang et al., 2024; Rackauckas, 2024) to improve QA systems.

Additionally, training and evaluating these systems rigorously remains crucial. This trend underscores the critical need for domain-specific QA datasets to facilitate the training and evaluation of such systems. Notably, while efforts have been directed towards releasing datasets across prominent and expansive domains such as Medicine (Pal et al., 2022; Pampari et al., 2018), Finance (Chen et al., 2021; Zhu et al., 2021), and Legal (Zhong et al., 2019; Chen et al., 2023a), there remains an apparent scarcity of such datasets in the area of software products.

To address this gap, our work investigates such industry-specific QA datasets, namely the Adobe HelpX datasets, and releases them for others to benchmark against and further improve their QA systems. These datasets comprise of user queries and their corresponding answers pertaining to Adobe products, specifically Acrobat and Photoshop. By providing these benchmark datasets, we aim to offer valuable resources for assessing the performance of domain-specific RAG-QA systems. The datasets will be released after obtaining relevant permissions from Adobe.

Furthermore, we introduce a novel LLM-based Knowledge-Driven RAG-QA framework designed to seamlessly accommodate domain knowledge into RAG-QA systems. This framework leverages comprehensive knowledge bases for query expansion, thereby enhancing both retrieval and generation in domain-specific QA tasks.

Through extensive experimentation, we've determined that performing accurate retrieval over these datasets poses a unique challenge. Even introducing this concept of query augmentation using knowledge directly from the corpora only helped improve the model so much. This illustrates how these datasets are challenging ones - as even complex frameworks such as the one we've proposed, could only result in so much improvement.

By contributing these datasets and proposing an innovative framework, we aim to advance LLM technology and its application in domain-specific QA tasks, ultimately improving user experiences and operational efficiency across various industries.

Proceedings of the 3rd Workshop on Knowledge Augmented Methods for NLP, pages 15–29
August 16, 2024 ©2024 Association for Computational Linguistics

2 Related Work

2.1 Domain-specific question answering

Several research efforts have been made to curate domain-specific question-answering benchmarks and training datasets, spanning domains like biomedical (Pal et al., 2022; Pampari et al., 2018; Li et al., 2021), finance (Chen et al., 2021; Zhu et al., 2021), and legal (Zhong et al., 2019; Chen et al., 2023a). In contrast, our work focuses on product question-answering, which is valuable in many enterprise settings. Furthermore, unlike many of these existing datasets that provide a simpler multiple-choice question-answer format, our work focuses on generative question-answering.

Among the research efforts in product-specific question-answering, Yang et al. (2023) also provides a dataset focused on answering user queries about Microsoft products. However, many of the question-answer pairs in this dataset require a yes/no answer, with only a small portion requiring more complex answers. The PhotoshopQuiA (Dulceanu et al., 2018) dataset is more closely related to our work in terms of domain, as it is also based on the Adobe Photoshop product. However, it specifically focuses on *why* questions. In contrast, our work centers on *how-to* queries, necessitating the model to generate a detailed sequence of steps to complete an operation. These answers are considerably more challenging to generate because their usefulness hinges on the accuracy of each individual step. If even one step in the generated answer is incorrect, the overall utility of the answer is compromised.

2.2 Augmenting LLMs

The Retrieval Augmented Generative (RAG) framework has been extensively worked on for years and (Gao et al., 2024; Zhao et al., 2024; Li et al., 2022) present a detailed examination of the progression of RAG paradigms (Ma et al., 2023; Ilin, 2024; Shao et al., 2023; Yu et al., 2023), and introduce the metrics and benchmarks for assessing RAG models (Chen et al., 2023b; Lyu et al., 2024). One suggested future direction involves identifying methods to fully harness the potential of Large Language Models (LLMs) to enhance domain-specific RAG systems, aligning with our aim of leveraging LLMs to answer queries related to Adobe products.

Recent efforts aim to enhance LLMs' contextual generation in specific domains by incorporating external knowledge (Mialon et al., 2023). Fatehkia et al. (2024) propose Tree-RAG where they utilize a tree structure to depict entity hierarchies in organizational documents and supplement context with textual descriptions for user queries. However, their approach is ineffective for documents lacking hierarchical organization such as ours. Another method to incorporate industry domain-specific information is presented by Yang et al. (2023). It involves getting a domain-specific language model with aligned knowledge and then feeding it to an LLM to generate enriched answers. We propose an alternative method to solve domain-specific RAG-QA through the construction of a comprehensive knowledge base consisting of triples and a multi-stage query reformulation pipeline. Zhu et al. (2024) evaluates LLMs for Knowledge Graph (KG) tasks across diverse datasets, highlighting their suitability as inference assistants. Additionally, Jagerman et al. (2023) explore query expansion by prompting LLMs through zero-shot, few-shot and Chain-of-Thought (CoT) learning. Our work takes it a step further by incorporating knowledge base tuples in query expansion.

3 Dataset Creation

3.1 Data Pre-processing

The corpus is sourced from the publicly available Adobe HelpX[1] web pages for Acrobat and Photoshop products, which explain how to use the functionalities present in these products.

A crawling script is employed to extract the content from the web pages, segmenting them into distinct sections based on H2 headings. Each of these sections typically represents a specific topic or task within the respective product. The resulting sections tend to be non-overlapping, facilitating targeted analysis.

Throughout the process, all clickable and in-section links within the web pages are transformed into plain text to maintain consistency, while images are omitted to ensure that the corpus comprises solely textual content.

3.2 Question-Answer Pairs with URLs Creation

Gold question-answer (QA) pairs are meticulously crafted for analysis. Product experts, recruited through Upwork for Adobe Acrobat and Telus International, are instructed to write how-to questions

[1] `https://helpx.adobe.com`

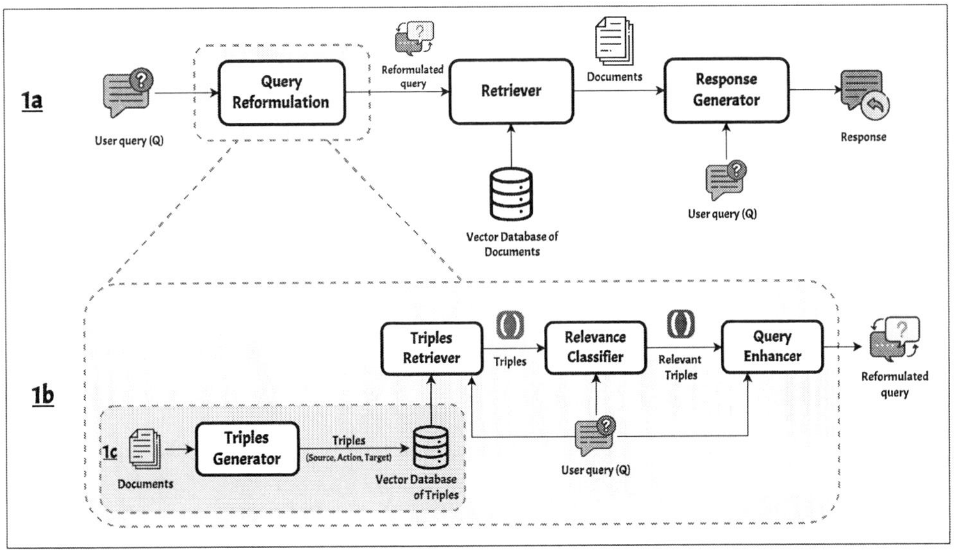

Figure 1: The figure represents our proposed framework. **1a** depicts the main RAG-QA pipeline consisting of a retriever and a generator, along with our proposed query reformulation sub-pipeline. **1b** gives a detailed view of the various components in our sub-pipeline. The process starts with the generation of knowledge base triples using the Triples Generator. Next, all matching triples to the user query are retrieved using the Triple Retriever, classified based on their relevance to the original query using the Relevance Classifier and finally reformulated using the Query Enhancer.

and answers that provide procedural steps to accomplish specific tasks using the software. Furthermore, each QA pair is mapped with its respective source web page.

The experts manually created question-answer pairs based on the respective HelpX web pages for Adobe Acrobat. Conversely, for Adobe Photoshop, GPT-4 initially generated question-answer pairs based on the web pages, which are subsequently reviewed and corrected by product experts to guarantee accuracy and relevance to the question and the answer.

This systematic approach of the question-answer pair generation ensures the integrity and usability of the dataset for evaluation and research in the domain of software products and support.

4 Data Analysis and Statistics

The Adobe Acrobat and the Photoshop datasets contain questions, answers, and corresponding source web page URLs. All questions in this dataset are how-to type asking steps to perform operations such as changing text font, editing text in a PDF, and creating certificate-based signatures. The gold answers to these questions provide procedural steps to accomplish these operations and the URLs of the web pages allow for independent verification of the answer. Table 1 provides insights into various metrics, such as the count of question-answer pairs, the average length of questions and answers, and the number of web pages and sections.

Answering these how-to queries presents significant challenges due to the critical nature of every step involved. It's essential to emphasize that for an answer to the "How to" query to be entirely accurate, each step must be precise, and all steps must be in the correct sequence. Even a minor mistake in the explanation of a step or its order can invalidate the entire utility of the answer. Moreover, the average number of steps per response for a query in the Adobe Acrobat dataset is 4.71, indicating that most queries

Metric	Acrobat	Photoshop
No. of QA pairs	131[a]	96
Avg. length of questions (words)	8.80	12.74
Avg. length of answers (words)	118.71	98.71
Total no. of web pages	146	349
Total no. of sections	1281	2478
Avg. no. of sections per web page	8.78	7.1
Avg. length of the section (words)	135.75	121.09

Table 1: Statistics for the Adobe Acrobat and Photoshop datasets.

[a] The count includes 22 composite questions. We focus on non-composite questions in this work (data analysis and experimentation). Composite Questions are an area for future exploration.

requires multi-step solutions. Below is an example highlighting the necessity for accurate and detailed instructions within every step of the response.

Sample Q&A from the dataset

Q: How to insert Images into a PDF?
A: 1. Open the PDF in Acrobat and go to the `Edit` menu.
2. Select `Image` from the `Add Content` submenu.
3. In the dialog box, choose the image file you want to insert.
4. Select the location where you want to insert the image or use the drag option to resize it as you insert.
5. A copy of the image file will appear on the page with the same resolution as the original file.

Adding to the complexity, a substantial portion of the Acrobat dataset, over 50%, is comprised of implicit questions, defined by their brevity and conversational tone, lacking clear indications of user intent, as shown in Table 2. Furthermore, close to a quarter of the questions of the Acrobat dataset are ambiguous, lacking clear context and leading to multiple potential interpretations of the ask. Our proposed QA framework has been designed considering these challenges and it effectively interprets the user ask.

To assess the generalizability of our proposed QA framework, we curated an additional synthetic dataset focused around Adobe Photoshop product, closely resembling Adobe Acrobat in terms of question type, question and answer lengths, as shown in Table 1. Additionally, the average number of steps per answer for Photoshop dataset is 4.6. However, since these are synthetically framed queries, they are well-formed, explicit, and unambiguous. By contrasting the characteristics of the synthetic dataset with those of Adobe Acrobat, we aim to evaluate the adaptability of our approach.

Moreover, both datasets serve as evaluation benchmarks, representing real-world user queries (both implicit and ambiguous) in Adobe Acrobat and controlled questions in the synthetic Adobe Photoshop dataset. They offer question-answer pairs for diverse scenarios, making them valuable resources for research in the software product domain.

5 Methodology

As summarized by (Zhao et al., 2024; Li et al., 2022; Gao et al., 2024; Lewis et al., 2021), in a standard RAG-QA process, upon receiving an input query, the retriever identifies and retrieves pertinent data sources, which are subsequently utilized by the response generator to enrich the overall generation process. To enable Adobe domain-specific QA, we add an initial query reformulation stage which enhances the user query using knowledge base triples. Query reformulation or rewriting (Anand et al., 2023; Ma et al., 2023) encompasses a set of techniques to transform a user's original query into one that's better aligned with the user's intent, thereby enhancing the retrieval outcomes. Our proposed query reformulation pipeline consists of multiple steps as shown in Fig.1. It starts with the generation of knowledge base triples using the Triples Generator. Next, all matching triples to the user query are retrieved using the Triple Retriever, classified based on their relevance to the original query using the Relevance Classifier and finally reformulated using the Query Enhancer. Refer to Appendix E for the LLM prompts used at various stages. Given below is a detailed outline of the different components in our pipeline:

Step 1: Triples generation. The goal is to represent each document as a collection of triples, each of which represents the key information contained within a document. Each triple is of the form (Source, Action, Target) to mimic what might be asked through a query i.e. assistance to act on a target. E.g., one of the generated triples from a document about editing text and text boxes is (rotation handle, rotate, text box) - the source of the action (rotate) is the rotation handle, which acts on a text box. Similarly, for each document, the LLM contextualizes input text using its vast knowledge base, identifying entities, actions, and relationships, before generating triples by selecting relevant phrases as sources, actions, and targets, informed by inferred context and linguistic patterns. The number of triples for each document varies (approximately 1 to 35 triples) based on the document's content and the model's comprehension. Each triple is then encoded into a numerical vector representation using a pre-trained sentence encoder model which converts the textual elements of the triple into dense vec-

Category	Count of questions (%)	Question Example
Explicit	48 (42.10%)	I need to increase image in PDF towards right direction, how to do that in Acrobat?
Implicit	66 (57.89%)	resize jpg in Acrobat
Ambiguous	28 (24.56%)	Unable to delete PDF content need help.

Table 2: Question Categories with examples in the Acrobat dataset.

tors. These are organized into a high-dimensional index structure, enabling efficient similarity search.

Step 2: Triples Retrieval. This stage accepts the user query as input and then searches the vector store to retrieve all triples related to the query by calculating the similarity scores between the query vector and the vectors of stored triples, utilizing a similarity search algorithm. For every user query, it over-retrieves numerous triples.

Step 3: Relevance Classification. Through the previous step, we obtain numerous triples that have some relevance to the user query. In this stage, we use the capabilities of an LLM to identify only those triples that are the most relevant to the user query. The content of the document along with the list of the triples retrieved in Step 2 are passed to the LLM as a prompt with the instruction that it identifies and return only those triples that are the most relevant to the user's query. Only the triples that are classified as relevant are considered in the subsequent steps.

Step 4: Query Enhancement. Here the user query is reformulated to ensure that it has all the necessary information within it that can help the retriever fetch the correct associated documents. This reformulation is a form of query enhancement where the user query is augmented with words that are used interchangeably in the Adobe products domain. This gives more information for the retriever to use through which it can perform a more accurate search over its vector store and return the documents that are more likely to be relevant. The relevant triples along with the original user query are passed as the prompt to the LLM which rephrases the query.

6 Experiments

We conducted a variety of experiments (as shown in Tables 3 and 4) on the Adobe datasets, where the main datasets formed the corpus of texts to be retrieved from, a selected few of which would be passed in as part of the prompt to the LLM; and the gold set was used for measuring performance. They ranged from using different retrievers to incorporating multiple components and techniques into the RAG-QA pipeline to achieve a performance gain. Throughout the processes we used GPT-3.5 0301 and GPT-4 0314 from Azure OpenAI.

6.1 Baselines

BM25 retriever + LLM: We utilize a BM25 retriever to scan the document corpus and select the top k (k=3) most relevant documents based on the user's query. The relevance of each document is calculated by considering the frequency of query terms within the document and the document's length relative to the entire corpus. These selected documents then serve as contextual input for subsequent response generation tasks.

DPR + LLM: The Dense Passage Retrieval (DPR) method utilizes embeddings to represent passages and queries as vectors, which are then indexed using a similarity search algorithm. When a query is received, DPR compares the vector representation of the query with those of passages in the store, selecting the top k documents with the highest similarity scores as context for answer generation.

General purpose LLM (or QR with no Triples): We add an intermediate step of query reformulation using an LLM to the second baseline. The LLM is instructed to improve the original user query directly without any additional information, i.e. without the addition of domain knowledge into the query.

6.2 Evaluation Methods

We use different metrics to evaluate the performance of the two main components of the RAG-QA pipeline. For retrieval, we employ the Hit Rate

	Retriever	Query reformulation method	Retriever Hit Rate	Answer Similarity Score		
				ROUGE-L	BERTScore	G-Eval
Baselines	BM25	None	41.2%	0.301	0.835	0.412
	DPR	None	73.6%	0.409	0.859	0.574
Ours	DPR	**augmentation with domain-specific triples**	**74.7%**	**0.416**	**0.860**	**0.578**
Ablation	DPR	via general purpose LLM (w/o triple retriever and relevance classifier)	70.2%	0.393	0.855	0.562
	DPR	w/o triple relevance classifier	65.7%	0.385	0.852	0.557
Oracle	DPR	w/o triple retriever (triples obtained from gold documents)	80.7%	0.455	0.870	0.649

Table 3: Performance of baseline methods, our proposed method, and the ablation experiments over Acrobat test set. In all the above experiments, we use GPT3.5 as the LLM for triple generation and answer generation. The semantic similarity scores are computed between the gold and the generated answer. Among ablations, in *w/o triple relevance classifier* setting, we provide all retrieved triples to the query expansion model; in *via general purpose LLM* setting, we only use LLM to reformulate query without including any triples. In the Oracle setting, *w/o triple retriever*, we use gold documents to generate triples and provide them to the relevance classifier. This setting gives us an upper bound on the performance when correct knowledge triples are known. The reported hit rate is the top-3 hit rate.

or the number of times the Gold document was correctly retrieved as the metric. To measure the quality of the generated answers, multiple metrics are explored. As supported by Yang et al. (2023), ROUGE-L (Lin, 2004) was utilized for measuring the lexical overlap between the generated answers and Gold answers, and BERTScore (Zhang et al., 2020) for calculating the semantic overlap by measuring the distances of embeddings between both the answers. Additionally, we incorporate G-Eval with GPT-4 (Liu et al., 2023) as an LLM-based metric to measure the similarity, leveraging its capability to provide a highly adaptable and versatile evaluation with human-like accuracy, enhancing the comprehensiveness of our evaluation approach. Apart from these, we also perform human evaluation to ensure correctness since there is a lack of good metrics for long-form answers (Yang et al., 2023; Fan et al., 2019).

7 Results

7.1 Performance on the Adobe dataset

Table 3 presents the results for baseline methods, our proposed method, and the ablations of different components in our proposed method. We observe that our proposed method outperforms (Hit Rate: 74.7%; GPTEval: 0.58) the baselines without any query reformulation when using BM25 (Hit Rate: 41.2%; GPTEval: 0.41) and DPR retrievers (Hit Rate: 73.6%; GPTEval: 0.57). Among the baseline retrievers, the DPR-based method performs better than the BM25 retrieval. Therefore, we present other results using the DPR retriever.

Our method also performs better than the baseline using simple LLM prompting (i.e., without including any domain-specific knowledge) to reformulate the query (Hit Rate: 70.2%; GPTEval: 0.56). On qualitative examination of reformulated queries, we observe that while query reformulation using a general-purpose LLM can make queries more grammatical or well-formed, it still cannot augment the queries with domain-specific knowledge. On the other hand, our method of using LLM-generated triples can help link entities that have similar meanings within the domain. For instance, for the query "How to convert word docs to pdf," our method retrieves triples that aid in reformulating the query to "How to convert files to pdf," thereby assisting in retrieving the correct document.

7.2 Ablation Studies

Next, we perform a series of ablations on our framework to evaluate the functions of various components in our pipeline.

Ablation on relevance classifier: We directly provide all the triples retrieved by the triples retriever to the query expansion model without filtering out any retrieved triples via the relevance classifier. This approach performs worse than our proposed model (Table 3), since the retrieved triples may include numerous noisy ones, which are then integrated into the query through the query expan-

	Retriever	Query reformulation method	Retriever Hit Rate	Answer Similarity Score		
				ROUGE-L	BERTScore	G-Eval
Baselines	BM25	None	79.17%	0.336	0.822	0.494
	DPR	None	**92.70%**	0.470	0.879	**0.828**
Ours	DPR	**augmentation with domain-specific triples**	**92.70%**	**0.480**	**0.880**	0.776
Ablation	DPR	via general purpose LLM (w/o triple retriever and relevance classifier)	83.33%	0.406	0.859	0.692
	DPR	w/o triple relevance classifier	91.67%	0.447	0.873	0.755

Table 4: Performance of baseline methods, our proposed method, and the ablation experiments over the Photoshop test set. In all the above experiments, we use GPT3.5 as the LLM for triple generation and answer generation. The semantic similarity scores are computed between the gold and the generated answer. The reported hit rate is the top-3 hit rate.

sion model, resulting in a noisy query. Thus, our results highlight the necessity for the relevance classifier to provide only highly relevant triples to the query expansion model.

Ablation on Triple Retriever: In this experiment, we only consider gold documents annotated for a given query in the Adobe dataset and generate triples from them. The generated triples are filtered via the relevance classifier and then fed to the query enhancer. As shown in Table 3, this setting performs the best due to the use of highly relevant triples for query reformulation. Our results highlight the importance of building an efficient triple retriever to improve overall performance.

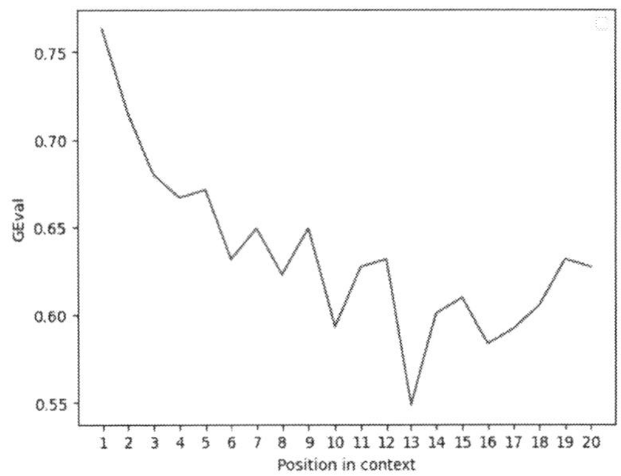

Figure 2: GEval score relative to the position the gold document is passed in as context over Acrobat test set.

7.3 Performance on the Photoshop dataset

Table 4 presents the results over the Photoshop test set. Once again, we observe that our proposed method is on par with the baseline, with a slight decrease in the GEval score. We attribute this to the fact that the Photoshop test set queries are already properly formulated; and reformulating these queries results in a slight deviation, hence the decrease in the G-Eval score. This illustrates that the performance of our proposed method is not dataset-specific. The pipeline is flexible enough to incorporate multiple different corpora - having created the respective knowledge bases.

7.4 Error analysis

While our method is able to link entities that are related in a particular domain, we also observe some cases of errors. For instance, the query 'Create PDFs of specific size by cutting a large PDF into a smaller file size.' was reformulated to 'How can I reduce the size of a PDF file?' as a result of retrieving the following triples :
1. (Reduce File Size command, reduces, size of PDF), 2. (PDF, reduce, size), 3. (PDF Optimizer, reduces, size of PDF files). These triples seemed to focus more on the keyword "size" and seemed to attribute the word "cutting" to reducing, while the intention of the original query was more towards splitting a PDF into multiple PDFs. This reformulation seemed to mis-interpret the original question, which resulted in incorrect retrieval. We attribute the source of such error to the noise originating from the retrieved triples that are irrelevant to the user query. Our analysis further highlights the importance of a high-precision triple retriever, as also suggested by our ablation study, which excludes the triple retriever and relies solely on triples from gold documents. Furthermore, another cause for concern was the similarity score metrics only slightly increasing when compared to their retrieval metric counterparts. We realized that hit rate may

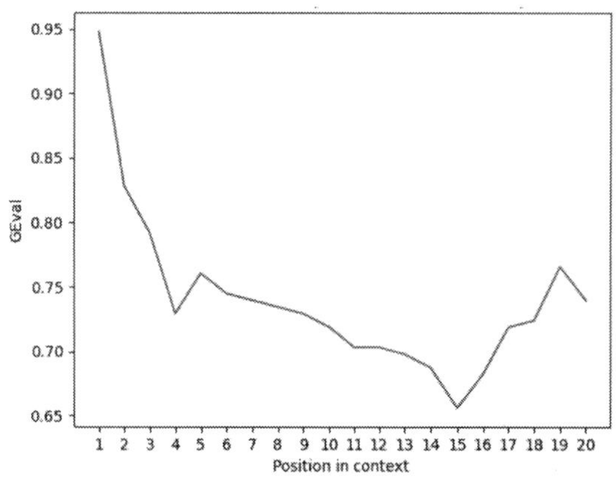

Figure 3: GEval score relative to the position the gold document is passed in as context over Photoshop test set.

not offer a holistic understanding of our retrievers performance. (Ravaut et al., 2024) suggests that LLM's are sensitive and exhibit different utilization of input tokens depending on their position within the context provided, which we also found to be the case as shown in Figure 2 3. It illustrates that the rank, or position, of the retrieved gold document impacts generation to a large extent, and is thus more indicative of proper retrieval than just hit rate alone. Following this, we decided to also consider NDCG as an evaluation metric, and the results are shown in Table 5.

Model	NDCG
Query Reformulation w/ Triples(Proposed Model)	0.447
Query Reformulation w/o Triples	0.453
No Query Reformulation (DPR Baseline)	0.507

Table 5: NDCG values for different models.

7.5 Performance using GPT-4o

Finally, we test our framework using a state-of-the-art model, GPT-4o, as well as different embeddings for the retriever to see how the performance would translate. In this experiment, we pass in a varying number of retrieved documents, and observe the corresponding NDCG and GEval values. Figures 4 and 5 present these results over the Acrobat test set. While the proposed model still outperforms the baseline in both of these metrics, vanilla query reformulation without triples seems to greatly outperform the aforementioned. Upon further qualitative analysis it was inferred that while GPT3.5 was more lax on introducing information from the triples into the query; GPT-4o tried to incorporate all of the information, which resulted in a far nosier query, thus leading to poorer retrieval.

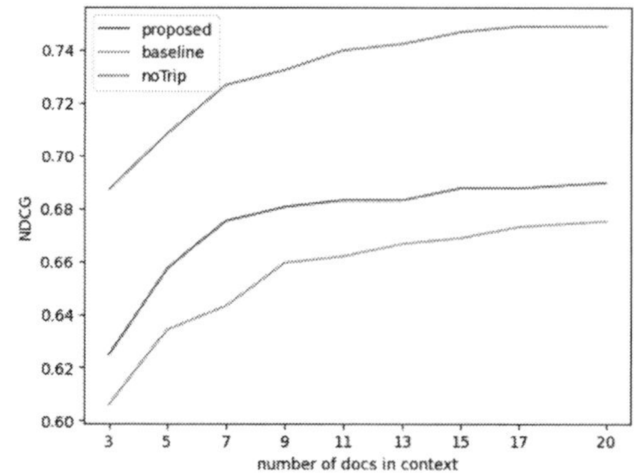

Figure 4: NDCG scores for our proposed model, the DPR baseline, and query reformulation without triples using an LLM (noTrip) over the Acrobat test set.

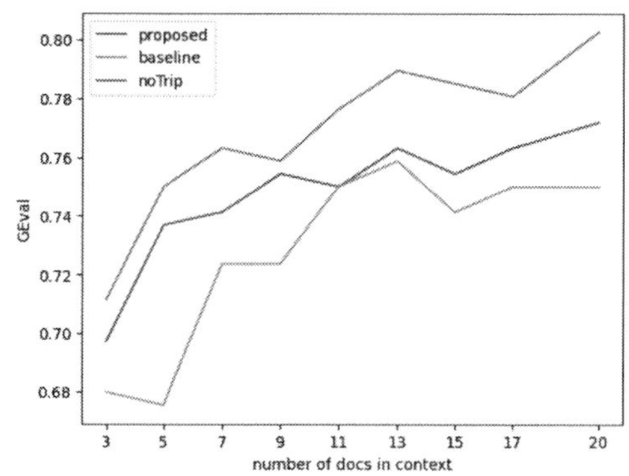

Figure 5: GEval scores for our proposed model, the DPR baseline, and query reformulation without triples using an LLM (noTrip) over the Acrobat test set.

Conversely, we observe the opposite results over the Photoshop dataset, as shown in Figures 6 and 7, which indicate that the baseline outperforms the proposed models in this setting. We attribute this to the fact that the Photoshop test set was synthesized using LLMs, which resulted in accurately formulated queries. In such scenarios, the proposed model under performs the baseline, as it tries to reformulate the query and deviates too much from the original meaning in doing so, thus resulting in poorer retrieval.

8 Conclusion

In this paper, we introduce two QA datasets focused on Adobe Acrobat and Photoshop products, that serve as benchmarks to evaluate an RAG-QA framework tailored for domain-specific procedural long-form QA datasets. We also introduce a novel and detailed pipeline with components directed to improve the retrieval and generation metrics in such QA datasets. It equips LLMs with domain-specific knowledge through the use of Knowledge Base triples to bridge the gap between general RAG-QA methods and industry demands. Through various experiments we showcase the effectiveness and limitations of our proposed pipeline in standard metrics.

9 Limitations

This research presents multiple opportunities for improvement that can be explored further. To enhance the versatility and applicability of our method, it would be advantageous to explore its effectiveness across a broader range of larger industry-specific datasets beyond those provided by Adobe. Additionally, although our RAG-QA framework exhibits advancements over the baselines and offers valuable insights, the noise introduced by the LLM during query reformulation makes room for enhancement in the retrieval process. Moreover, expanding the application of our framework beyond text-based QA scenarios to include multi-modal capabilities opens up exciting new possibilities and broadens its potential impact. Lastly, it's important to note that assessing long-form QA remains an ongoing area of research, highlighting the necessity for a well-defined and automated metric to ensure accurate evaluation. Addressing these limitations is crucial for advancing the efficiency and scope of future research endeavors.

10 Acknowledgments

The authors of this paper would like to thank Hamed Zamani and more generally the entire UMass COMPSCI 696DS course staff for their insightful feedback, as well as the anonymous reviewers for their constructive comments.

References

Abhijit Anand, Venktesh V, Vinay Setty, and Avishek Anand. 2023. Context aware query rewriting for text rankers using llm. *Preprint*, arXiv:2308.16753.

Andong Chen, Feng Yao, Xinyan Zhao, Yating Zhang, Changlong Sun, Yun Liu, and Weixing Shen. 2023a. Equals: A real-world dataset for legal question answering via reading chinese laws. In *Proceedings of the Nineteenth International Conference on Artificial Intelligence and Law*, pages 71–80.

Jiawei Chen, Hongyu Lin, Xianpei Han, and Le Sun. 2023b. Benchmarking large language models in retrieval-augmented generation. *Preprint*, arXiv:2309.01431.

Zhiyu Chen, Wenhu Chen, Charese Smiley, Sameena Shah, Iana Borova, Dylan Langdon, Reema Moussa, Matt Beane, Ting-Hao Huang, Bryan R Routledge, et al. 2021. Finqa: A dataset of numerical reasoning over financial data. In *Proceedings of the 2021 Conference on Empirical Methods in Natural Language Processing*, pages 3697–3711.

Andrei Dulceanu, Thang Le Dinh, Walter Chang, Trung Bui, Doo Soon Kim, Manh Chien Vu, and Seokhwan Kim. 2018. Photoshopquia: A corpus of non-factoid questions and answers for why-question answering. In *Proceedings of the Eleventh International Conference on Language Resources and Evaluation (LREC 2018)*.

Angela Fan, Yacine Jernite, Ethan Perez, David Grangier, Jason Weston, and Michael Auli. 2019. ELI5: Long form question answering. In *Proceedings of the 57th Annual Meeting of the Association for Computational Linguistics*, pages 3558–3567, Florence, Italy. Association for Computational Linguistics.

Masoomali Fatehkia, Ji Kim Lucas, and Sanjay Chawla. 2024. T-rag: Lessons from the llm trenches. *Preprint*, arXiv:2402.07483.

Yunfan Gao, Yun Xiong, Xinyu Gao, Kangxiang Jia, Jinliu Pan, Yuxi Bi, Yi Dai, Jiawei Sun, Qianyu Guo, Meng Wang, and Haofen Wang. 2024. Retrieval-augmented generation for large language models: A survey. *Preprint*, arXiv:2312.10997.

Ivan Ilin. 2024. Advanced rag techniques: an illustrated overview - towards ai. *Medium*.

Rolf Jagerman, Honglei Zhuang, Zhen Qin, Xuanhui Wang, and Michael Bendersky. 2023. Query expansion by prompting large language models. *Preprint*, arXiv:2305.03653.

Feihu Jiang, Chuan Qin, Kaichun Yao, Chuyu Fang, Fuzhen Zhuang, Hengshu Zhu, and Hui Xiong. 2024. Enhancing question answering for enterprise knowledge bases using large language models. *arXiv preprint arXiv:2404.08695*.

Patrick Lewis, Ethan Perez, Aleksandra Piktus, Fabio Petroni, Vladimir Karpukhin, Naman Goyal, Heinrich Küttler, Mike Lewis, Wen tau Yih, Tim Rocktäschel, Sebastian Riedel, and Douwe Kiela. 2021. Retrieval-augmented generation for knowledge-intensive nlp tasks. *Preprint*, arXiv:2005.11401.

Huayang Li, Yixuan Su, Deng Cai, Yan Wang, and Lemao Liu. 2022. A survey on retrieval-augmented text generation. *Preprint*, arXiv:2202.01110.

Jing Li, Shangping Zhong, and Kaizhi Chen. 2021. MLEC-QA: A Chinese Multi-Choice Biomedical Question Answering Dataset. In *Proceedings of the*

2021 Conference on Empirical Methods in Natural Language Processing, pages 8862–8874, Online and Punta Cana, Dominican Republic. Association for Computational Linguistics.

Chin-Yew Lin. 2004. ROUGE: A package for automatic evaluation of summaries. In *Text Summarization Branches Out*, pages 74–81, Barcelona, Spain. Association for Computational Linguistics.

Yang Liu, Dan Iter, Yichong Xu, Shuohang Wang, Ruochen Xu, and Chenguang Zhu. 2023. G-eval: Nlg evaluation using gpt-4 with better human alignment. *Preprint*, arXiv:2303.16634.

Yuanjie Lyu, Zhiyu Li, Simin Niu, Feiyu Xiong, Bo Tang, Wenjin Wang, Hao Wu, Huanyong Liu, Tong Xu, Enhong Chen, Yi Luo, Peng Cheng, Haiying Deng, Zhonghao Wang, and Zijia Lu. 2024. Crud-rag: A comprehensive chinese benchmark for retrieval-augmented generation of large language models. *Preprint*, arXiv:2401.17043.

Xinbei Ma, Yeyun Gong, Pengcheng He, Hai Zhao, and Nan Duan. 2023. Query rewriting for retrieval-augmented large language models. *Preprint*, arXiv:2305.14283.

Grégoire Mialon, Roberto Dessì, Maria Lomeli, Christoforos Nalmpantis, Ram Pasunuru, Roberta Raileanu, Baptiste Rozière, Timo Schick, Jane Dwivedi-Yu, Asli Celikyilmaz, Edouard Grave, Yann LeCun, and Thomas Scialom. 2023. Augmented language models: a survey. *Preprint*, arXiv:2302.07842.

Zooey Nguyen, Anthony Annunziata, Vinh Luong, Sang Dinh, Quynh Le, Anh Hai Ha, Chanh Le, Hong An Phan, Shruti Raghavan, and Christopher Nguyen. 2024. Enhancing q&a with domain-specific finetuning and iterative reasoning: A comparative study. *arXiv preprint arXiv:2404.11792*.

Ankit Pal, Logesh Kumar Umapathi, and Malaikannan Sankarasubbu. 2022. Medmcqa : A large-scale multi-subject multi-choice dataset for medical domain question answering. *Preprint*, arXiv:2203.14371.

Anusri Pampari, Preethi Raghavan, Jennifer Liang, and Jian Peng. 2018. emrqa: A large corpus for question answering on electronic medical records. *Preprint*, arXiv:1809.00732.

Zackary Rackauckas. 2024. Rag-fusion: a new take on retrieval-augmented generation. *arXiv preprint arXiv:2402.03367*.

Mathieu Ravaut, Aixin Sun, Nancy F. Chen, and Shafiq Joty. 2024. On context utilization in summarization with large language models. *Preprint*, arXiv:2310.10570.

Spurthi Setty, Katherine Jijo, Eden Chung, and Natan Vidra. 2024. Improving retrieval for rag based question answering models on financial documents. *arXiv preprint arXiv:2404.07221*.

Zhihong Shao, Yeyun Gong, Yelong Shen, Minlie Huang, Nan Duan, and Weizhu Chen. 2023. Enhancing retrieval-augmented large language models with iterative retrieval-generation synergy. *Preprint*, arXiv:2305.15294.

Fangkai Yang, Pu Zhao, Zezhong Wang, Lu Wang, Jue Zhang, Mohit Garg, Qingwei Lin, Saravan Rajmohan, and Dongmei Zhang. 2023. Empower large language model to perform better on industrial domain-specific question answering. *Preprint*, arXiv:2305.11541.

Wenhao Yu, Dan Iter, Shuohang Wang, Yichong Xu, Mingxuan Ju, Soumya Sanyal, Chenguang Zhu, Michael Zeng, and Meng Jiang. 2023. Generate rather than retrieve: Large language models are strong context generators. *Preprint*, arXiv:2209.10063.

Tianyi Zhang, Varsha Kishore, Felix Wu, Kilian Q. Weinberger, and Yoav Artzi. 2020. Bertscore: Evaluating text generation with bert. *Preprint*, arXiv:1904.09675.

Penghao Zhao, Hailin Zhang, Qinhan Yu, Zhengren Wang, Yunteng Geng, Fangcheng Fu, Ling Yang, Wentao Zhang, Jie Jiang, and Bin Cui. 2024. Retrieval-augmented generation for ai-generated content: A survey. *Preprint*, arXiv:2402.19473.

Haoxi Zhong, Chaojun Xiao, Cunchao Tu, Tianyang Zhang, Zhiyuan Liu, and Maosong Sun. 2019. Jec-qa: A legal-domain question answering dataset. *Preprint*, arXiv:1911.12011.

Fengbin Zhu, Wenqiang Lei, Youcheng Huang, Chao Wang, Shuo Zhang, Jiancheng Lv, Fuli Feng, and Tat-Seng Chua. 2021. Tat-qa: A question answering benchmark on a hybrid of tabular and textual content in finance. *arXiv preprint arXiv:2105.07624*.

Yuqi Zhu, Xiaohan Wang, Jing Chen, Shuofei Qiao, Yixin Ou, Yunzhi Yao, Shumin Deng, Huajun Chen, and Ningyu Zhang. 2024. Llms for knowledge graph construction and reasoning: Recent capabilities and future opportunities. *Preprint*, arXiv:2305.13168.

A Code Release

We will release the code along with the data at `https://github.com/daksh-dangi/KaPQA` upon getting the required permission from Adobe.

B Prompt Structures

In this section we have listed the high-level structure of all the prompts used for the components of our pipeline.

Triples Generator LLM prompt

System:
You are an assistant for the Adobe Acrobat application that helps create tuples of the form (source, action, target) based on the information given to you.

User:
You are given a section from an adobe help document. Extrapolate the most relevant relationships you can from the context and generate tuples of the form (source, action, target). Ensure that the sources, actions, and targets are directly present in the provided context.\n
You must use only the provided data in variable 'Context' to identify relationships.\n
You must not use any other information from any other source or from previous knowledge beyond the provided 'Context'.\n
Example: If the document contained the phrase "To edit the image, first click on the triple line menu", one relevant tuple would be (triple line menu, edit, image). Here, the source of the action (editing the image) is the triple line menu. The direct effect of this action is on the image, hence that is the target. In a similar manner, create tuples for the provided context.
Context: <CONTEXT>
Constraints:\n
1. The created tuples must form the same format as the example provided.\n
2. The source and target in the tuple must only reference objects or menu items, and no actions\n
3. Ensure that the tuples generated are all related to the title of the section: <SECTION HEADER>\n
4. Only generate the most relevant tuples for the provided document with the given section header\n
5. You must make the contents of the tuples short and concise\n
6. Ensure the words "Adobe", "PDF", and "Acrobat" are not in the generated tuples.\n

Relevance Classifier LLM prompt

System:
You are an assistant for the Adobe Acrobat application. You are designed to filter out the information provided and classify what is most relevant to the given query.

User:
A user has provided you with the following query: <USER QUERY>\n
Use the data given in the variable 'Context' to classify which of the data elements are most relevant to the user's query.\n
Data in the 'Context' variable is of the form (source, action, target), where the first value contains the source of the action that is directed towards the target.
Example: One data element could be (triple line menu, edit, image). If the query was asking about how to edit an image, this element would be relevant. However, if the query was instead asking how to edit a video, it would be very irrelevant, and hence should not be included. The presence of a query word in the tuple does not make it relevant, look at the meaning as well when you are considering relevance. In a similar manner, filter out the context for the provided provided document.
Context: <CONTEXT>
Constraints:\n
1. Retrieve the data elements that are most relevant to the action that the user is trying to do in the query provided.
2. Ensure that the source and target of the data elements retrieved are similar to what is present in the query. \n
4. Give the most relevant data elements in a numbered list, and only provide the data elements themselves. No explanation.\n

Query Enhancer LLM prompt

System:
You are an assistant that is designed to only enhance user queries.

User:
You are given a query by the user and you must enhance the query by only using the data provided in variable 'Tuples'. The 'Tuples' variable is of the form (source, action, target).\n
Constraints:\n
1. Rephrase the query using the provided tuples, but do not change the meaning of the initial query.\n
2. Only use information from the tuples that are relevant to the query to reform the query.\n
3. Make the rewritten query one sentence at most.\n
4. Re-write the query in a manner similar to how a human might search for an answer on a help page. Keep the query short.\n
5. Only reformulate the given query, without answering it.\n
6. You must not use any other information from any other source or from previous knowledge beyond the provided 'Tuples'.\n
7. Ensure the words "Adobe" and "Acrobat" are not in the query.\n
8. Only answer with one reformulated query. Example:\n
Given Query: 'how to remove letters from a text box'\n
Tuples: (text, delete key, remove),(page thumbnail, delete key, remove), (text, font item, edit), (text, font item, remove)\n
Reformulated Query: how to delete text
In a similar manner, reformulate the query below.
Given Query: <USER QUERY>
Tuples: <Tuples>
Reformulated Query:

DPR + General purpose LLM Prompt

System:
You are an assistant for the Adobe application that is designed to only enhance user queries. When asked about anything that does not relate to Adobe, only reply with 'Content not found'

User:
You are asked a question by the user and you must enhance the query. Do not answer the query, only change it's wording.\n
You must not use any other information from any other source or from previous knowledge beyond the query provided.\n
Understand what might be the cause of confusion, and rewrite the query by trying to model what the user could have been asking.\n
Ensure that the reformulated query is bound by the given constraints.\n
Query to be enhanced: "query" Constraints:\n
1. Make the rewritten query one sentence at most.\n
2. Make sure that the rewritten query does not have any excessive adjectives, and is short and to the point.\n
3. Only reformulate it, without answer it.\n
4. Only answer with the reformulated query.

C Graphs of Evaluation Metrics across models using GPT-4o

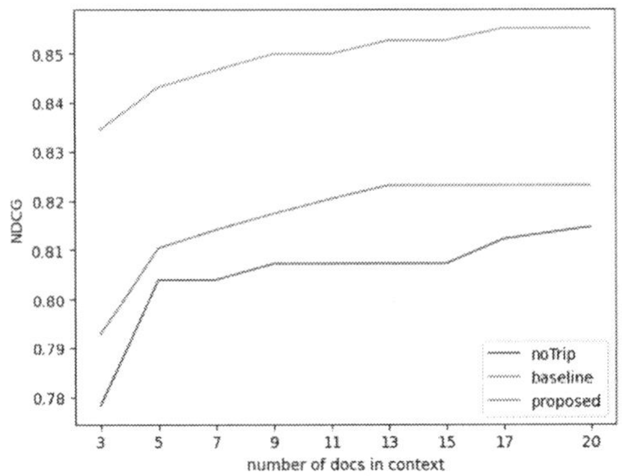

Figure 6: NDCG scores for our proposed model, the DPR baseline, and query reformulation without triples using an LLM (noTrip) over the Photoshop test set.

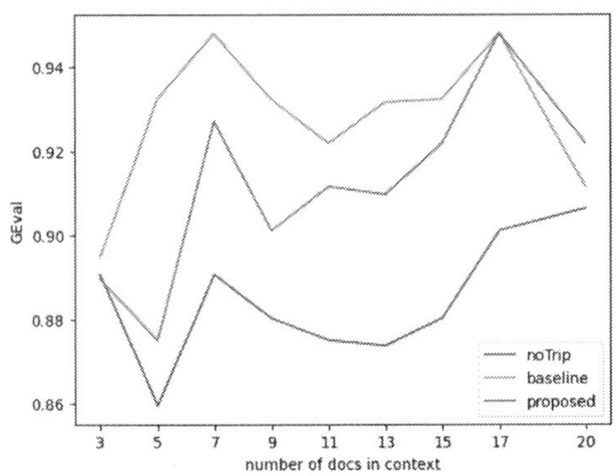

Figure 7: GEval scores for our proposed model, the DPR baseline, and query reformulation without triples using an LLM (noTrip) over the Photoshop test set.

D Examples of proposed method outperforming DPR + GPT3.5.

We have listed some examples in Table 6 where the proposed model using query reformulation outperforms the DPR + GPT3.5 baseline.

E Examples of proposed method under performing DPR + GPT3.5

We have listed some examples in Table 7 where the proposed model using query reformulation under performs the DPR + GPT3.5 baseline.

Original query	Reformulated Query	Generated Answer without QR	Generated Answer with QR	Gold Answer
test box resizing in acrobat	How to resize a text box or text in a PDF using the Edit panel in Acrobat?	To resize a box in Acrobat, follow these steps: 1. Open the PDF file in Acrobat.2. Choose the hamburger Menu (Windows), or the File menu (macOS) > Print. 3. Select Size, and choose one of the following options: - Scales small pages up and large pages down to fit the paper. [...] 4. If you don't see a Page Scaling options, click the arrow next to the Printer menu to expose more controls in the Print dialog box.	To resize a text box in Acrobat, follow these steps: 1. Select the text box you want to resize by clicking on it. 2. Drag one of the selection handles on the edge of the box to resize it. 3. To maintain alignment with other list items, press Shift as you drag. That's it! You have successfully resized the text box in Acrobat.	1. Choose 'Edit' from the mega verb bar. The PDF switched is to edit mode and the Edit PDF panel will be displayed. 2. Click on an edge of the text box to select it. 4. Drag any of the handles that appear on the corners or edges of the text box to resize it.
adding image on a pdf file	What are the different ways to add images to a PDF file?	To add an image to a PDF file, follow these steps: 1. Open the PDF file in Acrobat. 2. Choose Edit from the menu and select the image or object you want to edit. 3. If you want to edit multiple items together in the same file, select them all. 4. Under Adjust Objects in the Edit panel, select Edit using, and then choose an editor. 5. Make the desired changes in the editor. 6. Choose File > Save in the editor to save the changes. 7. The object is automatically updated and displayed in the PDF when you bring Acrobat to the foreground. If you want to copy and paste an image [...] file or a clipboard.	To add an image to a PDF file, follow these steps: 1. Open the PDF file in Acrobat. 2. Select Edit PDF̈from the right-hand pane. 3. Click on Image in the toolbar. 4. Select the image file you want to insert. 5. Choose where you want to insert the image or drag to resize it as you insert. 6. Once the image is added, you can move or resize it by hovering over the image and using the move or resize icons. 7. To adjust the image further, select Image from the left panel, [...] select File > Save.	1.Open the PDF in Acrobat and go to the 'Edit' mega verb. 2. Select 'Image' from the 'Add Content'. 3. In the dialog box that appears, choose the image file you want to insert. 4. Select the location where you want to insert the image or use the drag option to resize it as you insert. 5. A copy of the image file will appear on the page with the same resolution as the original file.
Are we allowed to crop images in a pdf file?	Can images be edited and added to a PDF file?	Yes, you can crop images in a PDF file using Adobe Acrobat. Here are the steps to do so: 1. From the top tools bar, select Edit. Alternatively, select the All tools menu > Edit a PDF.2. It displays the Edit toolset in the left panel. 3. From the Edit tools menu, select Crop Pages. 4. Drag a rectangle on the section that you want to crop. If necessary, drag the corner handles of the cropping rectangle until the page is the size you want.5. Double-click [...] 8. Select OK.	Yes, you can crop images in a PDF file using Adobe Acrobat. Here are the steps to do so: 1. Open the PDF in Acrobat and select Edit. 2. Choose the image you want to crop. 3. Under Adjust Objects in the Edit panel, select Crop Image. 4. Drag the cropping handles to adjust the size of the image. 5. Click outside the image to apply the crop. 6. Save the PDF.	1.Open the PDF in Acrobat and go to the Edit mega verb.2. select the image you want to crop.3. In the Adjust Objects section of the Edit panel, choose the Crop image tool.4. A selection handle will appear around the image. Drag the selection handles to adjust the cropping area.5. Once you have selected the desired area to crop, click outside the selection to apply the crop.The image will be cropped to the selected area.

Table 6: Examples of proposed method outperforming DPR + GPT3.5.

Original query	Reformulated Query	Generated Answer without QR	Generated Answer with QR	Gold Answer
How can I create PDFs from all non-pdfs stored in a directory? Is it possible to do it in one go.	Is it possible to convert all non-PDF files in a folder to PDFs with electronic features using Adobe Acrobat?	To create PDFs from all non-PDFs stored in a directory in one go, follow these steps:1. In Acrobat, select Create from the global bar.2. The Create a PDF tool opens. On the left rail, select Multiple files > Create multiple PDF files, and then select Next.3. Choose Add Files > Add Files or Add Folders, and then select the files or folder.4. Select OK. The Output options dialog box appears.5. In the Output Options dialog box, specify your target folder and filename preferences, and then select OK.[...]	To create PDFs from all non-PDFs stored in a directory, you can follow these steps:1. In Acrobat, select Create from the global toolbar.2. The Create a PDF tool opens. On the left rail, Single file is selected by default. Choose the Select a file button.3. In the Open dialog box, navigate to the directory where your non-PDF files are stored.4. Select all the non-PDF files you want to convert to PDF.5. Select Create to convert the files to PDF.6. Depending on the type [...] using this method.	1. You can create multiple PDFs from multiple native files, including files of different supported formats, in one operation. [...] 1. In Acrobat, select Create from the global bar.2. The Create a PDF tool opens. On the left rail, select Multiple files > Create multiple PDF files, and then select Next.3. Choose Add Files > Add Files or Add Folders, and then select the files or folder.4. Select OK. The Output options dialog box appears.5. Specify your target folder and filename preferences, and then select OK.
I need to create a link on a PDF.	How can I add a link to a PDF document?	To create a link on a PDF, follow these steps:1. In the source document, choose Edit > Link > Add or edit a link.2. Drag a rectangle to specify a location for the link.3. In the Create Link dialog box, set the link appearance.4. Select Go to a page view, and then select Next.5. In the target document, [...] create a link.	To create a link on a PDF, follow these steps:1. Choose the Select tool.2. Position the pointer over the linked area on the page until the pointer changes to the hand with a pointing finger. A plus sign (+) or a w appears within the hand if the link points to the web. Then click the link.3. In the Create Link [...] for a link to work correctly.	1. Choose Edit > Link > Add or edit a link. The pointer becomes a cross-hair, and any existing links in the document, including invisible links, are temporarily visible.2. Drag a rectangle where you want to create a link. This is the area in which the link is active.3. In the Create Link dialog, choose the options you want for the link appearance.4. Select one of the following link actions:- Go to a page viewSelect Next [...] associated with the link.
How to remove password from the PDF	How to remove password protection from a PDF?	To remove password from a PDF, follow these steps:1. Open the PDF in Acrobat.2. Go to All tools > Protect a PDF > Remove security.3. If prompted, type the permissions password. If you don't know the permissions password, contact the author of the PDF.4. Acrobat will remove the security from the PDF and you will be able to access it without a password.	To remove password from a PDF, follow these steps:1. Go to All tools > Protect a PDF > Protect with password from the Protect a PDF toolset in the left pane.2. Choose Editing.3. Type and retype your password. Your password must be at least six characters long. The password strength is displayed next to your password [...] using the password.	You can remove security from an open PDF if you have the permissions to do so. If the PDF is secured with a server-based security policy, only the policy author or a server administrator can change it.1. Open the PDF, then select All tools > Protect a PDF > Set security properties.2. In the Document Properties window, select the Security tab and then select Change settings.3. Your options vary [...] Select OK again to confirm the action.

Table 7: Examples of proposed method under performing DPR + GPT3.5.

Collecting High-quality Multi-modal Conversational Search Data for E-Commerce

Marcus D. Collins **Eugene Agichtein** **Oleg Rokhlenko** **Shervin Malmasi**
Amazon.com, Inc. Seattle, WA, USA
{collmr,eugeneag,olegro,malmasi}@amazon.com

Abstract

Continued improvement of conversational assistants in knowledge-rich domains like E-Commerce requires large volumes of realistic high-quality conversation data to power increasingly sophisticated LLM chatbots, dialogue managers, response rankers, and recommenders. The problem is worse for multi-modal interactions in realistic conversational product search and recommendation. Here, an artificial sales agent must interact intelligently with a customer using both textual and visual information, and incorporate results from external search systems, such as a product catalog. Yet, it remains an open question how to best crowd-source large-scale, naturalistic multi-modal dialogue and action data, required to train such an artificial agent. We describe our crowd-sourced task where one worker (the Buyer) plays the role of the customer, and other (the Seller) plays the role of the sales agent. We identify subtle interactions between one worker's environment and their partner's behavior mediated by workers' word choice. We find that *limiting* information presented to the Buyer, both in their backstory and by the Seller, improves conversation quality. We also show how conversations are improved through minimal automated Seller "coaching". While typed and spoken messages are slightly different, the differences are not as large as frequently assumed. We plan to release our platform code and the resulting dialogues to advance research on conversational search agents.

1 Introduction

In recent years, researchers have investigated new approaches to build automated agents capable of naturalistic conversations satisfying complex information needs. The need for such assistance is particularly acute in domains like E-Commerce, where customers may even know what questions to ask when shopping. Creating an automated agent to help such customers is challenging, as it must serve as a natural conversational interface to many specialized and general data sources, while maintaining context to return valuable responses or make proactive suggestions. In high-stakes domains like E-Commerce, experimentation on real customers is risky, presenting a significant barrier to training and validating such conversational agents. Most task-oriented conversation systems, especially for E-Commerce, have been evaluated on synthetic data even though such data may not reflect real world conversations (Gangadharaiah et al., 2018). Thus there is a clear need for high-quality and realistic data to be collected to allow training more natural automated agents. Moreover, it isn't clear *how to generate natural data that reflects real-world conversations in domains like E-Commerce*. Although Large Language Models such as ChatGPT can be used to generate conversation, these are not realistic as shopping conversations are dynamic and customer goals can change as new information is presented (Bernard and Balog, 2023).

We explore crowd task designs needed to collect the *right data* to train conversational search and recommender agents, roughly following a theoretical framework (Radlinski and Craswell, 2017). Such agents combine aspects of a mixed-initiative chat-like dialogues with goal oriented systems, creating a number of unique challenges. Consider Example 1. The Customer seeks help from the Agent with a specific goal, buying a TV set, but the conversation is open-ended. Unlike, say, airline reservation systems, there are few constraints on the utterances. In addition, Agent and Customer share initiative. The Agent must choose from several information sources to help construct a reply. Figure 1 shows a standard framework to provide such an experience. A language understanding module extracts information from customer utterances, used by the dialog manager to query sources, including product catalogs, QA databases, *etc.* A ranker selects among candidates to produce each system response.

Proceedings of the 3rd Workshop on Knowledge Augmented Methods for NLP, pages 30–43
August 16, 2024 ©2024 Association for Computational Linguistics

Example Dialog

Customer: I'm looking for a good sized TV for my living room.
Agent: Nice! How much are you looking to spend?
Customer: 400 dollars
Agent: Do you mostly watch TV shows, or maybe you want something for gaming?
Customer: I like to watch movies and play video games
Agent: How big? What about resolution?
Customer: at least 42 inches. what's resolution?
Agent: number of pixels per inch. Higher is better.
Customer: I don't care
Agent: Ok, do you care about refresh rate? Or brand?
Customer: I like Sony. It should be at least 120 frames per second.
Agent: OK, Sony has 3 TVs that match. Do you have another criteria you care about?
Customer: Not really.
Agent: Here's some options for you, what do you think of these? (pastes in links or uses sharing widget)
Customer: Ooh, there's one I like. I'll take a look.
[One of the shared options; system evaluates it, workers may continue if they like it.]

Example 1: An example dialog illustrating a desirable E-Commerce conversation with an automated agent (when we refer to an Agent, we mean an automated agent).

To train such an agent, we need a corpus of high-quality naturalistic, free-form, but goal-oriented conversations labeled with each action's intent and overall conversation success. Recently one such dataset was released (Moon et al., 2020) with a large number of conversations related to furniture and fashion. However, there is no exploration of the conversations' naturalness, or of how the multi-modal environment affects the results. Moreover, it isn't clear that such a corpus is ecologically valid (Vries et al., 2020), i.e., it isn't clear that the information and tools provided to the workers realistically emulate how customers would interact with automated or human sales agents. To ensure that, we aim here to understand how the conversation participants' multi-modal environment affects the conversation, and to add to the available conversational search and recommendation data.

We review prior work in the next section to put our contributions in context. Section 3 describes how we crowd-sourced conversations. Section 4 covers the development of our crowd-sourced annotations and automated measures of the conversation. We analyze the collected conversation data in Section 5, and demonstrate the effectiveness of the collected data to enable a robust conversational search and recommendation agent. Finally, we discuss future work and potential extensions in Section 6.

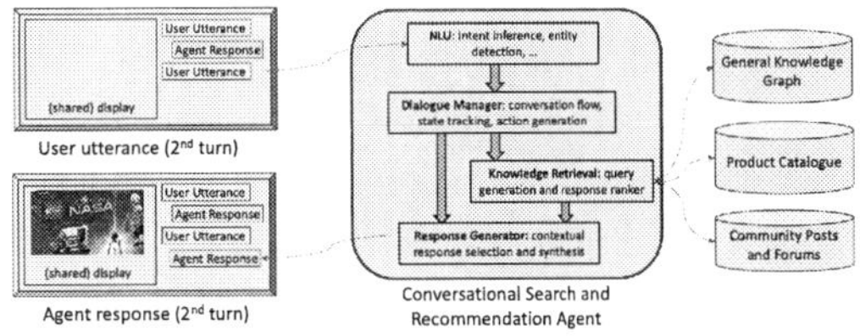

Figure 1: Illustration of a conversational search system that can act as the Agent in Example 1.

Contributions and Research Questions Multi-modal, conversational search opens up many questions. We focus on how the workers' environment — the information and tools provided to each worker — affects their interactions with each other. To that end, we aim to answer four research questions:

R1 How does one worker's environment affect their behavior and language use?

R2 Can one worker's *environment* alter the other's behavior including language and feature use?

R3 How much do spoken and typed utterances differ in a conversational search environment?

R4 What Buyer and Seller environments yield the most realistic conversations?

Our work for the first time explores and analyzes the most effective conditions for priming workers in large-scale, crowd-sourced conversational data collection, with multiple interaction modalities, and introduces quantitative evaluation metrics for dialogue quality, which, as we demonstrate, could be used to train a conversational E-Commerce search and recommendation agent.

2 Related Work

Automated conversational agents have been an active area of study, and their use has exploded following the success of voice-based conversational agents such as Siri, Alexa, and Google Home Assistant. A long-term goal for dialogue systems is to coherently and engagingly converse with humans on a variety of topics (Guo et al., 2018; Venkatesh et al., 2018; Khatri et al., 2018). However, such systems require extensive engineering or extensive training data collection and annotation, or both. Below, we review prior approaches to collecting and annotating data for training conversational agents. We focus mostly on task-oriented agents in complex domains such as search and recommendation, i.e., information-oriented and transactional tasks (Radlinski and Craswell, 2017; Zhang et al., 2018).

2.1 Task Completion Agents

For well-structured tasks like travel reservations (Bobrow et al., 1977) or movie ticket purchases, rule-based dialogue systems can be effective, but require significant engineering to design possible responses and appropriate dialogue flow. Beginning with early systems such as Eliza, rule-based dialogue management (DM) systems (Bobrow et al., 1977) have been steadily improving in sophistication and flexibility (Chen et al., 2017).

Recently, end-to-end learning for automated conversational agents approaches has grown in popularity, due in part to improvements in neural architectures and the availability of general-purpose training data, e.g. (Serban et al., 2018). The idea of conversation has also been introduced as a way to elicit user interests for item recommendation (Christakopoulou et al., 2016). For example, Sun and Zhang (2018) introduced an end-to-end reinforcement learning framework for a personalized conversational sales bot, and Li et al. (2018) use a combination of deep-learning based models for conversational movie recommendation.

2.2 Knowledge-grounded Agents

Corpus-based chatbots mine human-human conversations, often collected via crowd-sourcing or by scraping online resources. (Serban et al., 2018) summarizes available corpora up to 2017, including online human-human chats, Twitter, and in-movie dialog. However, these resources are not helpful to train knowledge-, task- or information-oriented conversational agents to provide or recommend useful information for a specific topic like a purchasing decision. To improve the knowledge retrieval process, several teams have recently introduced frameworks to incorporate external knowledge in response generation as well as actively learn concepts through conversations (Dinan et al., 2018; Luo et al., 2019; Jia et al., 2017; Ghazvininejad et al., 2018). Despite these advances, the underlying knowledge is essentially encoded, e.g. in a neural network. This is not feasible for extensible, large, or frequently updated domains, such as product information, or sources lacking a rich search mechanism. The closest effort to this is a system outlined in (Gur et al., 2018), which learned to query a reservations system from extensive logs of human interactions with the system. Such logs are naturally not available for privacy reasons. Thus, to train such agents, a conversation collection tool must be specifically designed to incorporate dynamically retrieved external knowledge from a search engine, with the associated queries and actions.

2.3 Previous Conversation Collections

Recently, a number of shared tasks and challenges have pushed researchers to develop more intelligent chat bots capable of in-depth conversations on numerous topics, not just *small talk*. Resulting conversations have been evaluated both by crowd workers and live users as part of the Alexa Prize Conversational AI challenge (Venkatesh et al., 2018). Some public datasets have been made available as a by-product of the challenge. (Dinan et al., 2018) introduced a valuable resource for crowd-sourcing conversations in a "Wizard of Oz" interface, used to collect restaurant reservation dialogs (CamRest676 dataset) (Wen et al., 2017); the Frame corpus in a more complex travel booking domain (El Asri et al., 2017), and a corpus of in-car navigation conversations (KVRET corpus) (Eric et al., 2017). Later, this approach was extended to conversations on multiple topics (Budzianowski et al., 2018). (Gopalakrishnan et al., 2019) complemented that work with a large corpus of topical conversations between crowd workers asked to discuss an assigned topic, but without specific suggestions or aspects to discuss.

A data set of *coached* movie discussions between a "Wizard" and an "Apprentice" was introduced by (Radlinski et al., 2019). Conversations did not have a specific goal, but unlike previous efforts the "Wizards" were instructed to follow a general script and ask prescribed questions about movie preferences. The resulting data set may be helpful for recommender systems. In other work, searchers asked "intermediaries"–other workers–to find information for them on complex tasks via voice input and output, with only the "intermediary" having access to the search engine (Trippas et al., 2017, 2018). The resulting data set, while valuable, was limited to a small number of participants in the laboratory study. The study's open-ended nature makes it hard to scale to sufficiently large and robust data collection required to train effective automated search agents.

While there has been substantial recent work in leveraging Large Language Models (LLMs) such as ChatGPT and GPT-4 to generate conversations (Brown et al., 2020; Han et al., 2021; Li et al., 2023), these approaches have not had much success in the E-Commerce domain due to the dynamic range of customer behavior, which is quite different from info-seeking scenarios where LLMs excel. This trend is reflected in Bernard and Balog (2023), where the authors release a collection of 64 high-quality shopping conversations encompassing various goals. The size of this data also reflects the challenges in scaling data collection in this domain, a key factor that we try to address. Most recently, Joko et al. (2024) used LLMs to provide workers with guidance on what to say, ostensibly to simplify collection of these complex conversations, but they collected less than half the conversations we have.

These previous efforts provide large corpora of human-human conversations grounded on specific topics, but are neither sufficient to learn to *search and retrieve*, nor to *incorporate* external, dynamically retrieved information, nor to lead the dialogue towards a task completion, which is the focus of our work. Furthermore, the ability to share rich information items, such as product descriptions or picture, is critical for an effective search-oriented conversational system. Prior work left as open questions *how* to collect such conversation and action data for complex search and recommendation tasks; how interaction modality variations affect the richness, and ultimately overall quality, of the resulting dialogue; and even how to measure dialogue quality in such crowd-sourced efforts.

3 Crowdsourced Conversation Task

Our crowd tasks pair "Buyers" with "Sellers" in a E-Commerce search simulation. Our goal is to simulate the in-store experience of asking a salesperson for assistance. Therefore, we wanted to learn how Seller behavior changes when Buyers come with varied shopping-related knowledge and needs. It has been long-held that voice and text interactions are very different, but this has largely been tested for simple text search, not conversation. To answer our research questions, we tested several product search and display features, and additionally the impact of a voice interface for the Buyer. We collected 1,500 conversations, on which we based on our analysis. We then collected 1503 more conversations under what we found were the best conditions, described in Table 1, which we publicly release.[1]

Below we describe key features of our conversation task. Further details, including the modified ParlAI/Mechanical Turk (Miller et al., 2017) framework, audio transcription, and the catalog used, may be found in the Appendices.

3.1 Layout and Conversation Flow

Each worker's interface (Figure 2) displays products at left, and a chat pane right for interacting with their partner. Both are given instructions before beginning the chat, but can view them again at any time. In particular, both workers are made aware they will be chatting in real time with another person, that the text and other interactions will be stored for future research use. The Seller first picks product categories they are familiar with. To increase variety, we kept track of each worker's choices, which they could not repeat within one week, unless they work through all categories in that time. The Buyer then chooses the category from the Seller's options, and opens the conversation with a request.

Buyer view In the left pane, the Buyer sees context about why and for what they are shopping (their "persona"), and three target products which match their context. The Buyer's goal is to guide the Seller to one of those products by asking and answering questions. The info shown varies depending on the experimental conditions (Section 3.3), but can include product title, details (price, age range, etc.), description, and images. The personas describe a shopping mission, e.g., "My four year old daughter loves Star Wars", or "I want really good headphones for home listening to classical music, but I don't have an unlimited budget". Each persona is specific to a particular product category.

Seller view Seller have a search box at upper right, and a limited interface for sorting and scanning search results. They have several options for

Topic	Count	Mean Turns
books	135	6.5
headphones	303	6.9
Lego	252	6.3
pet food	209	6.6
running shoes	187	6.8
smartwatches	294	6.6
vitamins	123	6.7

Table 1: Statistics of the data we will release. One turn is an exchange between the two users. These were collected under condition B.IIc, see Section 3.3 for details.

[1] https://github.com/marcuscollins/woa-ecommerce-conversations

Figure 2: A screenshot of the worker chat windows: Buyer view (top), in priming condition B (Section 3.3) with no product details available, and Seller view (bottom), in a "coached" condition. Search results, search box, message history, and the Seller checklist are shown.

sharing products, set by the experimental conditions. In all conditions, sellers can describe the product or provide a product URL to the Buyer. In some conditions, Sellers are allowed to copy/paste the URL directly from the product description. Another option is to click "Share Now" on the product and enter a message; product details and message are then immediately displayed to the Buyer. We experimented with a "recommendation list" that allowed the Seller to display several products at once to the Buyer for comparison. In one setting Sellers were "coached" with a variety of actions before, visible in Figure 2, and described below.

Ending the conversation The conversation continues at least until Buyer and Seller meet a minimum number of turns (usually 5). The Seller can then make a formal guess (by pressing the "Guess" button), which the Buyer can confirm or reject. The Buyer may also end the conversation at any point after the minimum number of turns. Or, the two can continue the conversation as long as they wish.

3.2 Product Search and Catalog

We selected seven categories: Lego, smartwatches, books, vitamins, running shoes, headphones, and pet food, each with 3-4 personas and 2,207 total products. We chose these categories to cover diverse but still common interests (gifts, technology, recurring purchases), but we did not do any statistical analysis showing them to be the most common amongst real shoppers. The exact products were chosen by searching Amazon.com using queries based on each of the personas, taking the top 100 results, and removing duplicates. More details are in Appendix A.3.

3.3 Experimental Settings

We tested four variables: Buyer *priming*, Seller sharing tools, coaching Sellers, and Buyer voice versus text message entry, each detailed below. To save cost and maximize benefit, we only tested voice transcription and seller coaching with some base conditions. These settings represent different ideas of what information a customer would have when shopping, and the tools a salesperson could use to make effective suggestions. For instance, salespeople are usually trained, and even scripts of how to interact with customers, reflected in our "coaching" condition. Buyers come to the store with different prior knowledge. Indeed, as we'll show, the aspects we condition them to focus on heavily influence their behavior.

Buyer Priming Priming describes what the Buyer is shown about their persona and target products. We used three settings:

A. one product image per product, with no other details or persona.

B. one product image per product and the persona.

C. full product details and persona.

D. a single image, with a pop-up displaying additional images, and the persona.

Seller sharing settings Sellers are assigned one of three levels for how they can share products. At each level Seller has all tools in the lower levels. So, Sellers in condition *II* can still share URLs in message text in addition to sharing a product in a modal dialog.

I. Only URLs can be shared, and only by including them in the message text.

II. All attributes of a single product can be shared in a modal dialog shown to the Buyer, with an optional message from the Seller.

III. The Seller can create a list of multiple products to share in a similar modal dialog.

Seller coaching "Coached" Sellers first choose an action from a list (Table 3, Figure 2) before sending a message to the Buyer. This yields dialog act labels and suggests important actions Sellers should take. To develop the list we consulted a separate set of Mechanical Turk workers about retail sales. We used coaching only with priming *B* and sharing *II* and refer to it as condition B.IIc.

Voice transcription We finally tested voice transcription for condition B.IIc. only. For privacy reasons no audio was stored, only the text transcript. Workers are asked to test their audio transcription first, shown how to correct the transcription if it has errors, and reminded that only text, no audio, will be stored. See Appendix A.2 for further details.

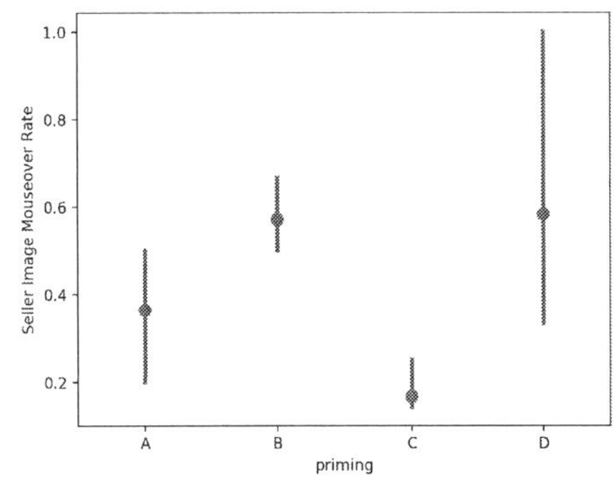

Figure 3: Median and 95% confidence bounds for the product image mouse-over rate per conversation turn, for each of the four priming conditions.

4 Evaluation

Noting that evaluating conversations remains difficult and subjective, we use a variety of measures to understand workers' behavior in our crowd-sourced conversations. We quantify conversations with automated linguistic measures, language modeling, worker surveys, and manual annotation.

4.1 Automated Measures

We computed a number of common language features derived from tri-gram language models and parsing. We use SpaCy[2] for dependency parsing and POS tagging. From the parse tree, we compute utterance-level mean and maximum token depths. We computed perplexity using the NLTK `lm` module.[3] We build the language model from all available conversations, and compute mean perplexity per word at the conversation level, sometimes limited to just Buyer or Seller utterances.

4.2 Language Modeling

To show that Buyer priming influences *Seller* behavior we developed a Poisson regression of word usage in different priming conditions; model details are in Appendix B.

4.3 Manual Annotation

Separate crowd workers evaluated several aspects of conversation quality at both chat and message level. They labeled many chats at once to improve task understanding and consistency of results. Herein, we focus on annotations of overall chat quality. Often these are highly subjective, so we focused on questions that were either quantitative, e.g. "Did the Buyer ask questions about the products?" or had unconventional framing, e.g. "Would you hire this Seller, if you owned the store?". These proved to be the questions that most clearly distinguish between different experimental conditions. We built a Plackett-Luce ranking model (Plackett, 1975; Luce, 1959) to learn a quantitative score for each condition. More details are in Appendix B.

In comparing coached/un-coached Sellers, annotators chose the better Seller from two randomly-paired conversations in the same product category. We modeled the ordered pair data with a Logistic Regression accounting for the presentation order.

5 Results

Below, we answer our research questions. We show in particular that Buyers' priming (i.e., their *environment*) significantly alters their behavior and language use (R1), that Buyers' environment significantly alters *Sellers'* behavior (R2). Finally, we find that while there are some differences between spoken and typed conversational messages, these differences are not as large as would be expected from studies of keyword-style spoken and typed search queries (R3). We address what are the "best" conditions (R4) throughout this section.

5.1 Buyer priming influences Seller behavior

When Buyers were given the most details (priming *C*), *Sellers* viewed fewer products and scrolled less over product images (Figure 3). We guessed that Buyers focused on the first attributes they saw, and mention only these to Sellers, who naturally

[2] www.spacy.io

[3] www.nltk.org/api/nltk.lm.html

Budget words		Brand and rating words	
word	*coefficient*	*word*	*coefficient*
around $	-3.0	stars	-2.7
dollars	-2.4	adidas	-2.3
pay	-1.8	apple watch	-2.5
pay $	-2.8	audio-technica	-3.5
something $	-3.5	pegasus	-3.4
us	-3.3	plantronics	-3.8
usd	-4.4	saucony	-2.6

Table 2: Interaction coefficients between priming with details and specific words. The model is log-linked (Eqn. 1), so a coefficient of -3.0 indicates the word is used e^3 20 times less often when showing fewer details.

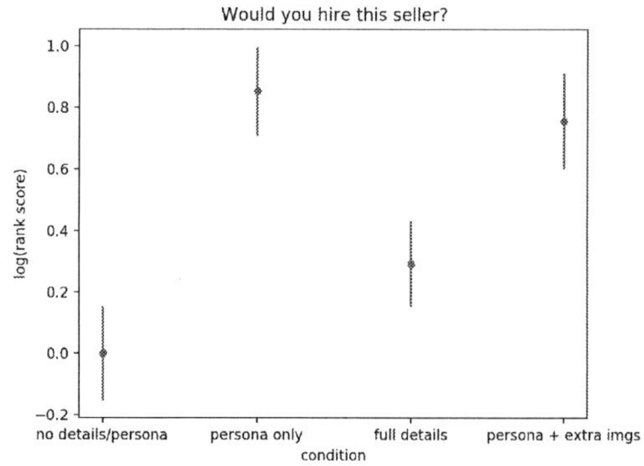

Figure 4: Plackett-Luce scores for the question "Would you hire this Seller, if you owned the store?" with 95 % confidence limits for the four priming conditions.

focus on what the Buyer says. To understand this, we investigated Buyers' word choice in different priming conditions.

The language model shows that Buyers *not* shown product details used budget- and brand-related words much less than Buyers who are shown product details. Table 2 lists words significantly ($p < 0.01$) influenced by product detail priming.

Buyers' word choice is clearly influenced by priming. To show that Buyer word choice led to the *Sellers'* behavior, we tested whether Buyer priming and Seller image mouse-overs are *conditionally independent* of each other, given Buyers' use of words identified by our language model. χ^2-tests of hover-rate and priming reveal that Buyers' word use is what influences Sellers. Specifically, we constructed the tables $P(h, p)$ and $P(h, p|\{w\}_{bb})$ with (binned) hover rate h, priming p, and words $\{w\}_{bb}$ from Table 2. The table conditioned on $\{w\}_{bb}$ yields a χ^2 p-value of 0.34, while without conditioning p is essentially zero, indicating that Buyer use of brand and budget words drives Sellers to ignore other details and images.

We conclude that providing certain product details results in more formulaic, less diverse language from Buyers, i.e., environment clearly influences their language use (R1). This leads Sellers to focus on fewer product aspects and examine fewer products to find a good fit for the Buyer, so one worker's environment clearly alters the other's behavior (R2). To generate the most natural and interesting conversations (R4), the Buyer should not see details like brand and price.

5.2 Sellers are rated higher if Buyers see fewer details

Annotators ranked priming condition B (personas and images but no product details) highest on the question "Would you hire this Seller, if you owned the store?" (Figure 4). Buyer priming affects not just click and hover actions, but overall Seller quality as well (R2). Our findings demonstrate that the best conversations come when we show Buyers only minimal product details.

5.3 Multi-modal sharing may impact the conversation

So far, we have focused on how the Buyer's priming affects both Buyer's and Seller's behavior. Do the Seller's options they have for sharing results have similar impact? We made a Plackett-Luce model of sharing conditions' impact on annotators responses to "Would you hire this Seller...?" We determined scores for conditions I, II, and III to be 0 ± 0.31, -0.19 ± 0.32, and -0.61 ± 0.37 respectively; that is, annotators felt Sellers did a better job when using only text to share products. However, we find that Buyers rated conversations as more natural in condition II, where Sellers were able to share a single product at a time with complete details. The ratings, on a scale of 1-4, were 2.61 ± 0.030, 2.67 ± 0.027, and 2.48 ± 0.066 for conditions I, II, and III respectively. For the best conversations (R4) we should limit Sellers to sharing simple, single results with perhaps one image.

5.4 Coached Sellers are Preferred

Specifically focusing on how to generate the highest quality conversations (R4), we hypothesize that some kind of coaching should improve Seller quality and indeed this proves true.

Coached Sellers are rated higher than uncoached Sellers We randomly sampled 30 conversations each from B.II with and without coaching and generated pairs of conversations in the same category. We then asked annotators to choose which Seller they preferred of two conversations from the same category. Annotators preferred coached Sellers in 60% of cases, $p \approx 0.013$.

Coaching Sellers results in better dialog from both Buyers and Sellers We analyzed both Buyer and Seller linguistic features to see what might make for more convincing Sellers. An example dialog from this experiment is shown in Appendix C. Coached Sellers used more long utterances (Mann-Whitney test $p \approx 0$), which we suspect indicate to Buyers that Seller is engaged. Coached Sellers' utterances have 12.6% higher perplexity in a 2-gram language model built over all conversations ($p \approx 7.7 \times 10^{-5}$). And, coached Sellers use slightly more complex language, measured by dependency tree depth (1.82 ± 0.049 average token depth versus 1.71 ± 0.035, $p = 0.012$.) We were surprised to find that the conversation partners weakly prefer simpler language. For instance both Buyers and Sellers rate their partner's message clarity slightly lower as the 2-gram perplexity per word increases. (Spearman's $\rho = -0.24$, $p = 0.00003$. Moreover, there is no correlation between annotators' "hire this Seller" rating and any of these linguistic features.

We examined detailed aspects of the dependency parsing and find that coached Sellers use fewer compound words and clausal compounds (e.g., "Let's see what **we can find**") but more compound descriptions, indicating language that is more descriptive but less complex. We observe that Buyers language use also appears to be different when Sellers are coached or not. At this point, we have no firm conclusions what, if any, linguistic features influence annotators ratings of conversation quality.

While we still don't have clear evidence explaining why coached Sellers do a better job, we do conclude that Seller coaching improves conversations overall, helping to answer R4.

5.5 Spoken and Typed Queries are Different

Experiments by Guy (2016), based on web searches in the Yahoo mobile app which had an option to speak the query, are frequently cited. In that study, voice queries were longer and there are noticeable differences in the queries used. In particular, the most distinctive tri-grams in voice reflect fully formed natural language questions, while text queries more strongly resemble keyword queries. Voice queries are much more likely to start with "wh-" question words.

Do those findings hold true in conversational systems (R3)? We tested a variant of priming condition B with voice transcription for Buyers only; Sellers still typed queries. Our findings are quite different than previous work. Perplexity is not significantly different between voice and typed utterances. Buyer voice utterances are on average a word shorter than typed utterances (10.0 vs. 9.0, $p \approx 0$). Surprisingly, Seller utterances are also shorter (10.3 vs. 8.7 words, $p \approx 0$), even though Sellers only type their responses; again Sellers seem to adapt to Buyer language. Finally, unlike Guy (2016) we find at most small differences in parts-of-speech usage between Buyers with and without voice transcription. The largest difference is that 11.7% of Buyer tokens are pronouns with voice, versus 11.0% without voice, just a 0.7% absolute difference. We see a much lower fraction of nouns than in search queries. Search queries were largely dominated by nouns, while we see roughly equal fractions of nouns, pronouns, and verbs.

Taken together, we find that while there are significant differences in voice and typed utterances in a task-oriented conversation, they are not as marked as for individual web search queries. Conversation in general likely leads to more complete and structured sentences, and the use of back-references like anaphora, while people typing web queries will focus on keywords and not use anaphora.

5.6 Results Summary

We have shown in a number of ways that worker environment (i.e., Buyer priming, multi-modal sharing, and coaching sellers) impacts worker behavior (R1). For instance, Buyers view fewer images when presented with other product details, and their language is altered by what they view; when we similarly prime Sellers by coaching them on what questions to ask, they use longer sentences and more diverse language. And we showed that at least

Buyer priming does impact Seller behavior (R2), although it still isn't clear whether the opposite is true, that Seller coaching or different forms of result sharing impact Buyer behavior or language. We found minimal differences in language use for Buyers who spoke or typed their messages (R3) in contrast to general search queries, which are quite different when spoken or typed. Most importantly, we found several ways in which to improve overall conversational quality (R4): limiting Buyer priming to personas and images, coaching Sellers, and limiting multi-modal sharing to single results, or simply sharing links or product titles.

6 Conclusions

We have highlighted several important results that should advance future efforts to crowd-source conversations for effective conversational multi-modal search. First, spoken and typed messages are not as different as previously thought. We attribute this to the conversational nature of the task. This suggests that transfer learning approaches that take advantage of the more plentiful text-based conversations are a promising avenue for voice systems as well.

Importantly, conversational partner's behavior– both "private" behaviors like mouse-overs as well as the language used to communicate–affects the other partner's behavior as well, and we found we can influence both behaviors through priming. Our results show that task design must both direct the desired behaviors as much as possible (e.g., Seller coaching) but must avoid providing too much information. We should look for opportunities to influence Seller behavior in the Buyer's environment as well. We emphasize that the more structure the Seller has, the better the resulting conversations.

Our findings have implications for voice assistants as well: workers will do what we've taught them to do, and ask questions only about the information we present to them. Therefore, to enable good conversational systems for search and exploration, strategies to prime customers with a knowledge of the actions they can take, and the information they can obtain are critical. For instance, if a system presents "price" as a key attribute to customers, our results show that customers are more likely to focus on price in their product exploration.

References

Nolwenn Bernard and Krisztian Balog. 2023. Mgshopdial: A multi-goal conversational dataset for e-commerce. In *Proceedings of the 46th International ACM SIGIR Conference on Research and Development in Information Retrieval (SIGIR '23), July 23–27, 2023, Taipei, Taiwan*, SIGIR '23.

Daniel G Bobrow, Ronald M Kaplan, Martin Kay, Donald A Norman, Henry Thompson, and Terry Winograd. 1977. Gus, a frame-driven dialog system. *Artificial intelligence*, 8(2):155–173.

Tom Brown, Benjamin Mann, Nick Ryder, Melanie Subbiah, Jared D Kaplan, Prafulla Dhariwal, Arvind Neelakantan, Pranav Shyam, Girish Sastry, Amanda Askell, et al. 2020. Language models are few-shot learners. *Advances in neural information processing systems*, 33:1877–1901.

Paweł Budzianowski, Tsung-Hsien Wen, Bo-Hsiang Tseng, Iñigo Casanueva, Stefan Ultes, Osman Ramadan, and Milica Gašić. 2018. MultiWOZ - a large-scale multi-domain wizard-of-Oz dataset for task-oriented dialogue modelling. In *Proceedings of the 2018 Conference on Empirical Methods in Natural Language Processing*, pages 5016–5026, Brussels, Belgium. Association for Computational Linguistics.

Hongshen Chen, Xiaorui Liu, Dawei Yin, and Jiliang Tang. 2017. A survey on dialogue systems: Recent advances and new frontiers. *Acm Sigkdd Explorations Newsletter*, 19(2):25–35.

Konstantina Christakopoulou, Filip Radlinski, and Katja Hofmann. 2016. Towards conversational recommender systems. In *Proceedings of the 22nd ACM SIGKDD international conference on knowledge discovery and data mining*, pages 815–824, New York, NY, USA. ACM, Association for Computing Machinery.

Emily Dinan, Stephen Roller, Kurt Shuster, Angela Fan, Michael Auli, and Jason Weston. 2018. Wizard of wikipedia: Knowledge-powered conversational agents. *arXiv preprint arXiv:1811.01241*.

Layla El Asri, Hannes Schulz, Shikhar Sharma, Jeremie Zumer, Justin Harris, Emery Fine, Rahul Mehrotra, and Kaheer Suleman. 2017. Frames: a corpus for adding memory to goal-oriented dialogue systems. In *Proceedings of the 18th Annual SIGdial Meeting on Discourse and Dialogue*, pages 207–219, Saarbrücken, Germany. Association for Computational Linguistics.

Mihail Eric, Lakshmi Krishnan, Francois Charette, and Christopher D. Manning. 2017. Key-value retrieval networks for task-oriented dialogue. In *Proceedings of the 18th Annual SIGdial Meeting on Discourse and Dialogue*, pages 37–49, Saarbrücken, Germany. Association for Computational Linguistics.

Rashmi Gangadharaiah, Balakrishnan Narayanaswamy, and Charles Elkan. 2018. What we need to learn if we want to do and not just talk. In *Proceedings of the 2018 Conference of the North American Chapter of the Association for Computational Linguistics:*

Human Language Technologies, Volume 3 (Industry Papers), pages 25–32, New Orleans - Louisiana. Association for Computational Linguistics.

Marjan Ghazvininejad, Chris Brockett, Ming-Wei Chang, Bill Dolan, Jianfeng Gao, Wen-tau Yih, and Michel Galley. 2018. A knowledge-grounded neural conversation model. In *Thirty-Second AAAI Conference on Artificial Intelligence*.

Karthik Gopalakrishnan, Behnam Hedayatnia, Qinlang Chen, Anna Gottardi, Sanjeev Kwatra, Anu Venkatesh, Raefer Gabriel, and Dilek Hakkani-Tür. 2019. Topical-Chat: Towards Knowledge-Grounded Open-Domain Conversations. In *Proc. Interspeech 2019*, pages 1891–1895.

Fenfei Guo, Angeliki Metallinou, Chandra Khatri, Anirudh Raju, Anu Venkatesh, and Ashwin Ram. 2018. Topic-based evaluation for conversational bots. In *NIPS*.

Izzeddin Gur, Ulrich Rueckert, Aleksandra Faust, and Dilek Hakkani-Tur. 2018. Learning to navigate the web. *arXiv preprint arXiv:1812.09195*.

Ido Guy. 2016. Searching by Talking: Analysis of Voice Queries on Mobile Web Search. In *Proceedings of the 39th International ACM SIGIR Conference on Research and Development in Information Retrieval*, page 35–44, New York, NY, USA. Association for Computing Machinery.

Ting Han, Ximing Liu, Ryuichi Takanabu, Yixin Lian, Chongxuan Huang, Dazhen Wan, Wei Peng, and Minlie Huang. 2021. Multiwoz 2.3: A multi-domain task-oriented dialogue dataset enhanced with annotation corrections and co-reference annotation. In *Natural Language Processing and Chinese Computing: 10th CCF International Conference, NLPCC 2021, Qingdao, China, October 13–17, 2021, Proceedings, Part II 10*, pages 206–218. Springer.

Panagiotis G. Ipeirotis, Foster Provost, and Jing Wang. 2010. Quality management on amazon mechanical turk. In *Proceedings of the ACM SIGKDD Workshop on Human Computation*, HCOMP '10, pages 64–67, New York, NY, USA. ACM.

Robin Jia, Larry Heck, Dilek Hakkani-Tür, and Georgi Nikolov. 2017. Learning concepts through conversations in spoken dialogue systems. In *Proc. of ICASSP*, pages 5725–5729. IEEE.

Hideaki Joko, Shubham Chatterjee, Andrew Ramsay, Arjen P de Vries, Jeff Dalton, and Faegheh Hasibi. 2024. Doing Personal LAPS: LLM-Augmented Dialogue Construction for Personalized Multi-Session Conversational Search. *arXiv*.

K. Sparck Jones, S. Walker, and S.E. Robertson. 2000. A probabilistic model of information retrieval: development and comparative experiments: Part 1. *Information Processing & Management*, 36(6):779 – 808.

Chandra Khatri, Rahul Goel, Behnam Hedayatnia, Angeliki Metanillou, Anushree Venkatesh, Raefer Gabriel, and Arindam Mandal. 2018. Contextual topic modeling for dialog systems. In *IEEE 2018 Spoken Language Technology (SLT)*. IEEE.

Raymond Li, Samira Ebrahimi Kahou, Hannes Schulz, Vincent Michalski, Laurent Charlin, and Chris Pal. 2018. Towards deep conversational recommendations. In *Advances in Neural Information Processing Systems*, pages 9748–9758.

Siheng Li, Cheng Yang, Yichun Yin, Xinyu Zhu, Zesen Cheng, Lifeng Shang, Xin Jiang, Qun Liu, and Yujiu Yang. 2023. AutoConv: Automatically generating information-seeking conversations with large language models. In *Proceedings of the 61st Annual Meeting of the Association for Computational Linguistics (Volume 2: Short Papers)*, pages 1751–1762, Toronto, Canada. Association for Computational Linguistics.

R. Duncan Luce. 1959. *Individual Choice Behavior: A Theoretical Analysis*. John Wiley and Sons, New York, NY, USA.

Liangchen Luo, Wenhao Huang, Qi Zeng, Zaiqing Nie, and Xu Sun. 2019. Learning personalized end-to-end goal-oriented dialog. In *Proceedings of the AAAI Conference on Artificial Intelligence*, volume 33, pages 6794–6801.

Alexander Miller, Will Feng, Dhruv Batra, Antoine Bordes, Adam Fisch, Jiasen Lu, Devi Parikh, and Jason Weston. 2017. ParlAI: A dialog research software platform. In *Proceedings of the 2017 Conference on Empirical Methods in Natural Language Processing: System Demonstrations*, pages 79–84, Copenhagen, Denmark. Association for Computational Linguistics.

Seungwhan Moon, Satwik Kottur, Paul A Crook, Ankita De, Shivani Poddar, Theodore Levin, David Whitney, Daniel Difranco, Ahmad Beirami, Eunjoon Cho, Rajen Subba, and Alborz Geramifard. 2020. Situated and Interactive Multimodal Conversations. *arXiv*.

Robert L. Plackett. 1975. The Analysis of Permutations. *Appl. Statist*, 24(2):193–202.

Filip Radlinski, Krisztian Balog, Bill Byrne, and Karthik Krishnamoorthi. 2019. Coached conversational preference elicitation: A case study in understanding movie preferences. In *Proceedings of the Annual SIGdial Meeting on Discourse and Dialogue*.

Filip Radlinski and Nick Craswell. 2017. A theoretical framework for conversational search. In *Proceedings of the 2017 conference on conference human information interaction and retrieval*, pages 117–126. ACM.

Skipper Seabold and Josef Perktold. 2010. Statsmodels: Econometric and statistical modeling with python. In *9th Python in Science Conference*, pages 92 – 96.

Iulian Vlad Serban, Ryan Lowe, Peter Henderson, Laurent Charlin, and Joelle Pineau. 2018. A survey of available corpora for building data-driven dialogue systems. *Dialogue & Discourse*, 9(1):1–49.

Yueming Sun and Yi Zhang. 2018. Conversational recommender system. In *The 41st International ACM SIGIR Conference on Research & Development in Information Retrieval*, pages 235–244. ACM.

Johanne R Trippas, Damiano Spina, Lawrence Cavedon, Hideo Joho, and Mark Sanderson. 2018. Informing the design of spoken conversational search: perspective paper. In *Proceedings of the 2018 Conference on Human Information Interaction & Retrieval*, pages 32–41. ACM.

Johanne R Trippas, Damiano Spina, Lawrence Cavedon, and Mark Sanderson. 2017. How do people interact in conversational speech-only search tasks: A preliminary analysis. In *Proceedings of the 2017 Conference on Conference Human Information Interaction and Retrieval*, pages 325–328. ACM.

Anu Venkatesh, Chandra Khatri, Ashwin Ram, Fenfei Guo, Raefer Gabriel, Ashish Nagar, Rohit Prasad, Ming Cheng, Behnam Hedayatnia, Angeliki Metallinou, Rahul Goel, Shaohua Yang, and Anirudh Raju. 2018. On evaluating and comparing conversational agents. In *NIPS*.

Harm de Vries, Dzmitry Bahdanau, and Christopher Manning. 2020. Towards Ecologically Valid Research on Language User Interfaces. *arXiv*.

Tsung-Hsien Wen, David Vandyke, Nikola Mrkšić, Milica Gašić, Lina M. Rojas-Barahona, Pei-Hao Su, Stefan Ultes, and Steve Young. 2017. A network-based end-to-end trainable task-oriented dialogue system. In *Proceedings of the 15th Conference of the European Chapter of the Association for Computational Linguistics: Volume 1, Long Papers*, pages 438–449, Valencia, Spain. Association for Computational Linguistics.

Yongfeng Zhang, Xu Chen, Qingyao Ai, Liu Yang, and W Bruce Croft. 2018. Towards conversational search and recommendation: System ask, user respond. In *Proceedings of the 27th acm international conference on information and knowledge management*, pages 177–186.

A Implementation details

A.1 ParlAI and Mechanical Turk frameworks

We modified ParlAI's (Miller et al., 2017) Mechanical Turk platform for our experiments. We incorporate features for logging worker click and scroll behavior, product search and sorting, and multi-modal product search result sharing. We also implemented audio transcription capabilities with Amazon AWS Transcribe. Finally, the entire system is configurable to easily deploy experiments with different combinations of conditions. We plan to release our code in the near future.

We required participants to use modern web browsers on non-mobile devices and originate in predominantly English-speaking countries: US, UK, Canada, Australia, and New Zealand. We required participants to have completed 1000 or more accepted HITs with $> 98\%$ acceptance rate on Mechanical Turk.

A.2 Voice transcription

Buyers were asked to test their voice transcription beforehand to ensure it worked correctly, as it did not work with all browsers. To begin, workers clicked a green "Start Transcription" button, which then flashes red and reads "Stop Transcription". A red flashing bar indicates that transcription is in progress. Transcription lags a few seconds, but is generally real time. Buyers can edit the transcription to correct any errors, but we found this was rare. We stored both raw and edited transcripts for later analysis.

For privacy reasons, no audio is kept. Sellers never used voice transcription.

A.3 Catalog

Each category has 3-4 personas (23 total), and each of those is assigned three target products. The catalog is completed with roughly 100 related products for each persona, some of which overlap (2,207 total). The product search feature is a very simple keyword search over product title and description; this is sufficient to locate products in our small catalog. Search is implemented using the `whoosh` Python package.[4] Sellers can sort search results by price and rating as well, to help them adapt to specific Buyer personas focused on value or quality.

A.4 Seller dialog acts

Table 3 lists all "coaching" actions available to Sellers in condition B.IIc. As shown in Figure 2 some "follow-up" actions are unavailable until others are used first.

B Evaluation details

B.1 Poisson word-usage model

We used `statsmodels` (Seabold and Perktold, 2010) to implement several different models describing word usage. Based on deviance, we found

[4] `https://whoosh.readthedocs.io`

#	text
1	Greet your partner, ask them how they are, what you can help them with.
2	Ask your partner if they are shopping for themselves, or someone else.
3	Ask your partner how they (or whoever they're shopping for) will use product.
3a	Learn more about the intended use, e.g. what breed of dog, do they have a favorite trail to run, etc...
3b	Share your thoughts or experiences relating to your partner's intended use of the product, e.g. a favorite podcast or musician, a child who likes a particular toy.
4	Ask your partner if they've owned something similar before.
4a	If they've owned something similar before, what did they like or dislike about what they've owned before.
5	Ask your partner if they're looking for particular features.
5a	(If more than one) which feature is most important to your partner?
6	Ask your partner how long they want to keep/own/use the product.
7	Ask your partner about their budget.
8	Ask your partner if they prefer a particular brand or brands.
9	Make a product recommendation with an explanation of why you think it is a good fit, and ask for their feedback.
9a	If your partner isn't completely satisfied with your recommendation, ask what wasn't right, or what could be better.
9b	After your partner accepts a recommendation, ask them how was their experience? Was there something that could have been better?
10	Thank your partner for their business.

Table 3: **Seller message actions.** Questions with a letter following the index number can only be asked as follow-ups to the corresponding unlettered question.

the best model to be

$$\log y = \boldsymbol{\theta}_w \cdot \boldsymbol{w} + \boldsymbol{\theta}_t \cdot \boldsymbol{t} + \boldsymbol{\theta}_{w} \boldsymbol{t} \cdot (\boldsymbol{w} \otimes \boldsymbol{t}) + \boldsymbol{\theta}_{pt} \cdot (\boldsymbol{p} \otimes \boldsymbol{t}) + \boldsymbol{\theta}_{wp} \cdot (\boldsymbol{w} \otimes \boldsymbol{p}), \quad (1)$$

where $\vec{w}$ are n-gram word features ($n \geq 3$), $\vec{p}$ the priming conditions, and $\vec{t}$ the chosen topic. $\otimes$ indicates the Cartesian product, and all $\vec{\theta}$ are (one-d) parameter vectors. Note that this model explicitly captures the interactions between the chosen topic and priming conditions. Statistical feature selection was performed to reduce the model dimension. We apply χ^2 tests to contingency tables of Buyer word occurrence and Seller behavior features to determine significant words.

B.2 Manual annotation details

As with the main crowd task, we took standard measures to ensure quality results, such as using "gold" test questions and excluding annotators with below 80% accuracy, and requiring a minimum time working on each task. Nonetheless, we found workers predictably over-rate the quality of conversations on any given aspect, resulting in skewed distributions and low variance. For example, annotators were probably overly accepting of conversation quality, as measured by the question "Would you hire this seller?" (Figure 5

Even filtering out low quality annotators (say, with the approach of (Ipeirotis et al., 2010)) simple statistical comparisons failed to reveal significant results, although they did provide some hints at differences between the conditions. To overcome the homogeneity of annotators' responses, we aggregated each worker's ratings to make a partial ranking over the experimental conditions. Workers who rate all chats the same are dropped, implicitly removing low-quality annotations. This partial ranking was then modeled using the Plackett-Luce framework mentioned in the main text.

B.3 Seller preference model

In evaluating Sellers in paired conversations, annotators showed a significant bias towards the second conversation of two presented; this *Context Effect* is probably most familiar in multiple-choice surveys, where it is addressed by randomly ordering the choices, as we have done here[5].

[5] https://methods.sagepub.com/reference/encyclopedia-of-survey-research-methods/n439.xml

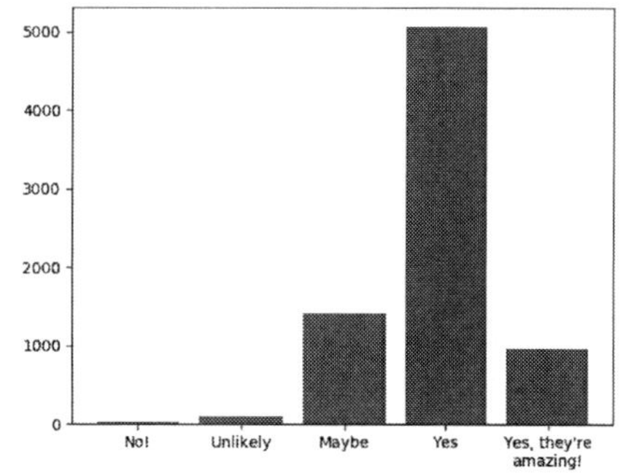

Figure 5: Distribution of responses to the question "Would you hire this Seller, if you owned the store?"

C Example dialog

Note. It has been suggested to us that the Buyer seems to "forget" the age of their child, and suggested this is an attempt to extend the conversation and meet the minimum number of turns. We suspect instead they failed at first to fully read their persona, which included the child being three years old, not six. In any event, we don't find this mistake particularly unnatural.

D Case Study: Retrieval-based Product Search and Recommendation Agent

We evaluated our data by creating a simple automated conversational search agent from it, as illustrated in Figure 1. Crowd workers tested the automated agent in a human-in-the-loop setting.

D.1 Conversational Agent Prototype

We collected 1,500 additional conversations in condition B.IIc. Our agent retrieves the most relevant archived response for the current context, using `whoosh` with BM25 ranking (Jones et al., 2000), for simplicity. It performs product search as needed. Queries are formed from Buyer utterances, with smaller weight for older utterances.

Heuristics improve the candidate responses. A simple bag-of-words logistic regression classifier identifies the product category; once known, our agent limits results to responses for just that category. We limit some dialog acts, like budget or brand questions, to be used at most once per conversation. (Recall Sellers labeled dialog acts as part of their task). Finally, we prevent similar responses from being given more than once.

After a minimum three turns, Product search is triggered if a candidate response is a product recommendation or mentions a product, or if no other

Conversation between a LEGO Buyer and a coached Seller

Buyer hi there, im looking for some legos for my kids. are these good for 6 year olds?
Seller They sure are! They are great for hand/eye coordination and problem solving skills! Do you know what kind of set you may be looking for? Do they have any specific likes or interests that may translate to a lego set we have for you?
Buyer awesome, they love trucks! anything out there with trucks?
Seller (*searches "lego truck set", "lego truck set 6"*) They do! I'll send a suggestion in just a moment. First, do you have a particular budget?
Buyer ok perfect, no particular budget, just don't want to break the bank. my child is actually 3, i got them mixed up with my niece somehow. didnt have enough coffee!
Seller (*searches "lego truck set 3"*) How about this? This has bigger LEGO pieces so it is less complicated. (*shares details for LEGO Duplo Big Construction Site 10813*)
Buyer That is perfect! thanks so much.
Seller Yay! I am so glad. Your child will love this set! Before you go, was everything to your satisfaction? Is there anything more I can do for you?
Buyer Absolutely everything went great. I'm sure they'll love it too. Thank you again!

Example 2: Conversation in condition B.II with coaching. Note that we use Seller and Buyer here, as this is a real conversation between two crowd workers in our task, *not* between an automated Agent and a real Customer.

suitable response is available. When the agent cannot retrieve a response, it constructs one using the following strategies, in order: find another response in the archive which mentions the desired product and still scores well; construct a response from product description highlights based on the current context; or use a default generic response. Despite the simplicity of the agent, we will show that due to the high quality of our conversational corpus, the agent often performs on par with experienced crowd-workers.

D.2 Results of Human-in-the-Loop Agent Test

The agent's best 3-5 candidate responses were presented to human crowd workers acting as Sellers, who could select one of the candidates, or create their own response. We can then evaluate conversation quality in two ways. We asked annotators to rate the conversations individually, as above. We also quantify how often Sellers used the agent-recommended responses in each conversation, i.e., whether the agents' response was accepted by the human crowd worker.

Figure 6 summarizes our findings. We grouped conversations by the fraction f of Seller responses generated by the computer agent. So, if the Seller used the agent response without editing in three of five turns, then $f = 0.6$. A significant fraction of Sellers appeared to either be unaware of how to use the agent recommendations or didn't want to use them. We separate these conversations into the '0' group. Fig. 6 shows that there is no statistically significant difference between the different bins in f. Furthermore, there is no statistical difference from conditions B.II or B.IIc, whose quartiles are shown in red and blue, respectively.

The distribution of f is shown at the bottom of Figure 6. About 10 % of conversations do not use the agent recommendations at all. Overall, slightly more than 40 % of responses used in all conversations were from the agent. Given our simple retrieval-based agent, the results are promising and demonstrate the value of our corpus. In future work we aim to improve our agent by exploring more sophisticated dialogue management, response ranking models, and generalization.

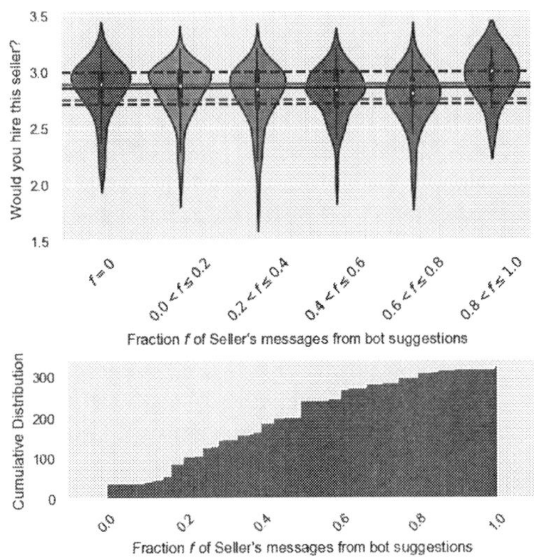

Figure 6: (Top) Violin plot of annotator ratings on the question "Would you hire this Seller?", grouped by the fraction of responses in each conversation generated by the retrieval agent. (Bottom) Cumulative Distribution of retrieval-agent response use fraction f.

Learning to Trust Your Feelings: Leveraging Self-awareness in LLMs for Hallucination Mitigation

Yuxin Liang*[1], Zhuoyang Song[2], Hao Wang[1], Jiaxing Zhang[2]

[1]X^2 Robot

[2]International Digital Economy Academy

liangyuxin42@gmail.com, wanghao@x2robot.com

{songzhuoyang, zhangjiaxing}@idea.edu.cn

Abstract

We evaluate the ability of Large Language Models (LLMs) to discern and express their internal knowledge state, a key factor in countering factual hallucination and ensuring reliable application of LLMs. We observe a robust self-awareness of internal knowledge state in LLMs, evidenced by over 85% accuracy in knowledge state probing. However, LLMs often fail to faithfully express their internal knowledge during generation, leading to factual hallucinations. We develop an automated hallucination annotation tool, DreamCatcher, which merges knowledge probing and consistency checking methods to rank factual preference data. Using knowledge preference as reward, We propose a Reinforcement Learning from Knowledge Feedback (RLKF) training framework, leveraging reinforcement learning to enhance the factuality and honesty of LLMs. Our experiments across multiple models show that RLKF training effectively enhances the ability of models to utilize their internal knowledge state, boosting performance in a variety of knowledge-based and honesty-related tasks.

1 Introduction

Large Language Models (LLMs), including notable examples such as GPT-3 (Brown et al., 2020), LLaMA (Touvron et al. (2023a), Touvron et al. (2023b)), and PaLM (Chowdhery et al., 2023), have emerged as a transformative tool in diverse fields due to their robust capabilities in various tasks. However, despite this significant progress and success, an inherent challenge continues to persist: their tendency to "hallucinate", i.e., generate content misaligned with actual facts. This issue is particularly problematic in critical applications, such as clinical or legal scenarios, where the reliability and accuracy of generated content is vital. Therefore, mitigating hallucinations in LLMs is a crucial step toward enhancing their practical application scope and improving the overall trust in these emerging technologies.

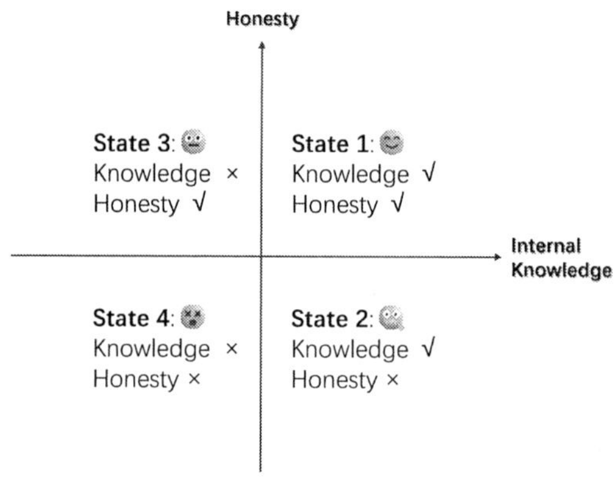

Figure 1: Internal knowledge state categorization of LLMs, based on the possession of corresponding internal knowledge and the capacity to express it honestly.

Hallucinations of LLMs can be categorized into three types (Zhang et al., 2023b): input conflict, context conflict, and factual conflict. This paper focus on the issue of fact-conflicting hallucination, where LLM produces fluent and seemingly plausible content, but conflicts with real-world facts, pose risks of misleading users and compromise the models' fact-based reasoning.

Commonly used hallucination mitigation methods, such as retrieval augmentation generation (RAG), address fact-conflict hallucination of LLM by bringing in external knowledge, but at the cost of introducing a retrieval system. In this paper, we propose to mitigate the factual hallucination problem from the perspective of enhancing the model's utilization of internal knowledge.

Previous works (Azaria and Mitchell (2023), Agrawal et al. (2023)) have shown that LLMs have the capability to discern the validity of factual statements, supported further by Kadavath et al. (2022) suggesting these models' capacity to assess their

*Work done in IDEA

Proceedings of the 3rd Workshop on Knowledge Augmented Methods for NLP, pages 44–58

ability in responding to specific questions. Nevertheless, the universality and extent of models' self-awareness of their internal knowledge remains an open question. In light of this, we conducted exploratory experiments to probe the knowledge state of various models across different scales, employing linear probes to ascertain the accuracy of models' self-awareness regarding their internal knowledge states. The results revealed that all models under analysis demonstrated proficient accuracy in recognizing whether they have the internal knowledge about certain facts.

However, during generation, such accurate judgments do not translate into honest output; instead, in the absence of specific internal knowledge, models often manifest a tendency towards hallucinations. Therefore, to mitigate factual hallucinations, it is crucial that models leverage their self-awareness of internal knowledge states.

We propose a training framework named reinforcement learning from knowledge feedback (RLKF) to improve the factuality and honesty of LLM with reinforcement learning using factual preferences as reward. Through the hallucination annotation method DreamCatcher – a blend of knowledge probing and consistency-based judgments – we rank the knowledge-based Question-Answering (QA) data adhering to a preference hierarchy delineated as: $factuality > uncertainty > hallucination$. This factual preference data is then utilized to train the reward model which is deployed to optimize the Large Language Model via Proximal Policy Optimisation (PPO) algorithm.

The primary contributions of this paper are articulated as follows:

1. Our comprehensive experiments evaluate the ability of various models to identify their internal knowledge. The findings reveal the remarkable proficiency of Large Language Models (LLMs) in discerning their internal knowledge state, achieving accuracy over **85%** in most settings, even with limited data.

2. We develop and open source **DreamCatcher**[1], an automatic hallucination detection tool for scoring the degree of hallucination in LLM generations. DreamCatcher integrates knowledge probing methods and consistency judgments, achieving 81% agreement with human annotator.

3. We introduce the Reinforcement Learning from Knowledge Feedback (RLKF) training framework to optimize LLM against the factual preference. The experiment results on multiple knowledge and reasoning tasks indicate that RLKF not only enhances the honesty and factuality of LLMs but also improves their general capabilities.

[1]https://github.com/liangyuxin42/dreamcatcher

2 Problem Setup

Hallucination, in the context of Large Language Models, refers to a set of inconsistencies in model generation. The central focus of this paper is exploring the fact-conflict hallucination which is defined as the inconsistency between the generated content and the established facts. Although the definition provides a description of the generation results, the causes underlying this phenomenon are multifaceted.

In general, LLMs encode factual knowledge into parameters during training and utilize this internal knowledge during inference. However, LLMs do not always honestly express the knowledge in its parameters, which is one of the major causes of fact-conflict hallucination.

For a given question that requires factual knowledge, the model output can be classified into one of four states, depending on the model's internal knowledge and its honesty. These states are illustrated in Figure 1:

State 1: The model has relevant internal knowledge and expresses it faithfully.

State 2: Despite having the relevant internal knowledge, the model fails to express it honestly. This discrepancy could be due to various factors such as the decoding strategy (Lee et al., 2022; Chuang et al., 2023), hallucination snowballing (Zhang et al., 2023a), or misalignment issues (Schulman, 2023).

State 3: The model lacks the necessary internal knowledge but honestly expresses unawareness.

State 4: The model lacks the necessary internal knowledge and produces a hallucinated response.

Outputs in **State 2** and **State 4** are both considered forms of hallucination, despite the differing conditions of internal knowledge.

In the upper section of Figure 1, the model's outputs are devoid of hallucinations, honestly mirroring its internal knowledge. Here, **State 1** stands out as the most desirable state, where the model

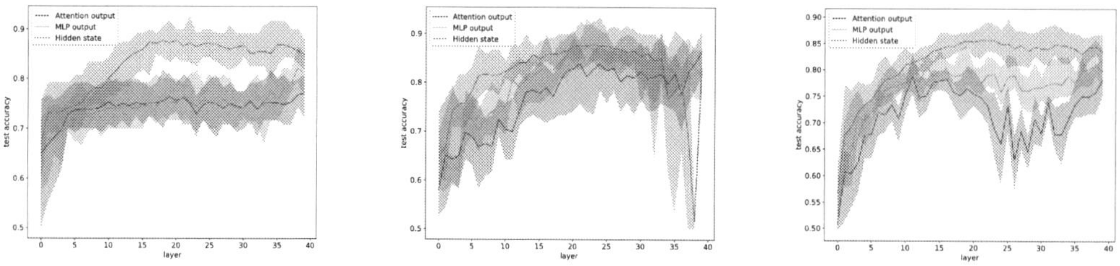

(a) Llama2-chat-13B (b) Qwen-chat-14B (c) Ziya-reader-13B

Figure 2: Accuracy of knowledge state probing across different models with different internal representations. The light-colored area in the figure shows the range of accuracy for ten repetitions of the experiment, and the solid line shows the mean accuracy. More results shown in A.2

both possesses and faithfully outputs the relevant knowledge.

Many efforts have been deployed to transition model toward state 1.

Retrieval-augmented generation (RAG) attempts to bypass the lack of internal knowledge by providing knowledge via context, thereby enabling the model to transition from **State 3/4** to **State 1**. On another front, certain strategies, like those of Li et al. (2023b) and Chuang et al. (2023), seek to move the model from **State 2** to **State 1** by intervening the model's internal representation or the decoding process during inference. While these methods improve the model's capacity to express existing internal knowledge, they disregard scenarios where the model lacks relevant internal knowledge. Also, interference at inference time can potentially lead to unpredictable effects on other types of tasks.

Without the introduction of external knowledge, the mitigation of the model's fact-conflict hallucination correspond to an upward movement of the state in Figure 1. In essence, this symbolizes the enhancement of the model's capacity to accurately express its internal knowledge state. A critical question, then, is how to discern the internal knowledge state of LLMs?

3 Knowledge State Probing

This section delves into the complexities of discerning a model's internal knowledge state. It comprises two perspectives. The first, an external perspective, discuss how to determine if a model possesses specific knowledge based on the model generations; The second perspective, an internal view, questions if it is possible to determine whether a model possesses specific knowledge by its internal activation.

For the following pilot experiments, we select three families of models with different sizes: Llama2-chat(Touvron et al., 2023b) (13B and 7B); Qwen-chat(Bai et al., 2023) (14B and 7B); Ziya-reader(Junqing et al., 2023) (13B).

As for data, We randomly select passages from Chinese and English Wikipedia and instruct GPT3.5 to generate a knowledge-related question-answer pair. The answer generated by GPT3.5 based on the original Wikipedia is considered as the correct answer. We refer to the QA pairs obtained by this method as **wiki-QA** in this paper. Examples of instructions and corresponding output are shown in Appendix A.1.

3.1 External perspective

Determining whether a model has specific knowledge through its generation is a straightforward way. But it is challenging to accurately assess the model's knowledge state through a singular generation result, due to the uncertainty of generation caused by sampling (Lee et al., 2022) and different generation tendencies (Chuang et al., 2023). Multiple generation results can more faithfully reflect the knowledge state of the model.

In the presence of a correct answer, the consistency of the model's multiple generation with the correct answer is a reliable method for assessing knowledge state. The consistency of model generation with the correct answer can be computed using methods such as unigram overlap and cosine similarity of text representation.

However, the correct answer is hard to obtain in many scenarios, in which case self-consistency becomes a critical tool for assessing the validity of the generation. As evidenced by multiple research (Manakul et al. (2023), Agrawal et al. (2023), Hase et al. (2023), Elaraby et al. (2023)), there is a general conclusion that higher consistency across multiple generations is often indicative of validity of the generation. Intuitively, if the model has the corresponding knowledge, multiple generation are likely to contain consistent facts, resulting in higher consistency. Whereas, the contents of the hallucinations often varies, leading to lower self-consistency. We evaluate the self-consistency of a certain generation by the average of the cosine similarity representations among other generated answers.

3.2 Internal perspective

Previous work (Azaria and Mitchell (2023), Kadavath et al. (2022), Li et al. (2023b)) prove that LLMs can discern the factual accuracy of certain statements, even when the false statements are self-generated. This supports the existence of state 2 in Figure 1 where the model has the corresponding knowledge but generates incorrect outputs. But are LLMs capable of discerning its own state of knowledge? The question can be rephrased as follows: for a given knowledge-related question, can a model discern its capability to output the correct answer before the actual generation of an answer? The following linear probing experiments on multiple models implies that the answer is yes.

We sample questions from the wiki-QA data, and use LLM to generate $k = 5$ answers for each question separately. We use the consistency method described earlier to pre-label the questions. The sum of these normalized consistency scores computed to derive the final score.

To categorize the questions, straightforward thresholds are utilized. The upper threshold is set at the 65th percentile score, and the lower at the 35th percentile score. Under this setup, responses with scores exceeding the upper threshold are labeled as correct, while those falling below the lower threshold are labeled as incorrect. If all of the k generated responses related to a specific question are deemed correct, the model is presumed to possess the relevant internal knowledge, and thus the question is labeled as 'Known'. Conversely, if all k responses are incorrect, the model is considered to lack the necessary internal knowledge, and hence the question is labeled as 'Unknown'.

A single linear layer classifier (probe) is trained on the internal representation corresponding to the last token of each question. Its task is to predict the corresponding Known/Unknown label.

For our experiments, we select three types of internal representations:

The attention output, which refers to the output of the dot product attention and before the attention linear layer in the decoder layer. This setup aligns with the probe's positioning within Li et al. (2023b); **The MLP output**, i.e., the feed-forward layer's output within the decoder layer, occurring prior to residual linkage; **The hidden states**, defined as each decoder layer's output.

The results of the internal knowledge probe experiment are shown in Figure 2, which presents the accuracy of the trained probes across different models with different internal representation and at different layers.

Comparative analysis of the experimental results across models of varying sizes yields consistent observations:

1. The linear probes of the internal state accurately predict the knowledge representation of the model. The probes' maximum accuracy surpasses 85% in most setups. This suggests that information about whether the model has the corresponding knowledge is linearly encoded in the internal representation of the model with high accuracy.

2. The accuracy of the probes increases rapidly in the early to middle layer, indicating that the model needs some layers of computation before it can determine its own knowledge states.

3. Hidden state probes exhibit the highest accuracy in discerning the knowledge state of the model, sustaining high accuracy from the middle layer to the output layer, which opens up the possibility of utilizing internal knowledge state when generating responses.

3.3 DreamCatcher

We integrated the above methods of knowledge state probing and consistency judgments to develop an automated hallucination annotation tool, DreamCatcher.

We start by collect the LLMs' generation for each question in the question set, in our case, the wiki-QA dataset. This process features two modes: normal generation and uncertainty generation. Normal generation is when the prompt contains only the question and model generates k responses, while uncertainty generation refers to where the prompt contains a request for the model to output answers that show uncertainty or lack of knowledge.

Subsequently, we assess the degree of hallucination of the generated responses using multiple scorers using the methods described above. Concretely, we compute the following scores:

$$\begin{aligned} s_{s2g} &= \text{avg}_{ij}(\cos(\mathbf{r}_{G_i}, \mathbf{r}_{G_j})) \\ s_p &= \text{probe}(\mathbf{r}_Q) \\ s_{o2a} &= \text{count}(token_{overlap})/\text{count}(token_A) \\ s_{s2a} &= \cos(\mathbf{r}_G, \mathbf{r}_A) \end{aligned}$$

where Q denotes the question, A the correct answer, G the generation and $\mathbf{r}$ the embedding representation of text.

s_{s2g} **(Similarity to Generation Score)**: computes the cosine similarity between the embedding of certain generation (G_i) and other generated responses (G_j), using the bge-large model (Xiao et al., 2023) for text embedding.

s_p **(Probe Score)**: rates the questions by utilizing the probes trained in Section 3.2, which are intended to discern the model's knowledge state for the corresponding questions.

s_{o2a} **(Overlap with Answer Score)**: calculates the ratio of token overlap between the generated output and the correct answer (A).

s_{s2a} **(Similarity to Answer Score)**: computes the cosine similarity between the embedding of the generated response (G) and the correct answer (A), using the bge-large model for text embedding.

The scores are normalized and summed to provide an overall factuality score for each generation. The generations are then classified as "correct" or "incorrect" based on whether their total score is above or below the median score, respectively. Questions are categorized as "Known", "Unknown", or "Mixed" based on whether the responses are consistently correct, incorrect, or a combination of correct and incorrect across multiple generations, with "Mixed" being a less frequent occurrence.

The categories correspond to three ranking hierarchies as shown in Figure 3: Known (corresponding to state 1 in Fig.1): factual > uncertainty; Mixed (state 2): factual > uncertainty > hallucination; Unknown (state 4): uncertainty > hallucination. Here, "factual" refers to the generation with the highest factuality score, while "hallucination" denotes the generation with the lowest score.

We randomly sampled 200 entries, half Chinese and half English, from the DreamCatcher labeled data. Then the human annotator annotate the same data, without access to the labels of DreamCatcher. The consistency between DreamCatcher and human annotator is shown in Table 1, with an overall accuracy of 81%.

Language	Accuracy	Precision	Recall
All	81%	77%	86%
Chinese	77%	79%	76%
English	86%	76%	98%

Table 1: The consistency between DreamCatcher and human annotator. For precision and recall, we treat "correct" as a positive label and "incorrect" as negative.

4 Method

From the above knowledge-probing experiments, we discover that LLMs are capable of evaluating their own knowledge states in response to specific knowledge-based questions. This implies that LLMs demonstrate a self-awareness of their knowledge state, which does not consistently translate into their generation.

Frequently, when faced with questions outside of internal knowledge, LLMs tends to generate hallucinations. Additionally, even with questions within internal knowledge, LLMs may potentially generate incorrect responses due to other influences. One possible explanation could be that LLMs did not learn to generate with respect to the internal knowledge state during model training. Instead, the fine-tuning process often requires the model to generate seemingly reasonable answers to all factual questions.

We therefore emphasize on enhancing the model's utilization of internal knowledge state so that the model can choose to rely on internal knowledge to answer or honestly express its lack of relevant knowledge.[2]

Consequently, we propose the RLKF (Reinforce Learning from Knowledge Feedback) training framework. This introduces model knowledge state assessments into the reinforcement learning feedback mechanism, enhancing model honesty and factuality. The RLKF training process shares similarities with the standard RLHF (Reinforce Learning from Human Feedback), and can integrate smoothly with the existing RLHF framework, but reduces data collection costs by substituting

[2]This intuition could also be used for efficient RAG, enabling direct responses when the LLM possesses relevant internal knowledge, while relying on the retrieval tool in case of a knowledge gap.

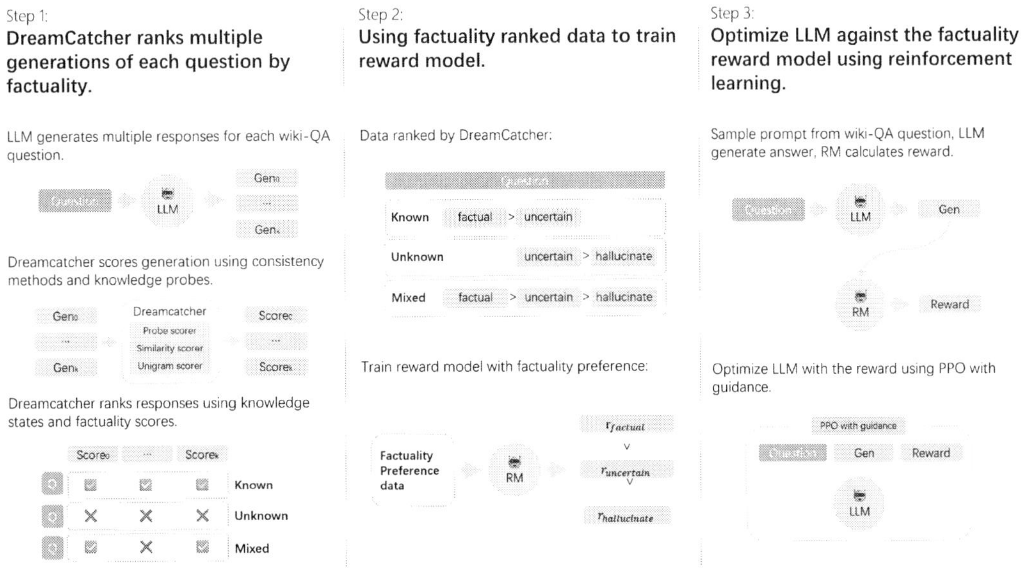

Figure 3: RLKF training framework

human labeling with automatic knowledge annotation.

The RLKF training framework consists of the following components, as shown in Figure 3.

Knowledge state annotation: We annotate factual preference data using the DreamCatcher tool.

Knowledge Feedback Modeling: Having obtained the factual preference data, we train the reward model following (Ouyang et al., 2022). The language modelling head in reward model is replaced with a linear layer to produce a scalar output, corresponding to the reward of the generated response. In line with (Köpf et al., 2023), an additional regularization parameter is introduced to prevents the predicted values from diverging too much.

By initiating the PPO Policy training and the reward model training from the same model, we can ensure that the reward model can leverage the same internal knowledge.

PPO Optimizing: Based on our factual reward model, we optimize the policy, i.e., the initial generative model, using the PPO algorithm once again following Ouyang et al., 2022. To improve the efficiency of model exploration towards honesty, we use guidance technique in reinforcement learning. Concretely, we concatenate the first few tokens of the preferred responses to the input prompts in a portion of the training data. The added tokens do not participate in the loss calculation, but can guide the model to generate desired responses, thus improving learning efficiency.

The core of the training framework is to establish the factual preference reward mechanism. The reinforcement learning algorithms in the RLKF framework can also be replaced by other optimization algorithms such as DPO (Rafailov et al., 2023), reject sampling, etc. We choose PPO to be consistent with the common practice in RLHF training.

5 Experiments

In the following experiments, We chose three different models of varying sizes: llama2-chat (13B and 7B); Qwen-chat (14B and 7B); and Ziya-reader (13B), which is consistent with the choice of models for the knowledge-probing experiments detailed in Section 3.

Model	Known	Unknown	Mixed
Qwen-chat-14B	82.7%	87.1%	77.8%
Qwen-chat-7B	65.7%	81.6%	61.1%
Llama2-chat-13B	85.4%	85.4%	60.0%
Llama2-chat-7B	78.9%	89.2%	57.6%
Ziya-reader-13B	93.5%	82.4%	64.5%

Table 2: Accuracy of trained reward model for each knowledge state category.

5.1 Data collection

We used the wiki-QA data collection method same as in Section 3, obtaining about 7,000 QA pairs

Models		MMLU	WinoGrande	ARC	BBH	GSM8K	MATH	C-Eval	CMMLU	Avg
Qwen-chat-14B	before	64.2%	53.8%	76.5%	34.5%	47.3%	18.9%	65.0%	64.1%	53.0%
	after	**64.5%**	**59.1%**	**87.2%**	**37.3%**	**49.9%**	**20.3%**	64.6%	**66.4%**	**56.2%**
Qwen-chat-7B	before	54.2%	49.6%	63.1%	28.8%	50.0%	12.6%	57.8%	58.1%	46.8%
	after	**55.3%**	**52.2%**	**75.4%**	28.1%	**50.9%**	12.5%	57.5%	56.0%	**48.5%**
Llama2-chat-13B	before	52.3%	51.9%	72.4%	21.7%	35.2%	3.2%	34.6%	34.5%	38.2%
	after	**52.8%**	**54.3%**	72.1%	**23.4%**	**35.6%**	3.1%	34.3%	**34.6%**	**38.8%**
Llama2-chat-7B	before	45.9%	51.5%	59.2%	23.3%	25.9%	1.6%	32.1%	31.6%	33.9%
	after	**46.2%**	**52.4%**	**61.1%**	**24.4%**	23.7%	**2.0%**	**34.0%**	**32.1%**	**34.5%**
Ziya-reader-13B	before	49.5%	50.8%	64.7%	44.7%	29.3%	4.3%	44.7%	46.1%	41.7%
	after	**50.3%**	**51.9%**	**67.9%**	42.6%	**33.2%**	3.8%	42.6%	45.1%	**42.2%**

Table 3: Evaluation of RLKF-trained models on various knowledge and reasoning related tasks: MMLU (Hendrycks et al., 2020), WinoGrande (Sakaguchi et al., 2021), ARC (Chollet, 2019), BBH (Suzgun et al., 2022), GSM8K (Cobbe et al., 2021), MATH (Hendrycks et al., 2021), C-Eval (Huang et al., 2023), CMMLU(Li et al., 2023a). Tasks are evaluated by the open-source evaluation tool TLEM (SUSTech, 2023), employing a 0-shot setting with greedy generation.

each for Chinese and English. To add variety to the questions, we have also modified the prompt to include multiple choice question types. Since our approach relies on the internal knowledge of the models and the boundaries of the internal knowledge are different for each model, we need to perform automatic annotation for each model individually. The generated responses are labeled using DreamCatcher to obtain factual preference data. The statistics of the factual preference data are shown in Table 7.

5.2 RLKF Training

We train the reward model using the factual preference data in Table 7. To maintain the generalization of the RM, we include same amount of general purpose data as the wiki-QA data in the training. Accuracy of the trained RM on factual preference data test set are shown in Table 2. Interestingly, the reward model is able to quickly achieve high accuracy for both known/unknown categories during training, suggesting that reward model may utilize the internal knowledge state of the initial model to determine whether the uncertainty response should be preferred.

Using the trained reward model, the RL process optimizes policy model using the PPO algorithm, where policy model is initialized from the same base model as reward model. The detailed training settings and hyper-parameters are described in A.4.

We conduct an evaluation of the trained model, focusing on its factuality and truthfulness. A comparative analysis of the models is performed between pre- and post- RLKF training on various tasks related to knowledge and reasoning as shown in Table 3. The RLKF-trained models demonstrate improvements on the majority of the benchmarks. While RLHF typically results in a reduction of benchmark performance, termed as 'alignment tax' (Askell et al., 2021), RLKF avoids this decline specifically on knowledge-related tasks, and even lead to improvements. Note that our training methodology does not employ any benchmark data, and the overall volume of training data utilized is small.

Models	TruthfulQA before	TruthfulQA after
Qwen-chat-14B	43.7%	**49.1%**
Qwen-chat-7B	49.1%	**50.3%**
Llama2-chat-13B	21.5%	20.9%
Llama2-chat-7B	27.5%	**28.3%**
Ziya-reader-13B	34.8%	**37.9%**

Table 4: Evaluation of RLKF-trained models on TruthfulQA, again using TLEM (SUSTech, 2023), employing a 0-shot setting with greedy generation.

Regarding the truthfulness of trained models, we evaluated their performance using the widely recognized TruthfulQA task. Notably, all models, with the exception of llama2-chat-13B, show increase in honesty, as shown in Table 4.

6 Related Work

Hallucination in large language models (LLMs) has been the focal point of research, spanning its causes, detection, and mitigation. Our work relates to all three aspects.

Causes of hallucination: Studies have linked

LLM hallucination to various causes. McKenna et al. (2023) ascribes it to memorization of training data, indicating a direct correlation between the training data and the resultant hallucination. Other works such as Schulman (2023) pinpoint improper model fine-tuning as contributive, and Perez et al. (2022) argues that RLHF induce model "sycophancy" which in turn degrades honesty.

Other studies link hallucinations to the generation process. For example, Lee et al. (2022) suggests that sampling-induced randomness could be responsible. One perspective provided by Chuang et al. (2023) proposes that "lower-level" prior layer information might overshadow factual information from subsequent layers. Furthermore, some works relate hallucinations to the overconfidence of LLMs (Ren et al., 2023).

Hallucination detecting: In terms of detecting hallucination, the consistency of multiple generations has been recognized as an effective indicator. SelfCheckGPT (Manakul et al., 2023) capitalizes on the consistent nature of internal knowledge-based generations compared to the variable nature of hallucination, propose several consistency checks to identify hallucinations. The idea is echoed by Agrawal et al. (2023), who suggest evaluating the generation consistency of generated references to spot hallucination. Similarly, Elaraby et al. (2023) proposes a metric involving the calculation of sentence-level entailment between response pairs as a measure of hallucination.

Employing large language models (LLMs) to recognize their own hallucinations has been suggested in Saunders et al. (2022), suggesting that discrimination is more accurate than generation for LLMs (G-D gap). This notion is furthered by Kadavath et al. (2022) and Agrawal et al. (2023) by directly prompting LLMs to assess the validity of their own output.

Another approach examines the factualness of statements by analyzing the model's internal representation. Studies Li et al. (2023b) and Burns et al. (2022) identify a "factualness" direction in the model's internal representation, with Li et al. (2023b) showcasing a high accuracy attention head through linear probing, and Burns et al. (2022) locating factualness direction through consistency of facts. Additionally, Kadavath et al. (2022) trains the model to predict the probability that it knows. Base on these works, we shifts focus onto the model's self-evaluation of knowledge state.

Hallucination mitigation: The common approach of hallucination mitigation involves enhancing the model with additional information. Elaraby et al. (2023) propose the use of larger models to provide additional information when hallucinations is detected.

Some research efforts focus on the optimization of decoding strategies to address hallucinations. Chuang et al. (2023) suggests that contrastive decoding can augment the factualness of model generation. Li et al. (2023b) enhances factualness by adjusting the output of attention heads along the direction of factualness during inference. Our work seeks to optimizes the utilization of the model's internal knowledge state, in line with the direction proposed by Schulman (2023) leveraging reinforcement learning to tackle hallucinations.

7 Conclusion

In our research, we thoroughly explore the capability of large language models (LLMs) to discern and express their internal knowledge, a key factor in mitigating factual hallucinations and ensuring reliable applications. Our research, manifested through a series of knowledge probing experiments, identifies the model's self-awareness of its knowledge state. We released the open-source tool DreamCatcher which scores and annotates the degree of hallucination in the LLM's response to knowledge-oriented question and rank responses based on their factuality.

We further validated our findings through the Reinforcement Learning from Knowledge Feedback (RLKF) training framework. Utilizing DreamCatcher to annotate factual preference data, we train a reward model and leveraging reinforcement learning to enhances LLM's factuality and truthfulness. Our results indicate RLKF's effectiveness in improving the model's utilization of its internal knowledge state, enhancing its performance in various knowledge and honesty related tasks. We posit that RLKF is a promising solution to address LLM's hallucination issues and, combined with RLHF, offers significant potential for enhancing the model's overall capabilities.

8 Limitations

Data limitation: Our Reinforcement Learning from Knowledge Feedback (RLKF) training relies on a relatively limited quantity and variety of data used. The factual question-answer data employed in our experiments predominantly resulted from using GPT3.5 to generate question-answer pairs from Wikipedia passages. Although this approach guarantees high factual precision and includes an extensive range of long-tail facts, it restricts diversity in writing style.

Given the time and cost considerations associated with the use of GPT api, the volume of data was also somewhat restricted. To enhance RLKF training, prospective research might contemplate compiling more intricate factual question-answer data that reflect real-world conditions.

Integration of Alternative Optimization Techniques: The essence of the RLKF framework lies in optimizing for factual preferences. After acquiring factual preference data, we opted for the Proximal Policy Optimization (PPO) method for optimization, given its demonstrated efficacy within the existing Reinforcement Learning from Human Feedback (RLHF) framework.

However, various other potential optimization methods exist, including reject sampling, DPO, mixed data supervised fine-tuning, among others. We anticipate future research will creatively incorporate factual preference data into their respective training frameworks, contributing to a comprehensive understanding of the LLM illusion phenomenon.

References

Ayush Agrawal, Lester Mackey, and Adam Tauman Kalai. 2023. Do language models know when they're hallucinating references? *arXiv preprint arXiv:2305.18248*.

Amanda Askell, Yuntao Bai, Anna Chen, Dawn Drain, Deep Ganguli, Tom Henighan, Andy Jones, Nicholas Joseph, Ben Mann, Nova DasSarma, et al. 2021. A general language assistant as a laboratory for alignment. *arXiv preprint arXiv:2112.00861*.

Amos Azaria and Tom Mitchell. 2023. The internal state of an llm knows when its lying. *arXiv preprint arXiv:2304.13734*.

Jinze Bai, Shuai Bai, Yunfei Chu, Zeyu Cui, Kai Dang, Xiaodong Deng, Yang Fan, Wenbin Ge, Yu Han, Fei Huang, et al. 2023. Qwen technical report. *arXiv preprint arXiv:2309.16609*.

Tom Brown, Benjamin Mann, Nick Ryder, Melanie Subbiah, Jared D Kaplan, Prafulla Dhariwal, Arvind Neelakantan, Pranav Shyam, Girish Sastry, Amanda Askell, et al. 2020. Language models are few-shot learners. *Advances in neural information processing systems*, 33:1877–1901.

Collin Burns, Haotian Ye, Dan Klein, and Jacob Steinhardt. 2022. Discovering latent knowledge in language models without supervision. *arXiv preprint arXiv:2212.03827*.

François Chollet. 2019. On the measure of intelligence. *arXiv preprint arXiv:1911.01547*.

Aakanksha Chowdhery, Sharan Narang, Jacob Devlin, Maarten Bosma, Gaurav Mishra, Adam Roberts, Paul Barham, Hyung Won Chung, Charles Sutton, Sebastian Gehrmann, et al. 2023. Palm: Scaling language modeling with pathways. *Journal of Machine Learning Research*, 24(240):1–113.

Yung-Sung Chuang, Yujia Xie, Hongyin Luo, Yoon Kim, James Glass, and Pengcheng He. 2023. Dola: Decoding by contrasting layers improves factuality in large language models. *arXiv preprint arXiv:2309.03883*.

Karl Cobbe, Vineet Kosaraju, Mohammad Bavarian, Mark Chen, Heewoo Jun, Lukasz Kaiser, Matthias Plappert, Jerry Tworek, Jacob Hilton, Reiichiro Nakano, et al. 2021. Training verifiers to solve math word problems. *arXiv preprint arXiv:2110.14168*.

Mohamed Elaraby, Mengyin Lu, Jacob Dunn, Xueying Zhang, Yu Wang, and Shizhu Liu. 2023. Halo: Estimation and reduction of hallucinations in open-source weak large language models. *arXiv preprint arXiv:2308.11764*.

Peter Hase, Mona Diab, Asli Celikyilmaz, Xian Li, Zornitsa Kozareva, Veselin Stoyanov, Mohit Bansal, and Srinivasan Iyer. 2023. Methods for measuring, updating, and visualizing factual beliefs in language models. In *Proceedings of the 17th Conference of the European Chapter of the Association for Computational Linguistics*, pages 2706–2723.

Dan Hendrycks, Collin Burns, Steven Basart, Andy Zou, Mantas Mazeika, Dawn Song, and Jacob Steinhardt. 2020. Measuring massive multitask language understanding. *arXiv preprint arXiv:2009.03300*.

Dan Hendrycks, Collin Burns, Saurav Kadavath, Akul Arora, Steven Basart, Eric Tang, Dawn Song, and Jacob Steinhardt. 2021. Measuring mathematical problem solving with the math dataset. *arXiv preprint arXiv:2103.03874*.

Yuzhen Huang, Yuzhuo Bai, Zhihao Zhu, Junlei Zhang, Jinghan Zhang, Tangjun Su, Junteng Liu, Chuancheng Lv, Yikai Zhang, Jiayi Lei, et al. 2023. C-eval: A multi-level multi-discipline chinese evaluation suite for foundation models. *arXiv preprint arXiv:2305.08322*.

He Junqing, Pan Kunhao, Dong Xiaoqun, Song Zhuoyang, Liu Yibo, Liang Yuxin, Wang Hao, Sun Qianguo, Zhang Songxin, Xie Zejian, et al. 2023. Never lost in the middle: Improving large language models via attention strengthening question answering. *arXiv preprint arXiv:2311.09198*.

Saurav Kadavath, Tom Conerly, Amanda Askell, Tom Henighan, Dawn Drain, Ethan Perez, Nicholas Schiefer, Zac Hatfield-Dodds, Nova DasSarma, Eli Tran-Johnson, et al. 2022. Language models (mostly) know what they know. *arXiv preprint arXiv:2207.05221*.

Andreas Köpf, Yannic Kilcher, Dimitri von Rütte, Sotiris Anagnostidis, Zhi-Rui Tam, Keith Stevens, Abdullah Barhoum, Nguyen Minh Duc, Oliver Stanley, Richárd Nagyfi, et al. 2023. Openassistant conversations–democratizing large language model alignment. *arXiv preprint arXiv:2304.07327*.

Nayeon Lee, Wei Ping, Peng Xu, Mostofa Patwary, Pascale N Fung, Mohammad Shoeybi, and Bryan Catanzaro. 2022. Factuality enhanced language models for open-ended text generation. *Advances in Neural Information Processing Systems*, 35:34586–34599.

Haonan Li, Yixuan Zhang, Fajri Koto, Yifei Yang, Hai Zhao, Yeyun Gong, Nan Duan, and Timothy Baldwin. 2023a. Cmmlu: Measuring massive multitask language understanding in chinese. *arXiv preprint arXiv:2306.09212*.

Kenneth Li, Oam Patel, Fernanda Viégas, Hanspeter Pfister, and Martin Wattenberg. 2023b. Inference-time intervention: Eliciting truthful answers from a language model. *arXiv preprint arXiv:2306.03341*.

Potsawee Manakul, Adian Liusie, and Mark JF Gales. 2023. Selfcheckgpt: Zero-resource black-box hallucination detection for generative large language models. *arXiv preprint arXiv:2303.08896*.

Nick McKenna, Tianyi Li, Liang Cheng, Mohammad Javad Hosseini, Mark Johnson, and Mark Steedman. 2023. Sources of hallucination by large language models on inference tasks. *arXiv preprint arXiv:2305.14552*.

Long Ouyang, Jeffrey Wu, Xu Jiang, Diogo Almeida, Carroll Wainwright, Pamela Mishkin, Chong Zhang, Sandhini Agarwal, Katarina Slama, Alex Ray, et al. 2022. Training language models to follow instructions with human feedback. *Advances in Neural Information Processing Systems*, 35:27730–27744.

Ethan Perez, Sam Ringer, Kamilė Lukošiūtė, Karina Nguyen, Edwin Chen, Scott Heiner, Craig Pettit, Catherine Olsson, Sandipan Kundu, Saurav Kadavath, et al. 2022. Discovering language model behaviors with model-written evaluations. *arXiv preprint arXiv:2212.09251*.

Rafael Rafailov, Archit Sharma, Eric Mitchell, Stefano Ermon, Christopher D Manning, and Chelsea Finn. 2023. Direct preference optimization: Your language model is secretly a reward model. *arXiv preprint arXiv:2305.18290*.

Ruiyang Ren, Yuhao Wang, Yingqi Qu, Wayne Xin Zhao, Jing Liu, Hao Tian, Hua Wu, Ji-Rong Wen, and Haifeng Wang. 2023. Investigating the factual knowledge boundary of large language models with retrieval augmentation. *arXiv preprint arXiv:2307.11019*.

Keisuke Sakaguchi, Ronan Le Bras, Chandra Bhagavatula, and Yejin Choi. 2021. Winogrande: An adversarial winograd schema challenge at scale. *Communications of the ACM*, 64(9):99–106.

William Saunders, Catherine Yeh, Jeff Wu, Steven Bills, Long Ouyang, Jonathan Ward, and Jan Leike. 2022. Self-critiquing models for assisting human evaluators. *arXiv preprint arXiv:2206.05802*.

John Schulman. 2023. Reinforcement learning from human feedback: Progress and challenges, 2023.

SUSTech. 2023. Introducing tlem: The future of language model evaluation.

Mirac Suzgun, Nathan Scales, Nathanael Schärli, Sebastian Gehrmann, Yi Tay, Hyung Won Chung, Aakanksha Chowdhery, Quoc V Le, Ed H Chi, Denny Zhou, et al. 2022. Challenging big-bench tasks and whether chain-of-thought can solve them. *arXiv preprint arXiv:2210.09261*.

Hugo Touvron, Thibaut Lavril, Gautier Izacard, Xavier Martinet, Marie-Anne Lachaux, Timothée Lacroix, Baptiste Rozière, Naman Goyal, Eric Hambro, Faisal Azhar, et al. 2023a. Llama: Open and efficient foundation language models. *arXiv preprint arXiv:2302.13971*.

Hugo Touvron, Louis Martin, Kevin Stone, Peter Albert, Amjad Almahairi, Yasmine Babaei, Nikolay Bashlykov, Soumya Batra, Prajjwal Bhargava, Shruti

Bhosale, et al. 2023b. Llama 2: Open foundation and fine-tuned chat models. *arXiv preprint arXiv:2307.09288*.

Shitao Xiao, Zheng Liu, Peitian Zhang, and Niklas Muennighoff. 2023. C-pack: Packaged resources to advance general chinese embedding.

Muru Zhang, Ofir Press, William Merrill, Alisa Liu, and Noah A Smith. 2023a. How language model hallucinations can snowball. *arXiv preprint arXiv:2305.13534*.

Yue Zhang, Yafu Li, Leyang Cui, Deng Cai, Lemao Liu, Tingchen Fu, Xinting Huang, Enbo Zhao, Yu Zhang, Yulong Chen, et al. 2023b. Siren's song in the ai ocean: A survey on hallucination in large language models. *arXiv preprint arXiv:2309.01219*.

A Appendix

A.1 Example of wiki-QA Instruction

A.2 More probing results

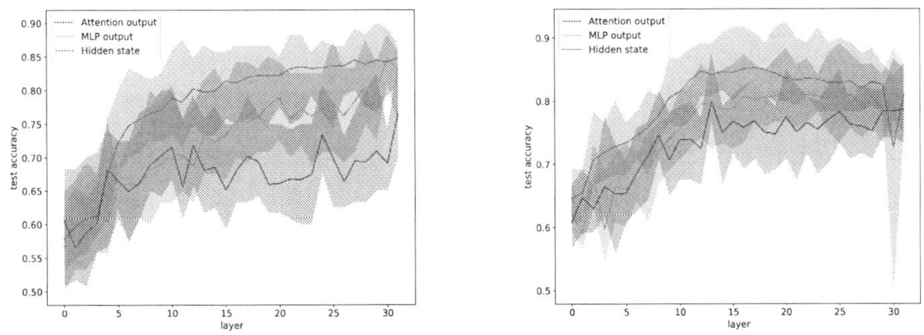

(a) Llama2-chat-7B (b) Qwen-chat-7B

Figure 4: Accuracy of knowledge state probing in 7B models. The light-colored area in the figure shows the range of accuracy for ten repetitions of the experiment, and the solid line shows the mean accuracy.

Instruction template:
Based on the following Wikipedia article snippet, ask a knowledge-based question and provide a corresponding answer.
Article snippet:
{Wikipedia passage}
Requirements:
1. there is a unique correct answer to the question, and the answer can be found in the given article fragment.
2. the question can be answered independently of the article fragment, i.e. the answer to the question cannot depend on contextual information, e.g. a question about a character in a literature needs to specify the work to which the character belongs, and a question such as "What is the article about?" cannot be asked.
3. Provide the question, answer, and category (e.g., literature, physics, etc.) at the same time, and reply in the following format: {"question":question,"answer":answer,"type":category}.
If you are unable to ask a question that meets the above requirements, you can simply reply "Unable to ask".
Reply:
Wikipedia passage:
House Arrest (1996 film) House Arrest is a 1996 American comedy film directed by Harry Winer, written by Michael Hitchcock, and starring Jamie Lee Curtis, Kevin Pollak, Jennifer Tilly, Christopher McDonald, Wallace Shawn, and Ray Walston with supporting roles done by Kyle Howard, Amy Sakasitz, Mooky Arizona, Russel Harper, and an up-and-coming Jennifer Love Hewitt. It tells the story of two children who trap their parents in their basement upon their plans for a separation as the other children they know get involved by trapping their respective problem parents as well. The film was released on August 14, 1996 and went on to gross just over $7 million at the box office. The film was panned by critics. The film was shot at various locations in the U.S. states of California and Ohio. Monrovia, California was the location for several exterior house scenes while most interior shots were done at the CBS/Radford lot in Studio City, California. The story was set in Defiance, Ohio, although another town, Chagrin Falls, Ohio, actually doubled for it.
GPT3.5 response:
{"question":"Who directed the film House Arrest?","answer":"Harry Winer","type":"film"}

Table 5: Example of instruction and corresponding GPT3.5 output of English wiki-QA.

Instruction template:
根据下面的维基百科文章片段，提出一个简短的知识型问题并给出对应回答，要求这个问题存在唯一正确答案，并且答案可以在给出的文章片段中找到。
文章片段：
{Wikipedia passage}
问题需要在脱离文章片段的情况下仍能够被回答，例如针对文学作品中人物提问需要指明所属的作品，以免引起歧义。问题的回答不能依赖于上下文的信息，不能提出类似"这篇文章的内容是什么？"的问题。
同时给出问题，回答和问题分类（比如文学类或物理类等），按如下格式回复：{"question":问题,"answer":回答,"type":分类}。如果无法提出满足上述要求的问题，可以直接回复"无法提问"。
回复：
Wikipedia passage:
M25
M25，也称为IC 4725，是一个由恒星组成，在南天人马座的疏散星团。Philippe Loys de Chéseaux在1745年对这个星团进行了第一次有记录的观测，查尔斯·梅西耶1764年将它收录进他的星云天体清单[6]。这个星团位于模糊的特征附近，因此有一条暗带通过中心附近[3]。
M25距离地球大约2,000光年，年龄约为6,760万岁[2]。这个星团在空间的维度大约是13光年，估计质量是1,937 M，其中大约24%是星际物质[4]。星团成员中的人马座U是一颗分类为造父变星的变星[7]，还有两颗红巨星，且其中一颗是联星系统[8]。
GPT3.5 response:
{"question":"M25是位于哪个星座的疏散星团？","answer":"南天人马座","type":"天文学"}

Table 6: Example of instruction and corresponding GPT3.5 output of Chinese wiki-QA.

A.3 Statistics of factual preference data

Model	Total	Known	Unknown	Mixed
Qwen-chat-14B	12799	49%	43%	8%
Qwen-chat-7B	7201	52%	40%	8%
Llama2-chat-13B	6600	48%	44%	8%
Llama2-chat-7B	6680	45%	45%	10%
Ziya-reader-13B	12558	49%	41%	10%

Table 7: Statistics of factual preference data and percentage of each knowledge state category used for reward modeling. The Llama2 models use English-only wiki-QA data, Qwen-chat-7B uses Chinese-only data, and Qwen-chat-14B and Ziya-reader-13B use a mixture of English and Chinese data.

A.4 RLKF Training details

We use the AdamW optimizer, with $\beta_1 = 0.9$, $\beta_2 = 0.99$, $eps = 1e - 5$ for all models. The learning rate for reward model training is $5e - 6$ with 1% warmup and linear decay scheduler. The batch size is 16 for 13/14B models and 64 for 7B models. We train the reward model for 1 epoch. For PPO training, we use learning rate of $1e - 6$ with cosine scheduler. The batch size is 32 for 13/14B models and 64 for 7B models. We set the KL penalty to 0 for all models.

A.5 More Observation

We observe that, some of the responses to the unknown questions are indicating uncertainty in RLHF-trained models, but there is also a significant percentage of responses that are hallucinations. This indicates an increase in model honesty achieved through RLHF, but there is still room for improvement.

Aggregating Impressions on Celebrities and their Reasons from Microblog Posts and Web Search Pages by LLMs

Hibiki Yokoyama[1], Rikuto Tsuchida[1], Kosei Buma[1], Sho Miyakawa[1], Takehito Utsuro[1], Masaharu Yoshioka[2],

[1]University of Tsukuba, [2]Hokkaido University,

s2320808@_u.tsukuba.ac.jp, s2110466@_u.tsukuba.ac.jp, s2313594@_u.tsukuba.ac.jp, s2320794@_u.tsukuba.ac.jp, utsuro@_iit.tsukuba.ac.jp, yoshioka@_ist.hokudai.ac.jp,

Abstract

This paper aims to augment fans' ability to critique and explore information related to celebrities of interest. First, we collect posts from X (formerly Twitter) that discuss matters related to specific celebrities. For the collection of major impressions from these posts, we employ ChatGPT as a large language model (LLM) to analyze and summarize key sentiments. Next, based on collected impressions, we search for Web pages and collect the content of the top 30 ranked pages as the source for exploring the reasons behind those impressions. Once the Web page content collection is complete, we collect and aggregate detailed reasons for the impressions on the celebrities from the content of each page. For this part, we continue to use ChatGPT, enhanced by the retrieval augmented generation (RAG) framework, to ensure the reliability of the collected results compared to relying solely on the prior knowledge of the LLM. Evaluation results by comparing a reference that is manually collected and aggregated reasons with those predicted by ChatGPT revealed that ChatGPT achieves high accuracy in reason collection and aggregation. Furthermore, we compared the performance of ChatGPT with an existing model of mT5 in reason collection and confirmed that ChatGPT exhibits superior performance.

1 Introduction

In recent years, social networking services (SNS) such as X (formerly Twitter) have become platforms where various opinions are expressed. As shown in Figure 1, a significant number of posts on these platforms contain impressions and critiques of celebrities, often triggered by events such as TV drama broadcasts, commercials, or news reports. Among celebrity fans, there are individuals who have a strong interest in this type of information. For example, when an event or an incident that is related to a popular celebrity occurs, people express their own thoughts regarding those events and incidents in SNS such as microblog (e.g., X) posts. Since a number of those posts are distributed through SNS, this makes it unexpectedly difficult to correctly identify what people actually intend to express in their posts. The reasoning behind these impressions is often implicit and can be influenced by various factors such as the stance of the writers of the posts, recently occurring related events, and the contexts provided by external sources like news articles and ads. However, such background information is not always detailed in the posts themselves. Therefore, it is necessary to utilize not only the information within the posts but also external information to gain comprehensive understanding.

Considering those situations, this paper aims to augment fans' ability to critique and explore information related to celebrities of interest. To achieve this overall goal, we first collect posts from X that discuss matters related to specific celebrities and gather major impressions on those celebrities.

Our ChatGPT-based approach overcomes the limitations of a previous research (Sugawara and Utsuro, 2022), allowing for a more flexible and comprehensive collection of aspects and impressions about celebrities. The details of our ChatGPT-based method for collecting and aggregating impressions are to be explained in Section 4. This approach allows us to more effectively identify and aggregate the major impressions on celebrities' aspects from the vast amount of information available in X posts, while taking into account the context of the posts. This enables a more comprehensive and nuanced understanding of the public's perceptions of celebrities, going beyond the limitations of the previous method. We then use the corresponding pair of a celebrity's aspect and an impression as a keyword for collecting detailed information and their reasons from Web pages.

After selecting the keyword, we search for Web

Proceedings of the 3rd Workshop on Knowledge Augmented Methods for NLP, pages 59–72

Figure 1: Numerous Posts on Celebrities triggered by Various Celebrities related Events

pages using the keyword as a query and collect the content of the top 30 ranked pages as the source for exploring the reasons behind the impressions.

Once the Web page content related to the keyword is collected, we explore detailed reasons for the impressions within the content of each page. For this part, we utilize ChatGPT as a large language model (LLM). A crucial aspect of our research is the use of RAG (Lewis et al., 2020) in this reason collection process, which plays a significant role in enhancing the reliability of LLM outputs. The RAG framework allows LLMs to refer to information retrieved from external databases, thereby improving the reliability of the generated content. In this paper, we aim to enhance the reliability of the collected results by leveraging the RAG framework to collect reasons for impressions based on the content of Web pages, compared to relying solely on the prior knowledge of LLMs. We also show that ChatGPT outperforms an existing model of mT5 (Xue et al., 2021) in reason collection.

The reasons for impressions obtained through this method, however, are highly duplicated and hence redundant, making it difficult for users to recognize the critiques and related information about celebrities at a glance. Therefore, we categorize and rank the multiple reasons for impressions obtained for each keyword, considering the frequency of the reasons. This allows users to easily understand the reasons behind the impressions on celebrities' aspects in an aggregated ranked format, enabling the exploration of critiques and relevant information on celebrity-related topics. We employ ChatGPT also for this part.

The followings give the contribution of this paper:

1. We proposed a novel approach using ChatGPT, a large language model, to effectively collect and aggregate impressions on celebrities' aspects from X posts.

2. In the RAG framework, we showed that ChatGPT is highly effective in collecting and aggregating reasons for the impressions on celebrities from Web pages.

3. In collecting reasons for impressions on celebrities, we demonstrated that ChatGPT outperforms mT5, highlighting the effectiveness of ChatGPT in extracting relevant information from Web pages.

2 Related Work

Previous work on assisting information access regarding celebrities includes studies on constructing large-scale celebrity profile datasets by combining Twitter and Wikidata (Wiegmann et al., 2019) and analyzing persuasion strategies in celebrities' language use on social media to predict their influence (Chang et al., 2021). Regarding assisting fans of celebrities, previous work includes studies on determining the relationship between celebrities and impressions in microblog posts (Nozaki et al., 2022) and those on mining impressions on celebrities' aspects in microblog posts (Sugawara and Utsuro, 2022). This paper differs from those previous work in that we search Web pages for reasons behind impressions on celebrities' aspects mined from microblog posts. This paper also differs from the previous work in that we employ ChatGPT, a large language model, to extract impressions on celebrities' aspects from microblog posts, while the previous studies relied on other methods such as co-occurrence frequency statistics.

Furthermore, one of the key characteristics of this paper is the use of RAG (Lewis et al., 2020), which improves the reliability of LLM-generated output by allowing reference to external information. RAG allows LLMs to refer to information

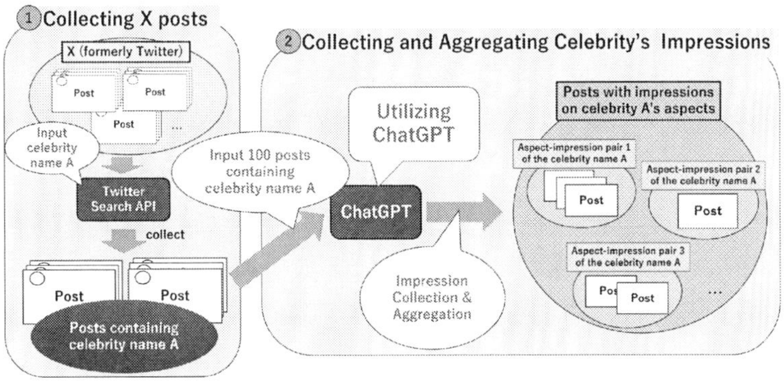

Figure 2: Overview of Collecting and Aggregating Impressions on Aspects of Celebrities from X Posts

retrieved from external databases, enhancing the accuracy and trustworthiness of the generated content. In this paper, we leverage RAG to collect reasons for impressions based on the content of Web pages, aiming to significantly improve the reliability of the collected results compared to traditional methods that rely solely on the knowledge stored within the LLMs. Recent studies have explored various RAG applications and improvements, such as context tuning for tool retrieval and plan generation (Anantha and Vodianik, 2024) improving open-domain table question answering with late interaction models and joint training (Lin et al., 2023), few-shot multilingual image captioning without requiring supervised training (Ramos et al., 2023), and incorporating additional components for more powerful question answering systems (Tan et al., 2023). Other works have focused on improving zero-shot performance on low-resource languages using prompts from high-resource languages (Nie et al., 2023), leveraging retrieval for non-knowledge-intensive tasks with a two-stage framework (Guo et al., 2023), and incorporating rich answer encoding for better generation quality in knowledge-intensive tasks (Huang et al., 2023).

ChatGPT-related research also includes entity linking (Peeters and Bizer, 2023), and dialogue analysis (Finch et al., 2023), and text summarization (Zhang et al., 2023b; Pu and Demberg, 2023; Zhang et al., 2023a). This paper differs in that we utilize ChatGPT for both collecting and aggregating impressions on celebrities' aspects, as well as collecting and aggregating the reasons for these impressions.

3 Aspect, Impression, and Reason

In this study, we define "aspect", "impression", and "reason" as follows:

aspect: a specific attribute, characteristics, or topic related to a celebrity. This can include physical features, skills or talents, specific works or performances, interactions or relationships, behaviors, or other notable elements of their public persona.

impression: a subjective opinion, evaluation, or feeling about a celebrity's aspect, often expressed through adjectives, descriptive phrases, or statements of recognition.

reason: the underlying explanations, justifications, or evidences that support a particular impression about a celebrity's aspect. Reasons are typically more detailed and context-rich than impressions, often found in longer-form content such as Web articles or detailed social media posts.

4 Collecting Impressions from X Posts using ChatGPT

This section describes the procedure of collecting posts containing celebrity names from X, identifying posts that mention impressions on specific aspects of celebrities, and aggregating them into aspect-impression pairs using ChatGPT. An overview is illustrated in Figure 2.

4.1 Collecting X posts

In this paper, we selected 10 celebrities who are frequently discussed on X and collected posts using their names as search queries from September 7,

celebrity name	number of posts	number of non-repost posts
Ryosuke Yamada	938,882	213,886
Kazunari Ninomiya	851,579	164,130
Fuma Kikuchi	1,131,863	185,823
Shun Oguri	425,188	120,583
Go Ayano	272,232	95,890
Kentaro Sakaguchi	284,622	64,472
Ryoma Takeuchi	83,368	31,670
Kasumi Arimura	370,956	105,084
Tomoya Nakamura	702,807	206,632
Mei Nagano	246,489	58,636
Total	5,307,986	1,246,806

Table 1: Numbers of Collected Posts for Each Celebrity Name

celebrity name	aggregated aspect	impression
Ryosuke Yamada	beauty	outstanding
	quality of dance	high
	interaction with Daiki Shigeoka	touching
	Karubi harassment	funny
	kidnapping of Jr.	cute
	eye contact with camera	charming
Kazunari Ninomiya	movie "Ragelee yori Ai wo Komete"	masterpiece and moving
	acting skills	recognized as a good actor
	activities during year-end and New Year	enjoyment for fans
	personality	loved and respected by fans
	radio program	enjoyment for fans

Table 2: Examples of Aspect-Impression Pairs aggregated by ChatGPT

2022 to April 9, 2023. This process is depicted in the "Collecting X posts" part of Figure 2. The Twitter Search API[1] was used for post collection. The numbers of posts and non-repost posts collected for each celebrity name are shown in Table 1. In this paper, we only use non-repost posts.

4.2 Collecting/Aggregating Impressions from Posts

Next, we perform two main tasks on the X posts containing a specific celebrity name collected in the previous section. First, we collect posts that mention impressions on specific aspects of that celebrity. Second, we aggregate the collected information into aspect-impression pairs. These tasks are illustrated in the "Collecting and Aggregating Celebrity's Impressions" part of Figure 2. As the framework for these tasks, we utilize ChatGPT[2] model, specifically `gpt-4-turbo-2024-04-09`. The specific prompts given to ChatGPT are shown in Figure 5 of Appendix A. Here, we show an example of a prompt targeting the celebrity "Ryosuke Yamada". The prompts begin by providing posts, and instruct to first collect posts that mention what aspects (impression targets) of Ryosuke Yamada and what kind of impressions are associated with those aspects. Next, it instructs to aggregate the collected posts based on the impression targets and their corresponding impressions. The desired output format is then specified, indicating to output the pairs of the impression target and the corresponding impression, along with the specific relevant posts. Due to the limitation of input token numbers, 100 posts are provided as an example. The prompts also instruct not to include the celebrity's name "<Ryosuke Yamada>" in the impression targets, and to be careful not to make the impression targets and their corresponding impressions redundant. Finally, before outputting, it instructs to double-check if there exist any remaining posts that were not collected nor aggregated.

To evaluate the performance of the proposed approach, we manually annotate a subset of the collected posts to create a reference dataset. The evaluation is conducted for both the collection and the aggregation tasks by comparing the outputs generated by ChatGPT with the reference. The results are summarized in Table 3. For the collecting task,

[1]https://developer.twitter.com/en/docs/tweets/search/api-reference/get-search-tweets

[2]https://platform.openai.com/docs/models/

celebrity name	total posts	collecting celebrity's impressions		aggregating celebrity's impressions	
		recall [# (ref ∩ collected) # ref]	precision [# (ref ∩ collected) # collected]	recall [# (ref ∩ aggregated) # ref]	precision [# (ref ∩ aggregated) # aggregated]
Ryosuke Yamada	100	0.42 (=10/24)	0.91 (=10/11)	0.82 (=9/11)	1.00 (=9/9)
Kazunari Ninomiya	100	0.73 (=8/11)	0.80 (=8/10)	0.38 (=3/8)	0.60 (=3/5)
Fuma Kikuchi	100	0.63 (=5/8)	0.71 (=5/7)	0.60 (=3/5)	0.60 (=3/5)
Shun Oguri	100	0.67 (=2/3)	0.40 (=2/5)	0.67 (=2/3)	0.50 (=2/4)
Go Ayano	100	0.69 (=9/13)	0.69 (=9/13)	0.50 (=3/6)	0.60 (=3/5)
Total/Micro Average	500	0.58 (=34/59)	0.74 (=34/46)	0.61 (=20/33)	0.71 (=20/28)

Table 3: Manual Evaluation Results of Collecting/Aggregating Impressions on Aspects of Celebrities

the evaluation results are shown in the "collecting celebrity's impressions" section of Table 3. The table presents the total number of posts used for evaluation in the "total posts" column. The "recall" and "precision" columns display the recall and precision of ChatGPT's performance for the collection task, respectively, where recall is calculated as [# (ref ∩ collected) / # ref] and precision as [# (ref ∩ collected) / # collected]. Similarly, for the aggregation task, the evaluation results are presented in the "aggregating celebrity's impressions" section of Table 3. The evaluation is conducted using the posts that were identified as containing impressions on aspects of celebrities by ChatGPT in the collection task. The "recall" and "precision" columns show the recall and precision of ChatGPT's performance for the aggregating task, respectively, where recall is calculated as [# (ref ∩ aggregated) / # ref] and precision as [# (ref ∩ aggregated) / # aggregated].

Table 2 shows examples of the aspect-impression pairs aggregated by ChatGPT for the celebrities Ryosuke Yamada and Kazunari Ninomiya. The table presents the aggregated aspects and their corresponding impressions for each celebrity. As can be seen from the examples in the table, ChatGPT is capable of capturing and aggregating a wide range of aspects and impressions for both celebrities. For Ryosuke Yamada, this includes physical appearance, performance skills, interactions with others, behavior on variety shows, roles in dramas, and even eye contact with the camera. For Kazunari Ninomiya, ChatGPT aggregates aspects such as his highly reputed movie, acting skills, activities during year-end and New Year, personality, and radio program. These examples demonstrate that our proposed method using ChatGPT can effectively address the limitations of the previous research (Sugawara and Utsuro, 2022), which considered the aspects of celebrities to be in the form of "A (celebrity name)'s B (noun)" and used a language model to determine whether an sentiment relation exists between the celebrity's aspect and the impression. By leveraging the advanced natural language understanding capabilities of ChatGPT, our approach allows for a more flexible and comprehensive analysis of celebrity aspects and impressions. Our method can identify and analyze aspects that may not fit the "A's B" format, capture impressions expressed in various parts of speech, not just adjectives, and consider the broader context of posts, leading to more accurate interpretation of sentiments. Our approach can better identify and aggregate the major impressions on celebrities' aspects from the vast amount of information available in X posts, while taking into account the context of the posts. This allows for a more comprehensive and nuanced understanding of the public's perceptions of celebrities, going beyond the limitations of the previous method.

5 Reason Collection/Aggregation

This section describes the procedure of collecting and aggregating reasons for impressions from Web pages using ChatGPT. Section 5.1 discusses the process of selecting pairs of aspects and their corresponding impressions from those collected and aggregated in Section 4, which will be used as keywords for searching for Web pages. Section 5.2 describes the method for searching for Web pages using the selected keywords and collecting the content of the Web pages. Section 5.3 explains the procedure for collecting reasons for impressions from the collected Web page contents and presents the results of manual evaluation. Section 5.4 discusses the procedure for aggregating the collected reasons for impressions and presents the results of manual evaluation.

5.1 Selecting Aspect-Impression Pairs

In this section, we describe the process of selecting pairs of aspects and their corresponding impressions from those collected and aggregated in

Section 4, which will be used as keywords for searching for Web pages. As will be explained in detail in Section 5.2, we use the Google search engine[3] for searching for Web pages in this study. Among the aspect-impression pairs collected and aggregated in Section 4, some may not yield sufficient number of Web pages when used directly as search keywords on the Google search engine. Examples of such pairs collected for the celebrity "Ryosuke Yamada" include "interaction with Daiki Shigeoka - touching" and "kidnapping of Jr. - cute" as shown in Table 2. Therefore, instead of simple Google searches, it is necessary to make significant efforts in the search process, such as collecting many Web pages related to the celebrity in advance and performing Semantic search or Embedding search (Reimers and Gurevych, 2019; Cer et al., 2018; Karpukhin et al., 2020) within those pages. This is a challenge that should be addressed in the future. Considering this, in this study, we use 10 aspect-impression pairs that are judged to be directly usable as search keywords on the Google search engine for the subsequent processes. These 10 pairs are listed in the "aggregated aspect" and "impression" columns of Table 4 of Appendix B. The aim of the following sections is to clarify whether it is possible to collect and aggregate reasons for impressions using these selected aspect-impression pairs as search keywords.

5.2 Web Page Search

First, we search for Web pages using the Google search engine with the keywords selected in the previous section. Next, we manually collect the content of the top 30 Web pages in the search results. This series of operations are performed for all the keywords. For example, in the case of "Ryosuke Yamada's acting performance - amazing", we first search for Web pages using "Ryosuke Yamada's acting performance - amazing" as the query and collect the content of the top 30 Web pages. Those Web pages are expected to contain reasons for the impressions expressed in the keywords such as "reasons why Ryosuke Yamada's acting performance is amazing".

5.3 Reason Collection

5.3.1 The Procedure

Next, we use the content of the Web pages collected in the previous section to collect reasons for impressions for each Web page. We use the ChatGPT model `gpt-4-0613` as the framework for collecting reasons for impressions. The entire prompt given to ChatGPT is shown in Figure 6 of Appendix B[4]. Here, we show an example of a prompt targeting the keyword "Ryosuke Yamada's acting performance - amazing". First, we use the prompt in Figure 6 of Appendix B to instruct ChatGPT to search for reasons for impressions based on the collected Web pages without using prior knowledge of ChatGPT itself but referring to the content of the retrieved Web pages as added as the context. If the added context information does not contain reasons for impressions, ChatGPT is instructed to output only "not included". By having ChatGPT search for reasons for impressions based on the content of Web pages rather than the prior knowledge of ChatGPT itself, we expect to suppress the output of information that differs from or does not exist in the Web search results at that moment, a phenomenon known as hallucination.

5.3.2 Manual Evaluation

Here, we evaluate the reasons for impressions collected by ChatGPT by comparing them with manually collected reference reasons for impressions, where the evaluation is performed with 10 sets of keywords.

Based on the content of Web pages obtained for each keyword in Section 5.2, the first author manually collected reasons for impressions. For example, for the keyword "Ryosuke Yamada's acting performance - amazing", the first author manually examined each collected Web page and extracted statements that correspond to reasons why "Ryosuke Yamada's acting is said to be amazing". These extracted reasons were compiled into a list for each Web page, serving as our reference data. We then assess whether ChatGPT can output corresponding reasons, allowing for variations in wording.

Based on the multiset[5] of reasons $S(d)$ output by ChatGPT for a given Web page d and the multiset of reference reasons $R(d)$ manually prepared

[3] `https://www.google.co.jp/`

[4] We confirmed through experimental ablation studies that, although all the prompts in Figure 6 of Appendix B and Figure 7 of Appendix B can be replaced with similar sentences, the performance of ChatGPT is severely damaged if any of them is removed.

[5] Note here that it can happen that ChatGPT redundantly outputs a single reason several times from a single Web page d. Similarly, it is allowed that reference reasons manually collected from a single Web page d may include a single reason several times, resulting in a multiset.

for the Web page d[6], the recall and precision are defined as follows:

$$\text{Recall} = \sum_d |R(d) \cap S(d)| / \sum_d |R(d)|,$$

$$\text{Precision} = \sum_d |R(d) \cap S(d)| / \sum_d |S(d)|$$

The evaluation is performed for each collected Web page, and the micro-average is used as the evaluation result for each keyword. The overall evaluation results are measured as the macro-average of the evaluation results for the total 10 keywords for evaluation. The overall evaluation results for reason collection are shown in Figure 3(a). As a result, in reason collection, high performance around 0.9 are achieved for recall, precision, and F1-score. As will be presented in Table 4 in section 6.2 and in Appendix B, half of the retrieved Web pages are without reasons. Thus, high performance of reason collection by ChatGPT reveals that ChatGPT is highly tolerant of noisy context such as those Web page retrieval errors, where ChatGPT does not collect incorrect reasons even from those noisy Web pages.

5.4 Reason Aggregation

5.4.1 The Procedure

Next, we aggregate the reasons for impressions collected in the previous section. Here, we use the ChatGPT model `gpt-4-1106-preview`. The entire prompt given to ChatGPT is shown in Figure 7 of Appendix B. Again, we show an example of a prompt targeting the keyword "Ryosuke Yamada's acting performance - amazing". First, the prompt in Figure 7 of Appendix B indicates that, the series of instructions are followed by summaries of Web pages related to the specified keyword. Furthermore, we instruct ChatGPT to perform reason aggregation by categorizing reasons given as the content mentioned in each Web page summary. Those instructions represent how ChatGPT aggregates reasons for impressions. In the example of Figure 7 of Appendix B, we begin by stating that we will provide ChatGPT with summaries of Web pages related to the keyword "Ryosuke Yamada's acting performance - amazing". Next, we present examples of categories and the corresponding sentences that are regarded as examples of reasons, instructing ChatGPT to categorize reasons of impressions following these examples. We also instruct ChatGPT to create new categories if the Web page summary includes categories that do not correspond to the provided examples.

By providing category examples in advance, we aim to stabilize ChatGPT's output. The actual category examples and corresponding sentences provided here are totally unrelated to the specified keyword "Ryosuke Yamada's acting performance - amazing". The subsequent instructions are further given with examples to simply guide the output format to obtain results in a format that is easy to automatically interpret. Details on the output format can be found in Appendix D.

5.4.2 Manual Evaluation Procedure

Here, we evaluate the reasons for impressions aggregated using ChatGPT by comparing them with manually aggregated reference reasons, where the evaluation is performed with 10 keywords. The manually aggregated reference reasons were created solely by the first author, who grouped similar reasons from the reference data used in the reason collection step. This process involved carefully examining the collected reasons for each keyword and combining those that expressed similar concepts or ideas, ensuring a concise yet comprehensive set of aggregated reasons. At this point, we define the following seven multisets/sets. Specifically, first, we define S' as the multiset of reasons aggregated by ChatGPT based on the collected reasons, and R as the set of distinct reference reasons prepared manually after aggregation[7]. Next, we define S'_r as the multiset of elements of S', where, for each of their elements, a corresponding reason exists in R. In contrast, we define $S'_{\neg r}$ as the multiset of the elements of S', where, for each of their elements, no corresponding reason exists in R. Then, we obtain S_r as the set of elements of S'_r by aggregating multiple reasons corresponding to a single reason in R into one reason. In contrast, we also obtain $S_{\neg r}$ as the set of elements of $S'_{\neg r}$ by aggregating multiple reasons into one reason. Finally, we define S as the union of S_r and $S_{\neg r}$.

Based on these multisets/sets, recall, precision, and redundancy are defined as follows. Here, redundancy measures how well ChatGPT can avoid redundancy in the aggregated reasons by comparing the number of redundant reasons before and after aggregation. The overall evaluation results are calculated as the macro-average of the evaluation

[6]See Appendix C.1 for details on the inter-annotator agreement in reason collection.

[7]See Appendix C.2 for details on the inter-annotator agreement in reason aggregation.

results for the total 10 keywords.

$$\text{Recall} = |S_r|/|R|, \ \ \text{Precision} = |S_r|/|S|,$$

$$\text{Redundancy} = |S'_r|/|S_r|$$

5.4.3 Manual Evaluation Results

We conducted an experiment to investigate the impact of providing category examples within the prompts on the manual evaluation results. The overall evaluation results for reason aggregation are shown in "w/ examples" of the "Reason Aggregation" section in Figure 3. As a result, in reason aggregation with examples, recall was 0.77, precision was 0.88, F1-score was 0.81, and redundancy was 1.40, where, overall, reason aggregation with examples outperforms that without examples in terms of recall and F1-score, while it was more redundant than that without examples, simply because it outputs more reasons than that without examples. These results suggest that by excluding category examples, ChatGPT can perform more concise and accurate categorization of reasons. However, it also tends to fail in detecting several reasons as illustrated in the damage in recall. In other words, providing examples allows ChatGPT to generate results closer to human annotations, but at the cost of potentially performing more redundant categorization.

6 Automatic Evaluation of Reason Detection/Collection

6.1 Task Definition: Reason Detection/Collection

In this section, we focus on two tasks for automatic evaluation: reason detection and reason collection. Given a keyword consisting of a celebrity name, an aspect and an impression such as "Ryosuke Yamada's acting performance - amazing" and a retrieved Web page in relation to the keyword, the reason detection task outputs a binary judgment whether or not there exist one or more reasons in the retrieved Web page for the question composed from the keyword as in "Why is Ryosuke Yamada's acting performance said to be amazing?". The output of the reason detection task is "YES" or "not included". The evaluation metrics for this task are recall, precision, and F1-score based on the reference judgment result.

The reason collection task aims to generate reasons for impressions from retrieved Web pages, where the inputs to the task are the same as the reason detection task. In the automatic evaluation, ROUGE-L is used as an evaluation metric for the reason collection results by ChatGPT and mT5, which measures the longest common subsequence between the generated reasons and the manually created reference reasons[8] . The sentences corresponding to reasons are rarely concentrated in one location but often span multiple parts within the text. Therefore, it is more appropriate to apply the procedure of generating reasons based on context rather than extracting reason chunks from the context. Here, we apply mT5 (Xue et al., 2021) as a comparison to ChatGPT for both tasks.

6.2 Evaluation

This section describes the automatic evaluation procedure for reason detection and reason collection by ChatGPT and mT5. The dataset for fine-tuning mT5[9] was created using the Web pages collected in section 5.2. Specifically, first, question sentences for fine-tuning of mT5 are set based on the keywords used for collecting Web pages. For example, for a Web page collected in relation to the keyword "Ryosuke Yamada's acting performance - amazing", the question sentence is set as "Why is Ryosuke Yamada's acting performance said to be amazing?" Next, the context for answering the question is set. Here, the collected Web pages are first split into sentences by periods, and then split sentences are concatenated as a chunk under the restriction of satisfying the input token length upper bound of mT5. After that, for each chunk, if it contains sentences that are the reasons for impressions, all the relevant sentences are manually extracted and combined to form the reference answer. If no chunk contains a sentence that is regarded as the reason for impressions, the Web page is judged as unanswerable to the question and "" (blank) is set as the reference answer. The statistics of the numbers of Web pages are shown in Table 4 of Appendix B.

For ChatGPT, as in Figure 6 of Appendix B, it is instructed to output "not included" if there is no reason. Thus, if only "not included" is output, it is treated as no reason is observed. For mT5, if the output is "" (blank), it is treated as no reason is observed. Moreover, there could be cases where

[8]While ROUGE-L relies on exact string matching, future work will explore metrics that better capture embedding based semantic similarity beyond string matching, such as BERTScore, BARTScore, and SentenceBERT, for a more comprehensive evaluation.

[9]https://huggingface.co/google/mt5-base

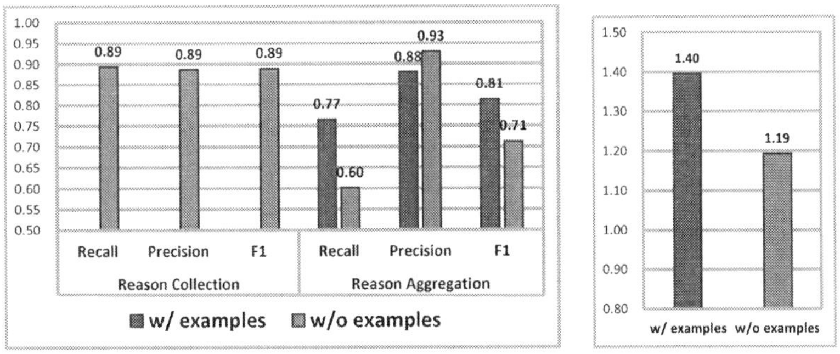

(a) Recall, Precision, and F1 Score

(b) Redundancy of Reason Aggregation

Figure 3: Manual Evaluation Results of Reason Collection/Aggregation by ChatGPT

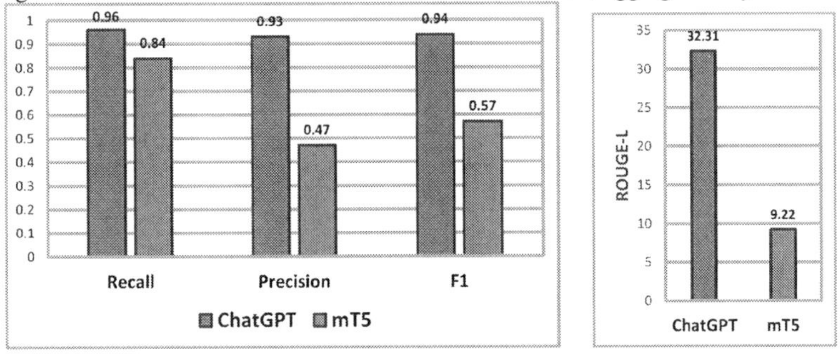

(a) reason detection

(b) reason collection

Figure 4: Automatic Evaluation Results of Detecting/Collecting Reasons for Impressions

mT5 outputs only symbols such as "." or "?", which are also treated as no reason is observed.

For the training and evaluation of mT5, 5-fold cross validation was performed based on the dataset shown in Table 4 of Appendix B, where each line is counted as the unit of 5-fold cross validation. In each fold of 5-fold cross validation, the dataset for 8 out of the 10 keywords shown in Table 4 was used as the training data[10], and the dataset for the remaining 2 keywords was used as the evaluation data. When generating answers to the evaluation data, answer generation is first performed on each chunk. Then, for each Web page, the generated answers are concatenated and then further used as the context when generating an answer for the whole Web page span again. Similar to reason collection by ChatGPT in section 5.3, this procedure allows for generating an answer for each Web page span[11].

ChatGPT outperformed mT5 for all evaluation results. In the evaluation of reason detection, as shown in Figure 4(a), ChatGPT outperformed mT5 in all the metrics, with a particularly large difference in precision. This means that mT5 tends to erroneously output reasons, corresponding to over detection of reasons. In contrast, ChatGPT achieved over 90% recall and precision. From the ROUGE-L evaluation results shown in Figure 4(b), on the other hand, ChatGPT is able to generate reasons much closer to the reference compared to mT5.

7 Conclusion

In this paper, we proposed a method to augment fans of celebrities to critique and explore information concerning celebrities. We conducted evaluation on the results obtained by the proposed method by comparing them with manually collected and aggregated reasons for impressions. We also evaluated the methods for reason collection with ChatGPT and mT5, confirming that ChatGPT shows higher performance. Beyond mT5, we plan to compare ChatGPT with larger models that have a comparable number of parameters, such as Mistral Large[12] or LLaMA 3 70B[13] , to provide a more meaningful evaluation of the proposed method.

8 Limitations

While our proposed method demonstrates promising results, it is important to acknowledge its lim-

[10]The number of training epochs is set as five.

[11]See Appendix C.3 for details on the inter-annotator agreement in reason detection.

[12]https://mistral.ai/news/mistral-large/

[13]https://ai.meta.com/blog/meta-llama-3/

itations. LLMs, including ChatGPT, are prone to hallucinations and may generate plausible but incorrect information. While our use of the RAG framework mitigates this risk, it does not eliminate it entirely. The manual aspects of our data collection and processing methods may pose challenges for exact reproducibility, despite our efforts to provide detailed descriptions.

Our approach relies on aspect-impression pairs that can be directly used as search keywords. For pairs that do not yield sufficient Web pages, more sophisticated information retrieval techniques, such as semantic or embedding search (Reimers and Gurevych, 2019; Cer et al., 2018; Karpukhin et al., 2020), may be necessary in future research.

9 Ethical Statements

The use of AI to analyze and aggregate information about celebrities raises several ethical concerns that we must address. While we use publicly available information, the aggregation and analysis of this data may have unintended consequences for the individuals involved. We emphasize the importance of using this information responsibly and respectfully. The potential for generating or amplifying false information is a significant concern. We acknowledge that our method, despite safeguards, could inadvertently contribute to the spread of misinformation if not used cautiously. There is also a risk that our system could reinforce existing biases or create echo chambers. We encourage users to seek diverse sources and perspectives beyond what our system provides.

We stress that the intent of this research is not to facilitate unwarranted criticism or invasion of privacy, but to promote more informed and nuanced understanding of public figures and media representation. We recognize the broader implications of developing tools that aggregate and analyze public sentiment. We call for ongoing dialogue about the ethical use of such technologies and their impact on public discourse.

In light of these considerations, we recommend that users of our system approach the generated information critically, cross-reference with reliable sources, and use the tool as a starting point for further exploration rather than as a definitive source of information. As researchers, we commit to continuing to refine our methods to address these limitations and ethical concerns, and to contribute to the responsible development of AI technologies in media analysis.

References

R. Anantha and D. Vodianik. 2024. Context tuning for retrieval augmented generation. In *Proc. UncertaiNLP*, pages 15–22.

D. Cer, Y. Yang, S. Kong, N. Hua, N. Limtiaco, R. S. John, N. Constant, M. Guajardo-Cespedes, S. Yuan, C. Tar, Y. Sung, B. Strope, and R. Kurzweil. 2018. Universal Sentence Encoder. *arXiv preprint arXiv:1803.11175*.

Y. Chang, P. A. Wang, H. Hung, K. Khóo, and S. Hsieh. 2021. Examine persuasion strategies in Chinese on social media. In *Proc. 35th PACLIC*, page 108–118.

S. E. Finch, E. S. Paek, and J. D. Choi. 2023. Leveraging large language models for automated dialogue analysis. In *Proc. 24th SIGDIAL*, pages 202–215.

Z. Guo, S. Cheng, Y. Wang, P. Li, and Y. Liu. 2023. Prompt-Guided Retrieval Augmentation for Non-Knowledge-Intensive Tasks. In *Findings ACL*, pages 10896—10912.

W. Huang, M. Lapata, P. Vougiouklis, N. Papasarantopoulos, and J. Pan. 2023. Retrieval Augmented Generation with Rich Answer Encoding. In *Proc. 13th IJCNLP and 3rd AACL*, pages 1012—1025.

V. Karpukhin, B. Oguz, S. Min, P. Lewis, L. Wu, S. Edunov, D. Chen, and W. Yih. 2020. Dense Passage Retrieval for Open-Domain Question Answering. In *EMNLP*, pages 6769–6781.

P. Lewis, E. Perez, et al. 2020. Retrieval-augmented generation for knowledge-intensive NLP tasks. In *Proc. 34th NeurIPS*, pages 483–498.

W. Lin, R. Blloshmi, B. Byrne, A. de Gispert, and G. Iglesias. 2023. LI-RAGE: Late Interaction Retrieval Augmented Generation with Explicit Signals for Open-Domain Table Question Answering. In *Proc. 61st ACL*, pages 1557—-1566.

E. Nie, S. Liang, H. Schmid, and H. Schütze. 2023. Cross-Lingual Retrieval Augmented Prompt for Low-Resource Languages. In *Findings ACL*, pages 8320—-8340.

Y. Nozaki, K. Sugawara, Y. Zenimoto, and T. Utsuro. 2022. Tweet review mining focusing on celebrities by MRC based on BERT. In *Proc. 36th PACLIC*, pages 757–766.

R. Peeters and C. Bizer. 2023. Using ChatGPT for entity matching. *arXiv preprint arXiv:2305.03423*.

D. Pu and V. Demberg. 2023. ChatGPT vs Human-authored Text: Insights into Controllable Text Summarization and Sentence Style Transfer. In *Proc. 61st ACL-SRW*, pages 1–18.

R. Ramos, B. Martins, and D. Elliott. 2023. LMCap: Few-shot multilingual image captioning by retrieval augmented language model prompting. In *Findings of ACL*, pages 1635—-1651.

N. Reimers and I. Gurevych. 2019. Sentence-BERT: Sentence Embeddings using Siamese BERT-Networks. In *EMNLP-IJCNLP*, pages 3982–3992.

K. Sugawara and T. Utsuro. 2022. Developing a dataset for mining reviews in tweets focusing on celebrities' aspects. In *Proc. 7th ABCSS*, pages 466–472.

W. Tan, Y. Li, et al. 2023. Reimagining retrieval augmented language models for answering queries. In *Findings of ACL*, pages 6131–6146.

M. Wiegmann, B. Stein, and M. Potthast. 2019. Celebrity Profiling. In *Proc. 57th ACL*, pages 2611–-2618.

L. Xue, N. Constant, et al. 2021. mT5: A massively multilingual pre-trained text-to-text Transformer. In *Proc. NAACL*, pages 483–498.

H. Zhang, X. Liu, and J. Zhang. 2023a. Extractive Summarization via ChatGPT for Faithful Summary Generation. In *Findings of EMNLP*, pages 3270–3278.

H. Zhang, X. Liu, and J. Zhang. 2023b. SummIt: Iterative text summarization via ChatGPT. In *Findings of EMNLP*, pages 10644–10657.

A Collecting/Aggregating Impressions from X Posts

Figure 5 presents the specific prompts given to ChatGPT for collecting and aggregating impressions on celebrities' aspects from X posts as described in Section 4.2.

B Reason Collection/Aggregation

Table 4 shows the selected aspect-impression pairs for Web page search and the numbers of Web pages in the dataset for reason detection and collection as described in Section 5.1 and Section 6.2, respectively.

Figure 6 shows the prompts given to ChatGPT for collecting reasons for impressions from Web pages, as described in Section 5.3.

Figure 7 presents the prompts given to ChatGPT for aggregating the collected reasons for impressions, as described in Section 5.4.

C Inter-annotator Agreement for Reason Collection, Aggregation and Detection

C.1 Reason Collection

The multiset $R(d)$ of reference reasons is manually prepared by the first author following exactly the same procedure as presented in the previous section for ChatGPT. Another annotator ID=SK also manually prepared $R(d)$ for 6 keywords out of the overall 10, where, out of all the 5,625 sentences within the retrieved Web pages, 242 agreed to be collected as specifying reasons, 5,200 agreed not to be collected as specifying reasons, while 183 not agreed (collected by only one of the two annotators), resulting in 97% agreement rate and Cohen's kappa coefficient as 0.71, which is sufficiently high agreement.

C.2 Reason Aggregation

R was prepared by the first author in the overall evaluation. Here, for 6 keywords out of the overall 10, R was prepared independently by the annotator ID=SK from one's own result of collecting reasons in the previous section, where the agreement rate between the first author and the annotator ID=SK was 71%.

C.3 Reason Detection

The reference data for reason detection is directly constructed from the multiset $R(d)$ of reference reasons for the Web page d prepared by the first author. The agreement rate between the first author and the annotator ID=SK was 98% and Cohen's kappa coefficient was 0.95. The reference text for reason collection is composed by concatenating reasons manually prepared by the first author for each Web page.

D ChatGPT Output Format for Reason Aggregation

Specifically, we instruct ChatGPT to output the estimated category names and the corresponding Web page IDs in a ranked format. Each category name represents a reason for an impression accompanied with Web paged IDs, where the corresponding reason is collected from each of those Web pages. Those categories each representing a reason are ranked in descending order of the frequencies of their observation, expecting users to more easily understand the reasons for impressions. The output format is specified to be in a JSON format.

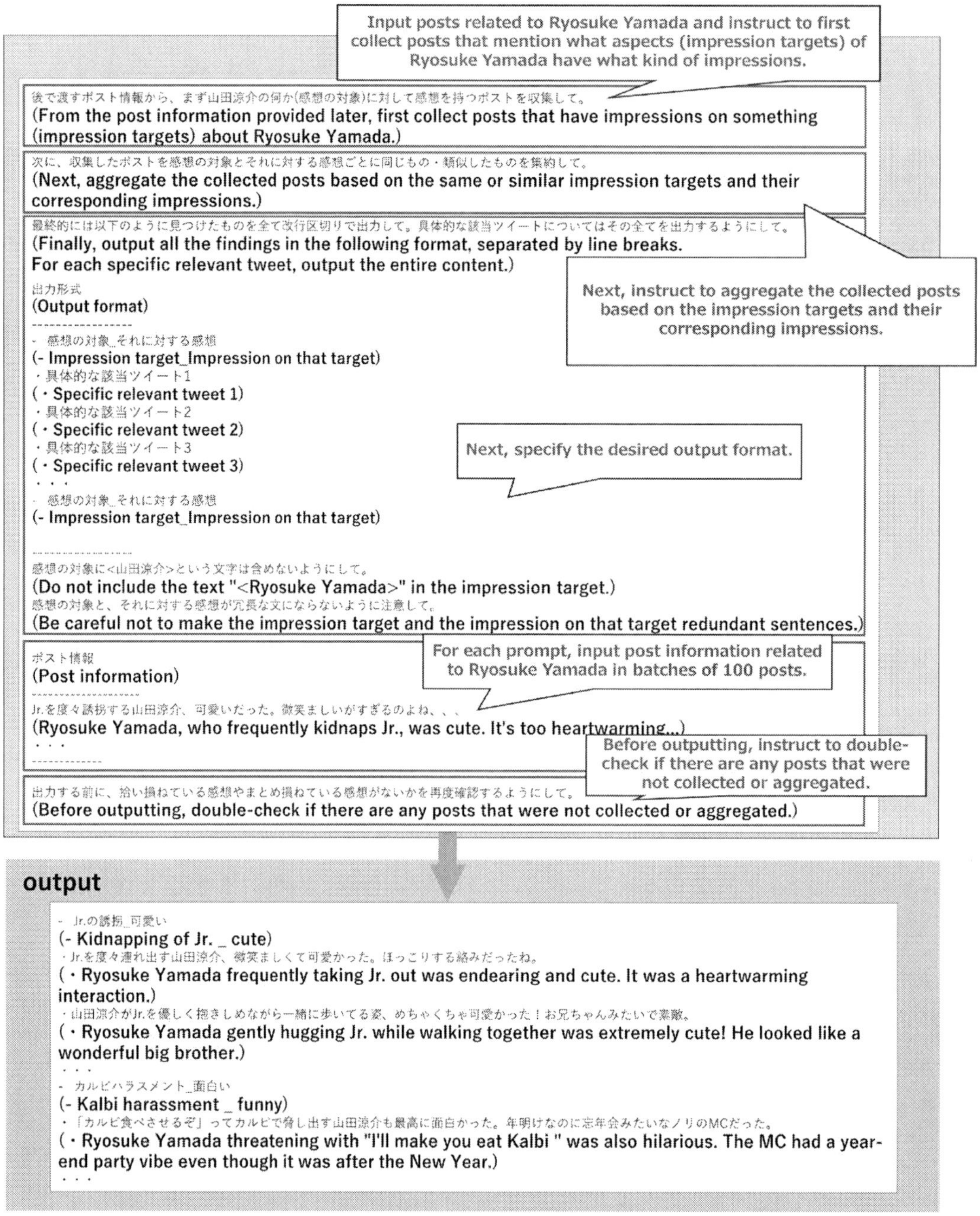

Figure 5: Prompts for Collecting/Aggregating Impressions from X Posts

celebrity name	aspect	impression	# Web pages		
			w/ reason	w/o reason	total
Ryosuke Yamada	acting performance	amazing	56	56	112
	drama	scary	22	22	44
		interesting	36	36	72
	face	good	20	20	40
Fuma Kikuchi	acting performance	amazing	33	33	66
	swamp	deep	8	8	16
Shun Oguri	acting performance	amazing	42	42	84
		bad	15	15	30
	face	good	12	12	24
	voice	good	13	13	26
total	—	—	**257**	**257**	**514**

Table 4: Selected Aspect-Impression Pairs and Numbers of Web Pages in the Dataset for Reason Detection/Collection

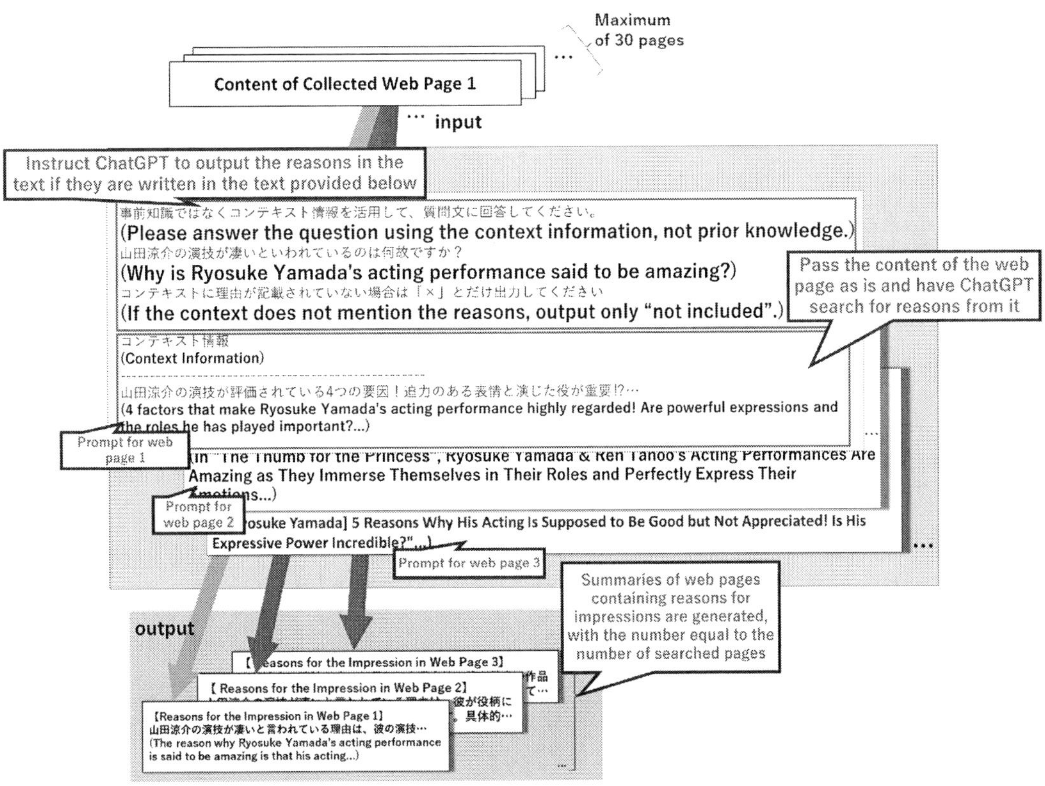

Figure 6: Prompts for Reason Collection by a Large Language Model (ChatGPT)

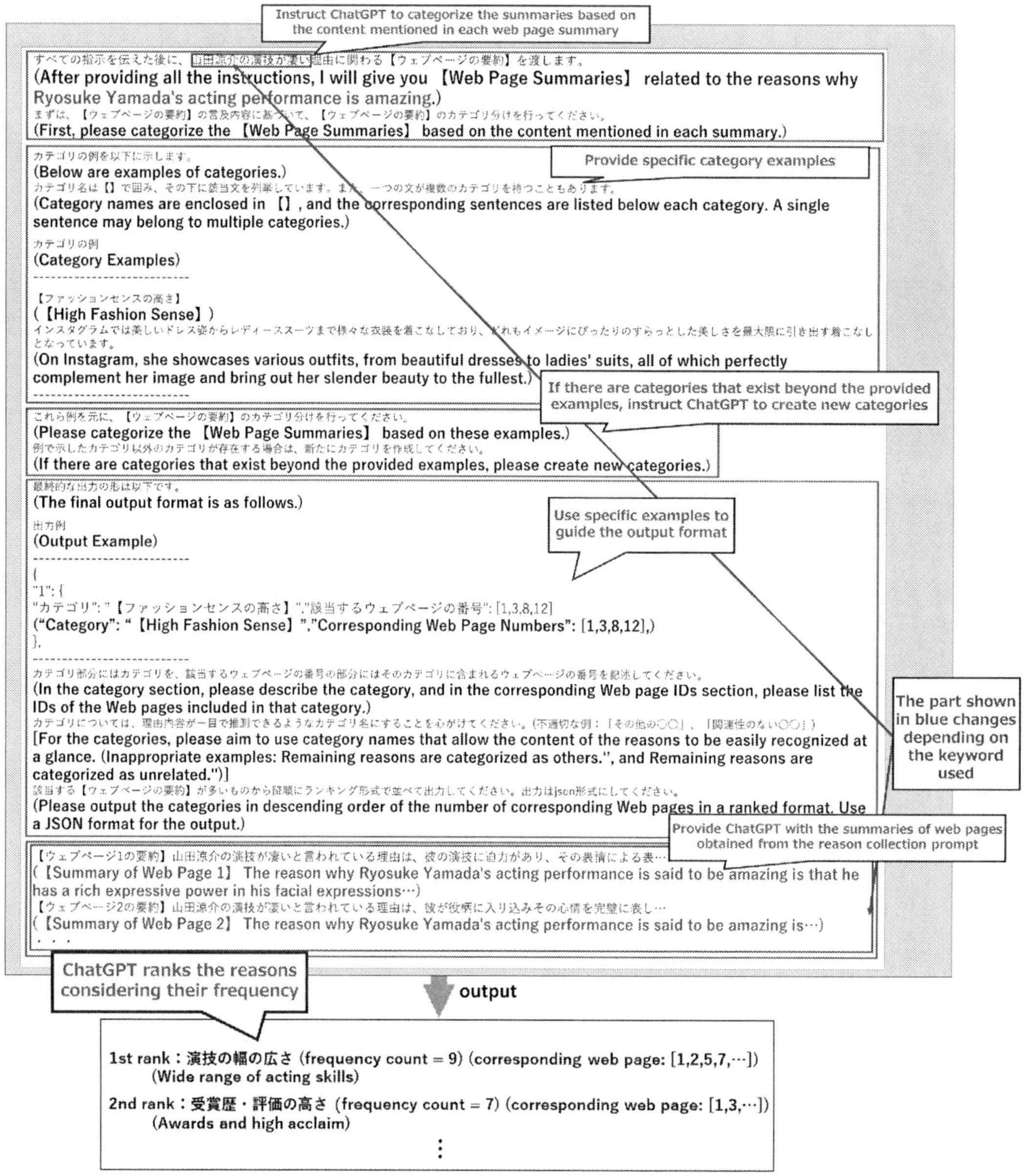

Figure 7: Prompts for Reason Aggregation by a Large Language Model (ChatGPT)

DSLR: Document Refinement with Sentence-Level Re-ranking and Reconstruction to Enhance Retrieval-Augmented Generation

Taeho Hwang Soyeong Jeong Sukmin Cho SeungYoon Han Jong C. Park*
School of Computing
Korea Advanced Institute of Science and Technology
{doubleyyh, starsuzi, nelllpic, seungyoonee, jongpark}@kaist.ac.kr

Abstract

Recent advancements in Large Language Models (LLMs) have significantly improved their performance across various Natural Language Processing (NLP) tasks. However, LLMs still struggle with generating non-factual responses due to limitations in their parametric memory. Retrieval-Augmented Generation (RAG) systems address this issue by incorporating external knowledge with a retrieval module. Despite their successes, however, current RAG systems face challenges with retrieval failures and the limited ability of LLMs to filter out irrelevant information. Therefore, in this work, we propose ***DSLR*** (**D**ocument Refinement with **S**entence-**L**evel **R**e-ranking and Reconstruction), an unsupervised framework that decomposes retrieved documents into sentences, filters out irrelevant sentences, and reconstructs them again into coherent passages. We experimentally validate *DSLR* on multiple open-domain QA datasets and the results demonstrate that *DSLR* significantly enhances the RAG performance over conventional fixed-size passage. Furthermore, our *DSLR* enhances performance in specific, yet realistic scenarios without the need for additional training, providing an effective and efficient solution for refining retrieved documents in RAG systems.

1 Introduction

Recent advancements in Large Language Models (LLMs) (Brown et al., 2020; OpenAI, 2023b; Touvron et al., 2023) have significantly expanded their capabilities across diverse knowledge-intensive tasks in Natural Language Processing (NLP), such as Question Answering (QA) (Kwiatkowski et al., 2019; Joshi et al., 2017; Rajpurkar et al., 2016). However, despite these capabilities, LLMs still face challenges such as generating plausible yet non-factual responses, known as hallucination, due to their reliance on limited parametric memory (Mallen et al., 2023). Also, it is noted that this parametric memory is static, as LLMs can learn knowledge only up to the specific date on which the training was completed. Therefore, these limitations restrict their adaptability to long-tailed or ever-evolving domains (Kasai et al., 2023) and to unseen knowledge outside their training data (Baek et al., 2023).

Retrieval-Augmented Generation (RAG) (Khandelwal et al., 2020; Lewis et al., 2020; Borgeaud et al., 2022; Shi et al., 2023b) has been introduced as an effective solution to address such problems. Specifically, RAG enhances LLMs by integrating non-parametric memories fetched from external knowledge bases using a retrieval module, which helps LLMs' responses grounded on factual evidence and makes them more up-to-date.

While the efficacy of RAG depends on the performance of the retrieval module, the instability of LLMs in incorporating the retrieved knowledge is also a critical challenge to RAG. To be specific, retrieved documents sometimes contain irrelevant information (Cho et al., 2023), and LLMs often struggle to effectively filter out such redundant details and focus on the most query-relevant knowledge (Shi et al., 2023a; Li et al., 2023; Liu et al., 2023; Wu et al., 2024), which leads to the failure of the overall RAG systems. Therefore, it is crucial to investigate how to effectively refine retrieved documents before augmenting them with LLMs, ensuring that the LLMs are not distracted by irrelevant information within retrieved documents.

Re-ranking the order of the retrieved document set (Nogueira et al., 2020; Qin et al., 2023a) or refining them into new documents (Wang et al., 2023; Xu et al., 2024) can be considered as solutions. However, they generally require high computational costs for training additional re-ranking or refining models. Another proposed solution is to reduce the retrieval granularity from passage-level to sentence-level which can help eliminate redun-

* Corresponding author

Proceedings of the 3rd Workshop on Knowledge Augmented Methods for NLP, pages 73–92
August 16, 2024

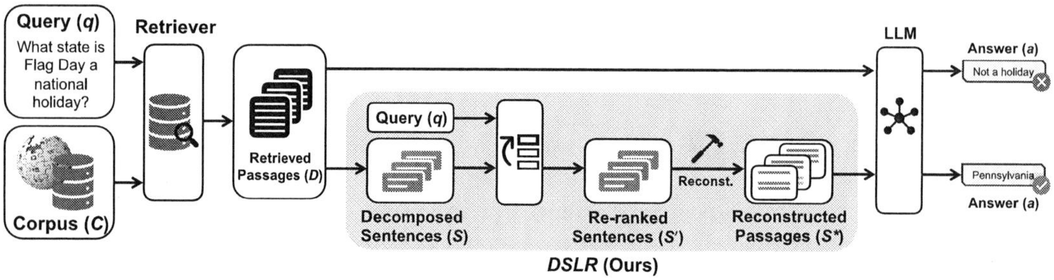

Figure 1: Comparison of the conventional RAG pipeline (top) and our sentence-level re-ranking and reconstruction framework (bottom) in an RAG system. Initially, both methods retrieve query-relevant documents at the passage level. The conventional approach directly utilizes these passages, which may contain redundant information leading to QA inaccuracies. By contrast, our method decomposes passages into sentences, re-ranks them based on relevance, and reconstructs them into coherent passages for more accurate LLM responses.

dant information within passages (Lee et al., 2021a; Chen et al., 2023). However, this might also inadvertently remove important contextual information, which is crucial for accurately answering the given queries (Choi et al., 2021). Therefore, we should explore a novel method that can effectively and efficiently filter out irrelevant information while maintaining the necessary contextual details.

In this work, we introduce an unsupervised ***DSLR*** (**D**ocument Refinement with **S**entence-**L**evel **R**e-ranking and Reconstruction) framework that consists of three steps: 1) decomposition, 2) re-ranking, and 3) reconstruction. Specifically, after retrieving the passage-level document, the *DSLR* framework operates by first decomposing the retrieved document into sentences for finer granularity and then filtering out the irrelevant sentences based on their re-ranking scores from the ranking models, including off-the-shelf retrievers and re-rankers. Finally, the remaining sentences are reconstructed into a single document to preserve the original contextual information. Note that *DSLR* is an unsupervised refinement framework, which does not require any additional training for re-ranking or reconstruction steps. The overall *DSLR* framework is illustrated in Figure 1.

We validate our framework across a diverse range of open-domain QA benchmarks, which include three general QA datasets and three specific QA datasets that require domain-specific or ever-evolving knowledge. Our experimental results show that *DSLR* significantly enhances the overall RAG performance and is comparable to, or even outperforms, the supervised baseline approaches. Specifically, when evaluated with specific QA datasets, *DSLR* shows high robustness in realistic settings. Furthermore, a detailed analysis demonstrates the effectiveness of each proposed step and how it contributes to the overall performance.

Our contributions in this work are threefold:

- We point out that recent RAG systems are largely vulnerable to redundant knowledge within fixed-size passage-level retrieved documents and that the existing refining strategies generally require additional training steps.
- We propose a *DSLR* framework that incorporates sentence-level re-ranking and reconstruction to effectively remove redundant knowledge that negatively affects the RAG system.
- We show that *DSLR* is highly effective and efficient even without additional training steps in both general and specific scenarios.

2 Related Work

Information Retrieval. Information Retrieval (IR) is the task of searching for query-relevant documents from a large corpus (Ponte and Croft, 1998), which has been widely applied for both search systems and various NLP tasks such as open-domain QA (Petroni et al., 2021). IR models can be categorized into sparse retrievers (Salton and Buckley, 1988; Robertson and Zaragoza, 2009), which use lexical metrics to calculate relevance scores between queries and documents, and dense retrievers (Karpukhin et al., 2020; Izacard et al., 2022), which embed queries and documents into a dense space that captures semantic relationships but requires significant computational resources (Jeong et al., 2022).

In order to further enhance retrieval performance, additional strategies have been proposed. Specifically, the re-ranking strategy improves retrieval performance by recalculating relevance scores using an additional re-ranking model (Nogueira and Cho, 2019; Nogueira et al., 2020; Zhuang et al., 2023), and then reordering the documents based on these scores. Recently, LLMs have shown remarkable re-ranking performance by generating relevance labels without requiring further fine-tuning (Liang et al., 2022; Qin et al., 2023b).

While the aforementioned work on IR (Wang et al., 2019; Karpukhin et al., 2020) generally assumes fixed-size, 100-word passages as the document length, some work has explored an optimal level of retrieval granularity (Seo et al., 2019; Lee et al., 2021a; Jeong et al., 2023; Chen et al., 2023). These approaches validate that a fine-grained level of granularity, containing only the knowledge needed to answer the query, can enhance the overall performance by excluding redundant details in the lengthy retrieved documents. However, reducing retrieval granularity to the sentence level can disrupt the original context and result in a loss of the document's coherence (Choi et al., 2021). In addition, sentence-level retrieval generally requires a much larger index size compared to passage-level retrieval (Lee et al., 2021b). By contrast, we investigate a novel framework for effectively re-ranking sentences within retrieved passage-level documents and then reconstructing the re-ranked sentences to preserve contextual integrity.

Retrieval-Augmented Generation. RAG has emerged as a promising solution for addressing LLMs' hallucination issues by leveraging external knowledge fetched by the retrieval module. Specifically, RAG incorporates retrieval modules that reduce the need to update the parameters of LLMs and help them generate accurate and reliable responses (Khandelwal et al., 2020; Lewis et al., 2020; Borgeaud et al., 2022; Shi et al., 2023b). Additionally, various real-world applications integrate RAG as a core component when deploying LLM-based services (OpenAI, 2023a; Chase, 2022; Qin et al., 2024). However, they still have limitations due to the imperfections of the retrieval module within RAG, where the retrieved documents containing query-irrelevant information can negatively lead the LLMs to generate inaccurate answers.

To address them, several studies have attempted to leverage the capabilities of LLMs to enhance their resilience against irrelevant knowledge. These approaches include crafting specialized prompts (Press et al., 2023; Cho et al., 2023), training plug-in knowledge verification models (Baek et al., 2023), adaptively retrieving the required knowledge (Jeong et al., 2024; Asai et al., 2024; Yu et al., 2023b), and augmenting knowledge using the capabilities of the LLM itself (Yu et al., 2023a). Among the promising solutions, recent studies show that further refining the retrieved documents into fine-grained knowledge can improve the RAG performance (Xu et al., 2024; Wang et al., 2024, 2023; Jin et al., 2024). However, such refinement strategies generally require additional fine-tuning on a specific dataset, which might result in limited generalizability and high computational cost. By contrast, our proposed refinement framework removes irrelevant information with unsupervised sentence-level re-ranking and reconstruction steps by using off-the-shelf ranking models without requiring additional training costs.

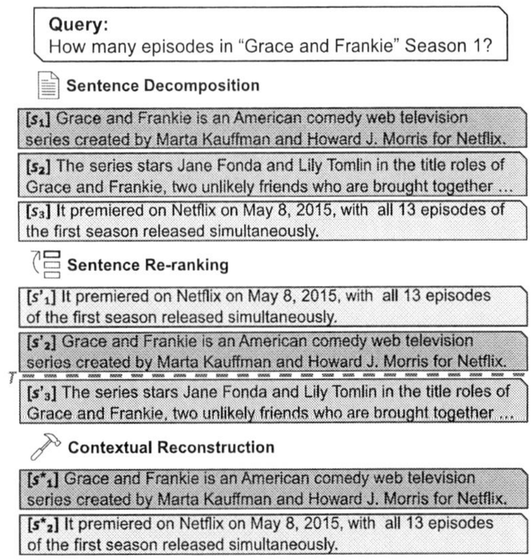

Figure 2: Examples of each step in the *DSLR* framework, which consists of three steps: 1) Sentence Decomposition 2) Sentence Re-ranking, and 3) Contextual Reconstruction.

3 Method

In this section, we describe a novel framework *DSLR* for enhancing the precision of retrieval results through sentence-level ranking and reconstruction, integrated into the RAG system. Note that *DSLR* does not require additional training.

3.1 Preliminaries

We first introduce the general RAG system, which consists of three steps: the retrieval step, the re-ranking step, and the generation step. Note that all steps focus on passage-level documents.

3.1.1 Retrieval Step

The retrieval step searches for a potentially relevant document set $\mathcal{D}$ to the given query q from a retrieval corpus $\mathcal{C}$ consisting of millions of documents. This retrieval step is conventionally performed using a sparse retriever S, such as BM25, which is widely used for processing large corpora due to its low latency. The sparse retriever S fetches the relevant documents having high relevant scores based on lexical values such as document length or unique word count. Formally, we define the retrieval step as:

$$\mathcal{D} = \text{Retrieve}(q, \mathcal{C}; S) = \{d_1, d_2, ..., d_n\}$$

where d_k represents a document having the top-k score among the retrieval corpus $\mathcal{C}$ for a given query q, and n denotes the size of $\mathcal{D}$, generally ranging from tens to hundreds.

3.1.2 Re-ranking Step

While the sparse retriever S can efficiently handle a large corpus, it cannot consider semantic similarities, thereby limiting its retrieval performance for lexically different but semantically relevant pairs. To address this, the re-ranking step aims for more precise retrieval results by reordering the retrieved document set $\mathcal{D}$ using the ranking model R. This model transforms $\mathcal{D}$ into a newly ordered document set $\mathcal{D}'$ based on relevance scores with a query q, capturing semantic meanings that could not be addressed in the retrieval step with S. Formally, we define the re-ranking step as:

$$\mathcal{D}' = \text{Re-rank}(q, \mathcal{D}; R) = \{d'_1, \ldots, d'_m\}$$

where d'_k represents the document that has top-k relevance score among $\mathcal{D}$ and $m \ll n$, indicating that the subset $\mathcal{D}'$ contains significantly fewer documents than the original set $\mathcal{D}$.

3.1.3 Generation Step

After the re-ranking step, the document set $\mathcal{D}'$ is augmented to the LLM M with the supporting documents to generate the correct answer a for the given query q. The generation step can be formalized as:

$$a = \text{Generate}(q, \mathcal{D}'; M)$$

In RAG systems, the three key steps are designed to retrieve the most query-relevant knowledge for LLMs, typically at the passage level. However, this fixed granularity can overlook finer relevance between queries and individual sentences. Therefore, in this work, we introduce a fine-grained, sentence-level ranking strategy in the re-ranking step, aiming to reduce distractions from irrelevant information and enhance answer accuracy.

3.2 Document Refinement with Sentence-Level Re-ranking and Reconstruction (DSLR)

We propose a novel unsupervised refinement framework, *D*ocument Refinement with *S*entence-*L*evel *R*e-ranking and Reconstruction (*DSLR*), designed to assess the fine-grained relevance of individual sentences within a passage and reconstruct to preserve the original contextual coherence. Figure 2 illustrates examples generated by each step in our *DSLR* framework.

3.2.1 Sentence Decomposition and Re-ranking

After the retrieval step (§3.1.1), we conduct sentence-level re-ranking for the documents within the retrieved set $\mathcal{D}$. First, each document $d_i \in \mathcal{D}$ is decomposed into a sentence set $\mathcal{S}_i = \{s_j\}_{j=1}^{l}$, where s_j represents the j-th sentence in document d_i and l is the number of sentences in d_i. Then, the passage-level retrieved set $\mathcal{D}$ is redefined to the sentence-level retrieved set $\mathcal{S} = \cup_{i=1}^{n} \mathcal{S}_i$. For instance, as illustrated in Figure 2, a passage retrieved for a query "How many episodes in "Grace and Frankie" Season 1?" is decomposed into three sentences s_1, s_2, and s_3 during the sentence decomposition step.

To extract sentences containing relevant information for a query q, we initially perform re-ranking to assess relevance scores at the sentence level. Sentences in $\mathcal{S}$ with scores below a predefined threshold T are deemed irrelevant and removed, resulting in a refined set $\mathcal{S}'$. The sentence-level re-ranking is formally defined as follows:

$$\mathcal{S}' = \text{Re-rank}(q, \mathcal{S}; R) = \{s'_1, \ldots, s'_m\}$$

where each s'_k is a sentence from $\mathcal{S}$ whose relevance score exceeds T. Figure 2 demonstrates the reordering of sentences, highlighting the exclusion of s'_3 due to its insufficient relevance score. Note that this step of the *DSLR* framework utilizes off-the-shelf ranking models, which are identical to those used in passage-level re-ranking.

3.2.2 Contextual Reconstruction

While the sentence decomposition and re-ranking steps select the top-m relevant sentences for the query q, these sentences may lack contextual relationships to one another, as these steps can disrupt the original contextual flow of the passage by discarding some sentences. Instead of following a widely used approach of simply concatenating these sentences in descending order of their relevance scores, we propose to reconstruct them into the contextually organized set, $\mathcal{S}^*$, to reflect the order in which they were originally positioned before being decomposed from passages, ensuring the original coherence and logical flow:

$$\mathcal{S}^* = \text{Reconstruction}(\mathcal{S}', \mathcal{S}) = \{s_1^*, \ldots, s_m^*\}$$

where s_i^* is the sentence included in S' and i denotes the relative position of s_i^* within $\mathcal{S}$. As shown in Figure 2, the remaining two sentences are reconstructed in their original order by switching their positions to preserve the context before the sentence re-ranking step. Then, LLM M generates the answer a for a given query q with $\mathcal{S}^*$ formalized as: $a = \text{Generate}(q, \mathcal{S}^*; M)$.

4 Experiment Setups

In this section, we describe the experimental setup for evaluating *DSLR* across various scenarios. We provide additional details in Appendix A.

4.1 Models

Retriever. We use BM25 (Robertson and Zaragoza, 2009) as a passage-level retriever, which is a widely used sparse retriever due to its notable performance with high efficiency. The retriever fetches the **top-1** passage-level query-relevant document from an external corpus, which serves as the baseline document.

Re-ranker. We operationalize a variety of ranking models as re-rankers, including off-the-shelf retrievers, fine-tuned re-rankers, and LLMs. **1) Sparse Retriever:** We use **BM25** (Robertson and Zaragoza, 2009) as a sentence-level re-ranker. Note that BM25 is only applied at the sentence level, as it is primarily utilized in the retrieval step. **2) Dense Retriever:** We utilize two representative dense retrievers, **Contriever** (Izacard et al., 2022) and **DPR** (Karpukhin et al., 2020), which are better at capturing the semantic similarity between documents and queries than sparse retrievers. **3) Supervised Re-ranker[1]:** We employ two supervised re-ranking models based on T5 (Raffel et al., 2020), **MonoT5** (Nogueira et al., 2020) and **RankT5** (Zhuang et al., 2023). These models are specifically trained for pointwise document ranking tasks. **4) Unsupervised Re-ranker[1]:** We explore **Relevance Generation (RG)** (Liang et al., 2022), a pointwise ranking method using the inherent ranking ability of LLMs, validating its effectiveness in scenarios lacking extensive labeled data. We use LLama2-13b-chat (Touvron et al., 2023) as a ranking model for **RG**.

Reader. We use the instruction-tuned, open-source LLM **LLama2-13b-chat** as our reader. To generate the final answer, the document is prepended to the system prompt.

4.2 Datasets

We evaluate our *DSLR* across 6 open-domain QA datasets, including both general and specific domains. First, we conduct our experiment using the development set of **Natural Questions (NQ)** (Kwiatkowski et al., 2019), **TriviaQA (TQA)** (Joshi et al., 2017), and **SQuAD (SQD)** (Rajpurkar et al., 2016), consisting of queries with general topics. Additionally, we incorporate specialized datasets such as **RealtimeQA (RQA)** (Kasai et al., 2023), **SciQ (SQ)** (Welbl et al., 2017), and **BioASQ (BASQ)** (Tsatsaronis et al., 2015; Krithara et al., 2023) for evaluating the generalizability of our proposed method. In detail, RQA includes questions that are updated periodically to test our system's ability to handle ever-evolving knowledge. In addition, SQ and BASQ are domain-specific datasets in science and biology, respectively. Specifically, for BASQ, we selectively use the questions from the BioASQ6 challenge (task b) that are suitable for yes/no and factoid responses. We report the effectiveness of our framework with **Accuracy (Acc)**, which determines whether the prediction contains golden answers, following Asai et al. (2024).

4.3 Implementation Details

The threshold T, used to remove irrelevant content, was determined empirically by sampling 1,000 random entries from each of the NQ, TQA, and SQD training sets and setting T to the relevance score at the 90th percentile. Detailed values of T for various models are provided in Table 5. The retrieval corpus for NQ, TQA, and SQD is a pre-processed Wikipedia dump from Dec. 20, 2018 following Karpukhin et al. (2020), and for BASQ

[1]It is important to note that the terms 'supervised' and 'unsupervised' in this context refer to the models being trained on document ranking tasks, and not on document refinement tasks.

Type	Re-ranker	NQ		TQA		SQD		RQA		SQ		BASQ		AVG.	
		# tok	Acc	# tok	Acc	# tok	Acc	# tok	Acc	# tok	Acc	# tok	Acc	# tok	Acc
							Baseline								
-	-	167	25.6	170	58.0	166	28.5	1277	41.1	162	33.9	444	56.7	398	40.6
							Ours								
Sparse Ret.	BM25	48	28.7	81	60.8	41	28.0	689	40.4	52	40.7	202	52.6	186	41.9
Dense Ret.	Contriever	68	29.2	60	62.0	61	29.1	418	41.2	69	40.8	308	57.2	164	43.2
	DPR	61	33.6	74	62.9	56	27.3	517	40.1	75	40.9	309	55.9	182	43.4
Supervised Re-r.	MonoT5	74	31.1	84	62.3	67	**30.4**	625	42.1	50	**41.1**	363	57.2	179	43.5
	RankT5	83	29.4	69	61.7	60	**30.4**	475	41.6	49	40.6	337	57.2	179	43.5
Unsupervised Re-r.	RG	46	**33.7**	76	**64.1**	51	29.5	534	**42.5**	97	38.9	291	**59.5**	183	**44.7**

Table 1: Performance comparison between the *Baseline* (original top-1 document) and *Ours* (*DSLR*-refined top-1 document) on various open-domain QA datasets. The table shows the average token count (# tok) and accuracy (Acc) for both sparse and dense retrievers, as well as for supervised and unsupervised re-rankers. Best results are in **bold**.

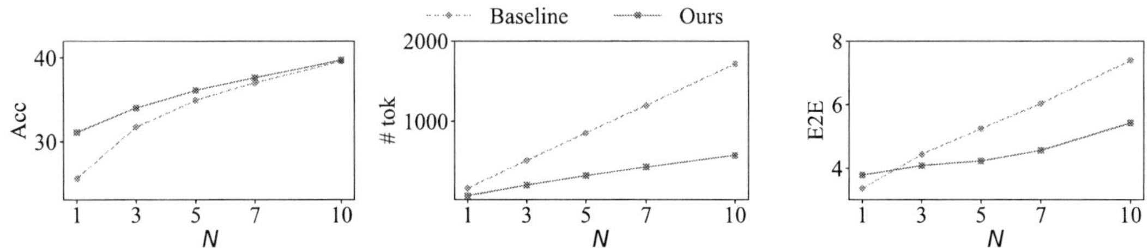

Figure 3: Comparison between the Baseline (original documents) and Ours (*DSLR*-refined documents using MonoT5) in the top-N multiple passages scenario on the NQ dataset. (Left) Accuracy (Acc) as top-N increases. (Center) Average token count (# tok) as top-N increases. (Right) Average end-to-end latency (E2E) as top-N increases, measured in seconds.

and RQA, we use their own retrieval corpora. To be specific, BASQ used the BEIR (v1.0.0) [2] BioASQ corpus, specializing in biomedical information retrieval. For the RQA dataset, spanning from 2022 to 2023, we use the search documents provided at the time of dataset creation through the Google Cloud Search (GCS) API to align the periods of the queries and answers. When implementing each component in *DSLR*, we decompose passage-level documents into sentences using the Sentencizer from Spacy[3]. All predictions in our experiments are generated via greedy decoding.

5 Experimental Results and Analyses

In this section, we show the overall experimental results with in-depth analyses of our framework.

Main Results. First of all, Table 1 shows that our *DSLR*-refined top-1 document consistently outperforms the original top-1 document across all datasets and scenarios, despite reduced token counts. This confirms our hypothesis that the redundant information within the fix-sized passages adversely affects the RAG performance and highlights the importance of providing only query-relevant information in RAG with finer-grained sentences.

Furthermore, *DSLR* also shows performance enhancement over specialized datasets, such as ever-evolving RQA and domain-specific SQ and BASQ datasets. Specifically, the re-rankers based on pre-trained models such as T5 and the LLM demonstrate remarkable performance improvement. Given that *DSLR* requires no additional training, the robust and effective performance suggests its applicability to diverse real-world scenarios, particularly where queries frequently change across different timelines and domains.

***DSLR* in Multiple Passages.** To assess the effectiveness and efficiency of *DSLR* in multiple passages, we gradually increased the number of documents N and compared the performance, token count, and end-to-end (E2E) latency[4] of the original top-N documents with those refined by *DSLR*.

As shown in the left panel of Figure 3, both sets of documents show consistent performance improvements as N increases. However, *DSLR* consistently outperforms the original documents across all N levels, with more notable differences

[2] https://github.com/beir-cellar/beir

[3] https://spacy.io/

[4] These experiments were conducted using four V100 GPUs.

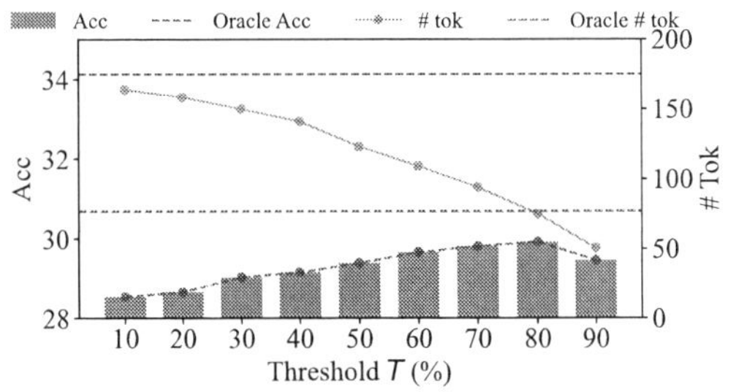

Figure 4: Variation in accuracy and token count (# tok) with adjustments to threshold T on the SQD dataset, with dashed lines indicating oracle accuracy and corresponding token count.

at lower N values. This suggests that *DSLR* can significantly enhance performance in RAG, even as the number of documents increases.

Due to the quadratic increase in memory and time requirements with the number of tokens in transformer-based LLMs, reducing the token count is crucial for improving efficiency (Vaswani et al., 2017). As depicted in the center and right panels of Figure 3, *DSLR* substantially reduces the token count compared to the original documents, with the difference becoming more significant as N increases. This reduction in tokens also decreases E2E latency in all scenarios except top-1. Notably, at top-10, while the performance difference is minimal (39.6 vs. 39.7), the token count reduction from 1,713 to 577 (nearly 2.97 times) and the corresponding E2E latency reduction from 7.382 seconds to 5.422 seconds (nearly 2 seconds) demonstrate that *DSLR* can enhance both performance and efficiency in RAG. Detailed results are available in Table 14.

Impact of Threshold Adjustment. To examine the impact of varying T, we adjusted the threshold in increments of 10, starting from the 10th percentile, and measured the resulting performance. Additionally, to explore the theoretical maximum performance of our method, we configured an oracle setting where any correct response, regardless of the threshold setting, was counted as correct.

As shown in Figure 4, increasing the threshold T generally improves performance by removing irrelevant content, thus reducing the number of tokens. However, our experimental results revealed that the performance at the 90th percentile threshold was 29.4, while a lower 80th percentile threshold yielded better performance at 29.9. This indicates that an overly stringent threshold can also remove essential information, suggesting that task-specific threshold fine-tuning could improve results.

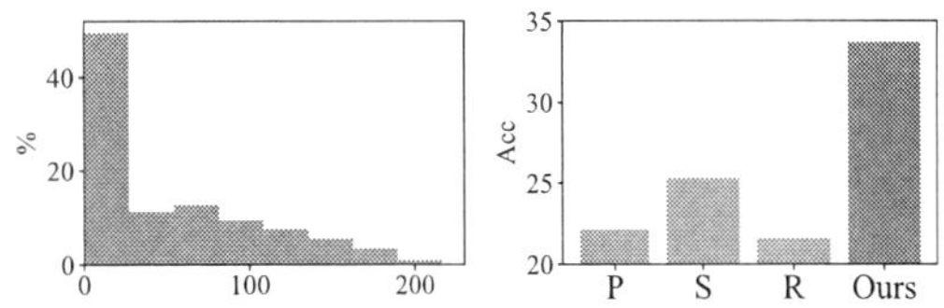

Figure 5: (Left) Distribution of token counts in *DSLR*-refined documents on the NQ dataset. (Right) Comparison of *DSLR* with document truncated to an average fixed length (P), document processed using sentence-level re-ranking to include only the most relevant sentences up to the average length (S), and document using random selection of sentences up to the average length (R).

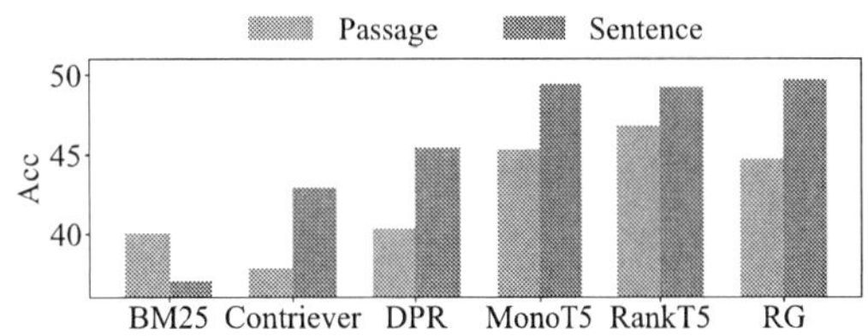

Figure 6: Comparative average performance of sentence-level and passage-level re-ranking across the dataset with a context length of 100 words.

Furthermore, in the oracle setting, accuracy significantly improved to 34.1, and the token count was reduced to 77. This shows a marked performance improvement over the best performing threshold (80th percentile), with a similar reduction in tokens. This result implies that dynamically adjusting the threshold based on the query could achieve substantial performance improvements with a comparable number of tokens, suggesting an area for future work. Detailed results are available in Table 15.

Token Distribution and Refinement Strategies. The left panel of Figure 5 displays the distribution of token counts in documents refined by *DSLR*. Unlike methods that trim passages to a fixed length, *DSLR* reduces token counts based on a relevance score threshold, resulting in a wide distribution of token counts, with many instances nearly devoid of external knowledge. The average token count post-refinement is 46. We analyzed performance by comparing this approach with cases where passages are consistently cut to 46 tokens: one where passages are simply truncated at 46 tokens, another using sentence-level re-ranking to select the most relevant sentences up to 46 tokens, and a third where sentences are randomly cut to 46 tokens.

As demonstrated in the right panel of Figure 5, *DSLR*, which trims content based on relevance, significantly outperforms methods that trim to a fixed length, improving scores from 25.3 to 33.7. This

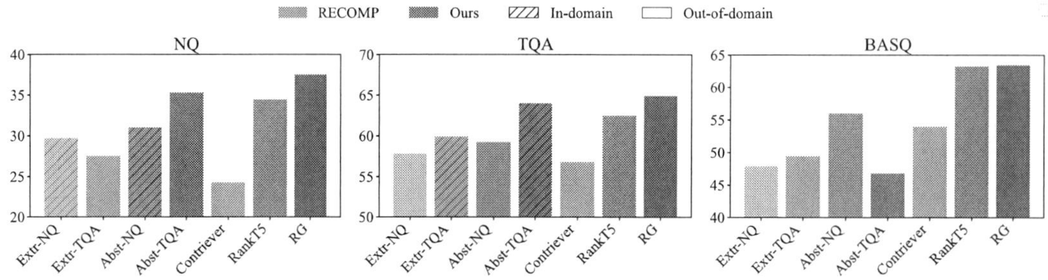

Figure 7: Performance comparison of *DSLR* and RECOMP (Xu et al., 2024) across multiple open-domain QA datasets, featuring models including Contriever, RankT5, and RG for *DSLR*, and extractive (Extr.) and abstractive (Abst.) models for RECOMP. The in-domain (Hatched) results refer to models specifically trained for the dataset.

	NQ	TQA
DSLR (Ours)	33.7	64.1
- sentence-level re-ranking	30.6	62.0
- reconstruction (descend)	33.6	63.8
- reconstruction (ascend)	33.6	63.9
- reconstruction (random)	33.5	63.8
Baseline	25.6	58.0

Table 2: Ablation studies on the NQ, TQA datasets, comparing *DSLR* with RG against the variants that exclude sentence-level re-ranking and reconstruction. The variants are ordered by relevance score (descend and ascend) or randomly (random).

suggests that trimming based on relevance score thresholds, rather than a fixed length, is more effective. This method accommodates the variability in the amount of relevant information per query, indicating that non-essential content should be dynamically removed.

Effectiveness of Sentence-Level Re-ranking. To assess the effectiveness of sentence-level re-ranking within our framework, we compared it to conventional passage-level re-ranking using the same context length in RAG, under an initial top-100 retrieval setting. Figure 6 demonstrates that sentence-level re-ranking markedly outperforms passage-level re-ranking by enhancing performance through increased information density at a finer granularity. Additionally, while dense retrievers and fine-tuned ranking models demonstrate improvements as re-rankers, BM25 as a re-ranker significantly decreases the performance. This highlights the limitations of keyword-matching approaches for assessing low-granularity, sentence-level relevance, underscoring the necessity for semantic understanding in sentence ranking tasks. Moreover, off-the-shelf ranking models, originally designed for passage-level relevance assessment, are also effective at determining relevance at the more granular level of individual sentences. Interestingly, even though it is not specifically trained for ranking tasks, the unsupervised re-ranker using LLMs shows remarkable performance in sentence-level re-ranking.

Ablation Studies on the Sentence-Level Re-ranking and Reconstruction Steps. To see how each step in *DSLR* contributes to the overall performance, we conduct the ablation studies, the results shown in Table 2, for the sentence-level re-ranking and reconstruction steps. These studies were uniquely tailored to the variable token counts reduced by *DSLR*, rather than using a fixed length.

First, we examine the impact of removing the sentence-level re-ranking step. In this scenario, after initially retrieving the top-1 passage, the results are decomposed into sentences. Subsequently, these sentences are randomly used as sources for generating answers. The performance drastically drops from 33.7 to 30.6 on the NQ, highlighting the crucial role of sentence-level re-ranking, which helps effectively filter out query-irrelevant information based on relevance scores.

Furthermore, we explore the effectiveness of the reconstruction step. The performance also drops from 64.1 to 63.8 on the TQA. This finding is similar to those from Choi et al. (2021), which suggests that removing contextual coherence negatively affects the performance. Therefore, in *DSLR*, reconstructing the order of sentences to reflect their original sequence within the retrieved passage is an essential step. Interestingly, the widely used approach of prepending external knowledge in descending order of relevance scores is not effective in our sentence-level refinement framework, showing similar results to a randomly ordered setting.

Query	Original Document	DSLR-Refined Document
the element which is the most abundant in the human body is (NQ)	[1] Nitrogen diatomic gas with the formula N. Dinitrogen forms about 78% of Earth's atmosphere, making it the most abundant uncombined element. Nitrogen occurs in all organisms, primarily in amino acids (and thus proteins), in the nucleic acids (DNA and RNA) and in the energy transfer molecule adenosine triphosphate. The human body contains about 3% nitrogen by mass, the fourth most abundant element in the body after oxygen, carbon, and hydrogen. The nitrogen cycle describes movement of the element from the air, into the biosphere and organic compounds, then back into the atmosphere. Many industrially important compounds, such as ammonia, nitric acid,	[1] Nitrogen diatomic gas with the formula N. Dinitrogen forms about 78% of Earth's atmosphere, making it the most abundant uncombined element. The human body contains about 3% nitrogen by mass, the fourth most abundant element in the body after oxygen, carbon, and hydrogen.
Predict	Nitrogen (X)	Oxygen (O)

Table 3: Case study with the top-1 document, where we represent query-irrelevant sentences in red and query-relevant sentences in blue.

Comparative Analysis of Document Refining methods: Evaluating RECOMP and *DSLR*. We further compare our *DSLR* to the concurrent supervised refinement method, RECOMP (Xu et al., 2024), which requires additional training steps for refining the retrieved documents. To be specific, RECOMP is designed to refine the retrieved passages by either abstractively or extractively summarizing them with additional models. Note that due to significant differences between supervised and unsupervised schemes, directly comparing *DSLR* with RECOMP on an apples-to-apples basis is difficult. However, to ensure as fair a comparison as possible, we evaluate both refining methods under the same conditions by adopting a two-sentence extraction context length, following the extractive setting used for RECOMP. Additionally, RECOMP's extractive compressor, which requires Contriever to be fine-tuned on specific datasets, shares similarities with our *DSLR* implementation that also uses Contriever, though ours is not additionally fine-tuned.

Figure 7 shows the results of the comparison between *DSLR* and RECOMP in both in-domain and out-of-domain settings. While RECOMP shows robust performance on the in-domain datasets where it is particularly trained, its performance drops drastically for the out-of-domain settings, notably for BASQ from 54 to 47.9. This indicates the challenges of dataset-specific tuning for the supervised refinement methods. On the other hand, our *DSLR* with RankT5 and RG shows robust performance even without additional training steps for refinement.

Case Study. We conduct a case study of the *DSLR* framework in Table 3. Specifically, a conventional fixed-size passage may contain distractors, such as unrelated knowledge and irrelevant conceptual details about Nitrogen (highlighted in red). Note that, although the retrieved passage-level document includes 'Oxygen', which is the correct answer to the given query, the LLM used as the reader fails to generate the accurate answer by being distracted by irrelevant information. On the other hand, *DSLR* effectively filters out such query-irrelevant sentences. Furthermore, *DSLR* also helps focus on the information closely related to the query (highlighted in blue), thus correctly generating the answer.

6 Conclusion

In this work, we present *DSLR*, a novel unsupervised document refinement framework that enhances the performance of RAG systems. The *DSLR* framework aids RAG systems to generate more accurate answers by decomposing passages into sentences, re-ranking them based on each relevance score, and then reconstructing them to preserve the continuity and coherence of the context. Our comprehensive experiments on multiple QA datasets show that *DSLR* consistently outperforms the conventional approaches of using fixed-size passage in RAG, especially in ever-evolving and domain-specific contexts. Our ablation studies highlight the importance of sentence-level reranking and contextual reconstruction for improvement on RAG. We believe that *DSLR* suggests a promising research direction for refining document retrieval without additional training, together with potential applications across a wide range of knowledge-intensive NLP tasks by integrating more diverse retrieval or ranking models.

Limitation

While our *DSLR* shows significant improvements in RAG performance, it is important to recognize that there is still room for further improvement. First, although we aim to preserve the original contextual integrity with the reconstruction step, there is a risk of unintentionally removing important sentences that might contain query-relevant information. We believe that developing more advanced re-ranking models to more accurately capture relevance scores could address this, which we leave as valuable future work. Second, since *DSLR* aims to refine the set of retrieved documents, there might be a bottleneck stemming from the initial retrieval step; the overall performance can be negatively affected by incorrectly retrieved documents. Therefore, future work may focus on developing a more precise retrieval module. Since the *DSLR* framework is composed of off-the-shelf modules, we believe that its overall performance will improve concurrently with the development of these modules.

Ethics Statement

The experimental results on *DSLR* validate the effectiveness of sentence-level re-ranking and reconstruction in RAG. However, since RAG requires processing a large amount of textual data, we should always be aware of the documents containing sensitive or private information when applying it to real-world scenarios. While it is not within the scope of our study, we believe that developing filtering strategies to mitigate such problems is essential.

Acknowledgments

This work was supported by Institute for Information and Communications Technology Promotion (IITP) grant funded by the Korea government (No. 2018-0-00582, Prediction and augmentation of the credibility distribution via linguistic analysis and automated evidence document collection), Basic Science Research Program through the National Research Foundation of Korea (NRF) funded by the Ministry of Education (RS-2023-00275747), and the Artificial Intelligence Industrial Convergence Cluster Development project funded by the Ministry of Science and ICT (MSIT, Korea) & Gwangju Metropolitan City.

References

Akari Asai, Zeqiu Wu, Yizhong Wang, Avirup Sil, and Hannaneh Hajishirzi. 2024. Self-RAG: Learning to retrieve, generate, and critique through self-reflection. In *The Twelfth International Conference on Learning Representations*.

Jinheon Baek, Soyeong Jeong, Minki Kang, Jong C. Park, and Sung Ju Hwang. 2023. Knowledge-augmented language model verification. In *Proceedings of the 2023 Conference on Empirical Methods in Natural Language Processing, EMNLP 2023, Singapore, December 6-10, 2023*, pages 1720–1736. Association for Computational Linguistics.

Sebastian Borgeaud, Arthur Mensch, Jordan Hoffmann, Trevor Cai, Eliza Rutherford, Katie Millican, George van den Driessche, Jean-Baptiste Lespiau, Bogdan Damoc, Aidan Clark, Diego de Las Casas, Aurelia Guy, Jacob Menick, Roman Ring, Tom Hennigan, Saffron Huang, Loren Maggiore, Chris Jones, Albin Cassirer, Andy Brock, Michela Paganini, Geoffrey Irving, Oriol Vinyals, Simon Osindero, Karen Simonyan, Jack W. Rae, Erich Elsen, and Laurent Sifre. 2022. Improving language models by retrieving from trillions of tokens. In *International Conference on Machine Learning, ICML 2022, 17-23 July 2022, Baltimore, Maryland, USA*, volume 162 of *Proceedings of Machine Learning Research*, pages 2206–2240. PMLR.

Tom B. Brown, Benjamin Mann, Nick Ryder, Melanie Subbiah, Jared Kaplan, Prafulla Dhariwal, Arvind Neelakantan, Pranav Shyam, Girish Sastry, Amanda Askell, Sandhini Agarwal, Ariel Herbert-Voss, Gretchen Krueger, Tom Henighan, Rewon Child, Aditya Ramesh, Daniel M. Ziegler, Jeffrey Wu, Clemens Winter, Christopher Hesse, Mark Chen, Eric Sigler, Mateusz Litwin, Scott Gray, Benjamin Chess, Jack Clark, Christopher Berner, Sam McCandlish, Alec Radford, Ilya Sutskever, and Dario Amodei. 2020. Language models are few-shot learners. In *Advances in Neural Information Processing Systems 33: Annual Conference on Neural Information Processing Systems 2020, NeurIPS 2020, December 6-12, 2020, virtual*.

Harrison Chase. 2022. LangChain.

Tong Chen, Hongwei Wang, Sihao Chen, Wenhao Yu, Kaixin Ma, Xinran Zhao, Hongming Zhang, and Dong Yu. 2023. Dense X retrieval: What retrieval granularity should we use? *arXiv preprint arXiv:2312.06648*, abs/2312.06648.

Sukmin Cho, Jeongyeon Seo, Soyeong Jeong, and Jong C. Park. 2023. Improving zero-shot reader by reducing distractions from irrelevant documents in open-domain question answering. In *Findings of the Association for Computational Linguistics: EMNLP 2023, Singapore, December 6-10, 2023*, pages 3145–3157. Association for Computational Linguistics.

Eunsol Choi, Jennimaria Palomaki, Matthew Lamm, Tom Kwiatkowski, Dipanjan Das, and Michael

Collins. 2021. Decontextualization: Making sentences stand-alone. *Trans. Assoc. Comput. Linguistics*, 9:447–461.

Gautier Izacard, Mathilde Caron, Lucas Hosseini, Sebastian Riedel, Piotr Bojanowski, Armand Joulin, and Edouard Grave. 2022. Unsupervised dense information retrieval with contrastive learning. *Trans. Mach. Learn. Res.*, 2022.

Soyeong Jeong, Jinheon Baek, Sukmin Cho, Sung Ju Hwang, and Jong C. Park. 2022. Augmenting document representations for dense retrieval with interpolation and perturbation. In *Proceedings of the 60th Annual Meeting of the Association for Computational Linguistics (Volume 2: Short Papers), ACL 2022, Dublin, Ireland, May 22-27, 2022*, pages 442–452. Association for Computational Linguistics.

Soyeong Jeong, Jinheon Baek, Sukmin Cho, Sung Ju Hwang, and Jong C. Park. 2024. Adaptive-rag: Learning to adapt retrieval-augmented large language models through question complexity. *arXiv.2403.14403*, abs/2403.14403.

Soyeong Jeong, Jinheon Baek, Sung Ju Hwang, and Jong Park. 2023. Phrase retrieval for open domain conversational question answering with conversational dependency modeling via contrastive learning. In *Findings of the Association for Computational Linguistics: ACL 2023, Toronto, Canada, July 9-14, 2023*, pages 6019–6031. Association for Computational Linguistics.

Jiajie Jin, Yutao Zhu, Yujia Zhou, and Zhicheng Dou. 2024. BIDER: bridging knowledge inconsistency for efficient retrieval-augmented llms via key supporting evidence. *arXiv.2402.12174*, abs/2402.12174.

Mandar Joshi, Eunsol Choi, Daniel S. Weld, and Luke Zettlemoyer. 2017. Triviaqa: A large scale distantly supervised challenge dataset for reading comprehension. In *Proceedings of the 55th Annual Meeting of the Association for Computational Linguistics, ACL 2017, Vancouver, Canada, July 30 - August 4, Volume 1: Long Papers*, pages 1601–1611. Association for Computational Linguistics.

Vladimir Karpukhin, Barlas Oguz, Sewon Min, Patrick S. H. Lewis, Ledell Wu, Sergey Edunov, Danqi Chen, and Wen-tau Yih. 2020. Dense passage retrieval for open-domain question answering. In *Proceedings of the 2020 Conference on Empirical Methods in Natural Language Processing, EMNLP 2020, Online, November 16-20, 2020*, pages 6769–6781. Association for Computational Linguistics.

Jungo Kasai, Keisuke Sakaguchi, Yoichi Takahashi, Ronan Le Bras, Akari Asai, Xinyan Yu, Dragomir Radev, Noah A. Smith, Yejin Choi, and Kentaro Inui. 2023. Realtime QA: what's the answer right now? In *Advances in Neural Information Processing Systems 36: Annual Conference on Neural Information Processing Systems 2023, NeurIPS 2023, New Orleans, LA, USA, December 10 - 16, 2023.*

Urvashi Khandelwal, Omer Levy, Dan Jurafsky, Luke Zettlemoyer, and Mike Lewis. 2020. Generalization through memorization: Nearest neighbor language models. In *8th International Conference on Learning Representations, ICLR 2020, Addis Ababa, Ethiopia, April 26-30, 2020*. OpenReview.net.

Anastasia Krithara, Anastasios Nentidis, Konstantinos Bougiatiotis, and Georgios Paliouras. 2023. BioASQ-QA: A manually curated corpus for biomedical question answering. *Scientific Data*, 10(1):170. Published 2023 Mar 27.

Tom Kwiatkowski, Jennimaria Palomaki, Olivia Redfield, Michael Collins, Ankur P. Parikh, Chris Alberti, Danielle Epstein, Illia Polosukhin, Jacob Devlin, Kenton Lee, Kristina Toutanova, Llion Jones, Matthew Kelcey, Ming-Wei Chang, Andrew M. Dai, Jakob Uszkoreit, Quoc Le, and Slav Petrov. 2019. Natural questions: a benchmark for question answering research. *Trans. Assoc. Comput. Linguistics*, 7:452–466.

Jinhyuk Lee, Mujeen Sung, Jaewoo Kang, and Danqi Chen. 2021a. Learning dense representations of phrases at scale. In *Proceedings of the 59th Annual Meeting of the Association for Computational Linguistics and the 11th International Joint Conference on Natural Language Processing, ACL/IJCNLP 2021, (Volume 1: Long Papers), Virtual Event, August 1-6, 2021*, pages 6634–6647. Association for Computational Linguistics.

Jinhyuk Lee, Alexander Wettig, and Danqi Chen. 2021b. Phrase retrieval learns passage retrieval, too. In *Proceedings of the 2021 Conference on Empirical Methods in Natural Language Processing, EMNLP 2021, Virtual Event / Punta Cana, Dominican Republic, 7-11 November, 2021*, pages 3661–3672. Association for Computational Linguistics.

Patrick S. H. Lewis, Ethan Perez, Aleksandra Piktus, Fabio Petroni, Vladimir Karpukhin, Naman Goyal, Heinrich Küttler, Mike Lewis, Wen-tau Yih, Tim Rocktäschel, Sebastian Riedel, and Douwe Kiela. 2020. Retrieval-augmented generation for knowledge-intensive NLP tasks. In *Advances in Neural Information Processing Systems 33: Annual Conference on Neural Information Processing Systems 2020, NeurIPS 2020, December 6-12, 2020, virtual.*

Daliang Li, Ankit Singh Rawat, Manzil Zaheer, Xin Wang, Michal Lukasik, Andreas Veit, Felix X. Yu, and Sanjiv Kumar. 2023. Large language models with controllable working memory. In *Findings of the Association for Computational Linguistics: ACL 2023, Toronto, Canada, July 9-14, 2023*, pages 1774–1793. Association for Computational Linguistics.

Percy Liang, Rishi Bommasani, Tony Lee, Dimitris Tsipras, Dilara Soylu, Michihiro Yasunaga, Yian Zhang, Deepak Narayanan, Yuhuai Wu, Ananya Kumar, Benjamin Newman, Binhang Yuan, Bobby Yan, Ce Zhang, Christian Cosgrove, Christopher D. Manning, Christopher Ré, Diana Acosta-Navas, Drew A.

Hudson, Eric Zelikman, Esin Durmus, Faisal Ladhak, Frieda Rong, Hongyu Ren, Huaxiu Yao, Jue Wang, Keshav Santhanam, Laurel J. Orr, Lucia Zheng, Mert Yüksekgönül, Mirac Suzgun, Nathan Kim, Neel Guha, Niladri S. Chatterji, Omar Khattab, Peter Henderson, Qian Huang, Ryan Chi, Sang Michael Xie, Shibani Santurkar, Surya Ganguli, Tatsunori Hashimoto, Thomas Icard, Tianyi Zhang, Vishrav Chaudhary, William Wang, Xuechen Li, Yifan Mai, Yuhui Zhang, and Yuta Koreeda. 2022. Holistic evaluation of language models. *arXiv preprint arXiv:2211.09110*, abs/2211.09110.

Nelson F. Liu, Kevin Lin, John Hewitt, Ashwin Paranjape, Michele Bevilacqua, Fabio Petroni, and Percy Liang. 2023. Lost in the middle: How language models use long contexts. *arXiv:2307.03172*, abs/2307.03172.

Alex Mallen, Akari Asai, Victor Zhong, Rajarshi Das, Daniel Khashabi, and Hannaneh Hajishirzi. 2023. When not to trust language models: Investigating effectiveness of parametric and non-parametric memories. In *Proceedings of the 61st Annual Meeting of the Association for Computational Linguistics (Volume 1: Long Papers), ACL 2023, Toronto, Canada, July 9-14, 2023*, pages 9802–9822. Association for Computational Linguistics.

Rodrigo Frassetto Nogueira and Kyunghyun Cho. 2019. Passage re-ranking with BERT. *arXiv, 1901.04085*, abs/1901.04085.

Rodrigo Frassetto Nogueira, Zhiying Jiang, Ronak Pradeep, and Jimmy Lin. 2020. Document ranking with a pretrained sequence-to-sequence model. In *Findings of the Association for Computational Linguistics: EMNLP 2020, Online Event, 16-20 November 2020*, volume EMNLP 2020 of *Findings of ACL*, pages 708–718. Association for Computational Linguistics.

OpenAI. 2023a. Chatgpt plugins.

OpenAI. 2023b. GPT-4 technical report. *arXiv:2303.08774*, abs/2303.08774.

Fabio Petroni, Aleksandra Piktus, Angela Fan, Patrick S. H. Lewis, Majid Yazdani, Nicola De Cao, James Thorne, Yacine Jernite, Vladimir Karpukhin, Jean Maillard, Vassilis Plachouras, Tim Rocktäschel, and Sebastian Riedel. 2021. KILT: a benchmark for knowledge intensive language tasks. In *Proceedings of the 2021 Conference of the North American Chapter of the Association for Computational Linguistics: Human Language Technologies, NAACL-HLT 2021, Online, June 6-11, 2021*, pages 2523–2544. Association for Computational Linguistics.

Jay M. Ponte and W. Bruce Croft. 1998. A language modeling approach to information retrieval. In *SIGIR '98: Proceedings of the 21st Annual International ACM SIGIR Conference on Research and Development in Information Retrieval, August 24-28 1998, Melbourne, Australia*, pages 275–281. ACM.

Ofir Press, Muru Zhang, Sewon Min, Ludwig Schmidt, Noah A. Smith, and Mike Lewis. 2023. Measuring and narrowing the compositionality gap in language models. In *Findings of the Association for Computational Linguistics: EMNLP 2023, Singapore, December 6-10, 2023*, pages 5687–5711. Association for Computational Linguistics.

Yujia Qin, Shihao Liang, Yining Ye, Kunlun Zhu, Lan Yan, Yaxi Lu, Yankai Lin, Xin Cong, Xiangru Tang, Bill Qian, Sihan Zhao, Lauren Hong, Runchu Tian, Ruobing Xie, Jie Zhou, Mark Gerstein, dahai li, Zhiyuan Liu, and Maosong Sun. 2024. ToolLLM: Facilitating large language models to master 16000+ real-world APIs. In *The Twelfth International Conference on Learning Representations*.

Zhen Qin, Rolf Jagerman, Kai Hui, Honglei Zhuang, Junru Wu, Jiaming Shen, Tianqi Liu, Jialu Liu, Donald Metzler, Xuanhui Wang, and Michael Bendersky. 2023a. Large language models are effective text rankers with pairwise ranking prompting. *arXiv:2306.17563*, abs/2306.17563.

Zhen Qin, Rolf Jagerman, Kai Hui, Honglei Zhuang, Junru Wu, Jiaming Shen, Tianqi Liu, Jialu Liu, Donald Metzler, Xuanhui Wang, and Michael Bendersky. 2023b. Large language models are effective text rankers with pairwise ranking prompting. *arXiv:2306.17563*, abs/2306.17563.

Colin Raffel, Noam Shazeer, Adam Roberts, Katherine Lee, Sharan Narang, Michael Matena, Yanqi Zhou, Wei Li, and Peter J. Liu. 2020. Exploring the limits of transfer learning with a unified text-to-text transformer. *J. Mach. Learn. Res.*, 21:140:1–140:67.

Pranav Rajpurkar, Jian Zhang, Konstantin Lopyrev, and Percy Liang. 2016. Squad: 100, 000+ questions for machine comprehension of text. In *Proceedings of the 2016 Conference on Empirical Methods in Natural Language Processing, EMNLP 2016, Austin, Texas, USA, November 1-4, 2016*, pages 2383–2392. The Association for Computational Linguistics.

Stephen E. Robertson and Hugo Zaragoza. 2009. The probabilistic relevance framework: BM25 and beyond. *Found. Trends Inf. Retr.*, 3(4):333–389.

Gerard Salton and Chris Buckley. 1988. Term-weighting approaches in automatic text retrieval. *Inf. Process. Manag.*, 24(5):513–523.

Min Joon Seo, Jinhyuk Lee, Tom Kwiatkowski, Ankur P. Parikh, Ali Farhadi, and Hannaneh Hajishirzi. 2019. Real-time open-domain question answering with dense-sparse phrase index. In *Proceedings of the 57th Conference of the Association for Computational Linguistics, ACL 2019, Florence, Italy, July 28-August 2, 2019, Volume 1: Long Papers*, pages 4430–4441. Association for Computational Linguistics.

Freda Shi, Xinyun Chen, Kanishka Misra, Nathan Scales, David Dohan, Ed H. Chi, Nathanael Schärli, and Denny Zhou. 2023a. Large language models can be easily distracted by irrelevant context. In *International Conference on Machine Learning, ICML 2023, 23-29 July 2023, Honolulu, Hawaii, USA*, volume 202 of *Proceedings of Machine Learning Research*, pages 31210–31227. PMLR.

Weijia Shi, Sewon Min, Michihiro Yasunaga, Minjoon Seo, Rich James, Mike Lewis, Luke Zettlemoyer, and Wen-tau Yih. 2023b. REPLUG: retrieval-augmented black-box language models. *arXiv.2301.12652*, abs/2301.12652.

Hugo Touvron, Louis Martin, Kevin Stone, Peter Albert, Amjad Almahairi, Yasmine Babaei, Nikolay Bashlykov, Soumya Batra, Prajjwal Bhargava, Shruti Bhosale, Dan Bikel, Lukas Blecher, Cristian Canton-Ferrer, Moya Chen, Guillem Cucurull, David Esiobu, Jude Fernandes, Jeremy Fu, Wenyin Fu, Brian Fuller, Cynthia Gao, Vedanuj Goswami, Naman Goyal, Anthony Hartshorn, Saghar Hosseini, Rui Hou, Hakan Inan, Marcin Kardas, Viktor Kerkez, Madian Khabsa, Isabel Kloumann, Artem Korenev, Punit Singh Koura, Marie-Anne Lachaux, Thibaut Lavril, Jenya Lee, Diana Liskovich, Yinghai Lu, Yuning Mao, Xavier Martinet, Todor Mihaylov, Pushkar Mishra, Igor Molybog, Yixin Nie, Andrew Poulton, Jeremy Reizenstein, Rashi Rungta, Kalyan Saladi, Alan Schelten, Ruan Silva, Eric Michael Smith, Ranjan Subramanian, Xiaoqing Ellen Tan, Binh Tang, Ross Taylor, Adina Williams, Jian Xiang Kuan, Puxin Xu, Zheng Yan, Iliyan Zarov, Yuchen Zhang, Angela Fan, Melanie Kambadur, Sharan Narang, Aurélien Rodriguez, Robert Stojnic, Sergey Edunov, and Thomas Scialom. 2023. Llama 2: Open foundation and fine-tuned chat models. *arXiv preprint arXiv:2307.09288*, abs/2307.09288.

George Tsatsaronis, Georgios Balikas, Prodromos Malakasiotis, Ioannis Partalas, Matthias Zschunke, Michael R. Alvers, Dirk Weissenborn, Anastasia Krithara, Sergios Petridis, Dimitris Polychronopoulos, Yannis Almirantis, John Pavlopoulos, Nicolas Baskiotis, Patrick Gallinari, Thierry Artières, Axel-Cyrille Ngonga Ngomo, Norman Heino, Éric Gaussier, Liliana Barrio-Alvers, Michael Schroeder, Ion Androutsopoulos, and Georgios Paliouras. 2015. An overview of the BIOASQ large-scale biomedical semantic indexing and question answering competition. *BMC Bioinform.*, 16:138:1–138:28.

Ashish Vaswani, Noam Shazeer, Niki Parmar, Jakob Uszkoreit, Llion Jones, Aidan N. Gomez, Lukasz Kaiser, and Illia Polosukhin. 2017. Attention is all you need. In *Advances in Neural Information Processing Systems 30: Annual Conference on Neural Information Processing Systems 2017, December 4-9, 2017, Long Beach, CA, USA*, pages 5998–6008.

Yuhao Wang, Ruiyang Ren, Junyi Li, Wayne Xin Zhao, Jing Liu, and Ji-Rong Wen. 2024. REAR: A relevance-aware retrieval-augmented framework for open-domain question answering. *arXiv preprint arXiv:2402.17497*, abs/2402.17497.

Zhiguo Wang, Patrick Ng, Xiaofei Ma, Ramesh Nallapati, and Bing Xiang. 2019. Multi-passage BERT: A globally normalized BERT model for open-domain question answering. In *Proceedings of the 2019 Conference on Empirical Methods in Natural Language Processing and the 9th International Joint Conference on Natural Language Processing, EMNLP-IJCNLP 2019, Hong Kong, China, November 3-7, 2019*, pages 5877–5881. Association for Computational Linguistics.

Zhiruo Wang, Jun Araki, Zhengbao Jiang, Md. Rizwan Parvez, and Graham Neubig. 2023. Learning to filter context for retrieval-augmented generation. *arXiv.2311.08377*, abs/2311.08377.

Johannes Welbl, Nelson F. Liu, and Matt Gardner. 2017. Crowdsourcing multiple choice science questions. In *Proceedings of the 3rd Workshop on Noisy User-generated Text, NUT@EMNLP 2017, Copenhagen, Denmark, September 7, 2017*, pages 94–106. Association for Computational Linguistics.

Zhenyu Wu, Chao Shen, and Meng Jiang. 2024. Instructing large language models to identify and ignore irrelevant conditions. *arXiv.2403.12744*, abs/2403.12744.

Fangyuan Xu, Weijia Shi, and Eunsol Choi. 2024. RECOMP: Improving retrieval-augmented LMs with context compression and selective augmentation. In *The Twelfth International Conference on Learning Representations*.

Wenhao Yu, Dan Iter, Shuohang Wang, Yichong Xu, Mingxuan Ju, Soumya Sanyal, Chenguang Zhu, Michael Zeng, and Meng Jiang. 2023a. Generate rather than retrieve: Large language models are strong context generators. In *The Eleventh International Conference on Learning Representations, ICLR 2023, Kigali, Rwanda, May 1-5, 2023*. OpenReview.net.

Wenhao Yu, Zhihan Zhang, Zhenwen Liang, Meng Jiang, and Ashish Sabharwal. 2023b. Improving language models via plug-and-play retrieval feedback. *arXiv.2305.14002*, abs/2305.14002.

Honglei Zhuang, Zhen Qin, Rolf Jagerman, Kai Hui, Ji Ma, Jing Lu, Jianmo Ni, Xuanhui Wang, and Michael Bendersky. 2023. Rankt5: Fine-tuning T5 for text ranking with ranking losses. In *Proceedings of the 46th International ACM SIGIR Conference on Research and Development in Information Retrieval, SIGIR 2023, Taipei, Taiwan, July 23-27, 2023*, pages 2308–2313. ACM.

A Additional Experimental Setups

A.1 Datasets

Dataset	Number of Queries
NQ	8,758
TQA	8,837
SQD	8,886
RQA	3137
SQ	1,000
BASQ	1,235

Table 4: Detailed number of queries for each dataset used in the experiment.

Table 4 shows the number of queries of the datasets utilized in our experiments. Following (Karpukhin et al., 2020), we used the development sets of the NQ, TQA, and SQD datasets. The SQ dev-set was also employed. For RQA, we selected answerable queries from documents available on GCS spanning from 2022 to 2023. In BASQ, we selectively employed questions from BioASQ6 challenge (task b) that permitted either factoid or yes/no responses to ensure accuracy.

A.2 Models

To construct the retrieval system for our RAG model, we employed BM25 with Pyserini[5], using pre-indexed corpora provided by the framework. To improve answer generation across datasets, we include document titles to provide context to the LLM, following Asai et al. (2024). Additionally, recognizing that sentences alone may offer insufficient context, we also included document titles in the reranking process to further ensure contextual richness.

To select models for our re-ranking experiments, we considered a range of realistic scenarios and selected representative models from three key categories: dense retrieval, supervised re-ranking, and unsupervised re-ranking. Specifically, for dense retrieval, we chose DPR and Contriever. In the category of supervised re-ranking, we used the established pointwise ranking models MonoT5 and RankT5. For unsupervised re-ranking, we employed RG, a widely used pointwise re-ranking method. Additionally, acknowledging the significance of latency in practical settings, we favored pointwise methods to efficiently manage the computational overhead associated with processing and decomposing passages into sentences.

[5] `https://github.com/castorini/pyserini`

Model	T
BM25	7.6389
Contriever	0.9341
DPR	71.4338
MonoT5	0.098
RankT5	-3.597
RG	0.9998

Table 5: Threshold T values used for each model in the main experiments.

A.2.1 Model Weights

All model weights were sourced from Hugging Face, and the models were used without any additional training. Below, we list the specific Hugging Face model names corresponding to the weights employed in our experiments:

DPR:

- `facebook/dpr-question_encoder-multiset-base`
- `facebook/dpr-ctx_encoder-multiset-base`

Contriever:

- `facebook/contriever`

MonoT5:

- `castorini/monot5-base-msmarco`

RankT5:

- `Soyoung97/RankT5-base`

RECOMP:

- `fangyuan/nq_abstractive_compressor`
- `fangyuan/nq_extractive_compressor`
- `fangyuan/tqa_abstractive_compressor`
- `fangyuan/tqa_extractive_compressor`
- `fangyuan/hotpotqa_abstractive_compressor`
- `fangyuan/hotpotqa_extractive_compressor`

LLama2-13b-chat:

- `meta-llama/Llama-2-13b-chat-hf`

A.2.2 Threshold T for Each Model

As shown in the Figure 8, the distribution of relevance scores varies significantly across models. Experimentally, we sampled 1,000 entries each from the training sets of the NQ, TQA, and SQD datasets to set the 90th percentile threshold T. Sentences scoring below this threshold were removed. Although it is possible to sample from the training set in each experiment to establish new thresholds, our experiments conducted in Section 5 across various thresholds consistently yielded better performance than using the top-1 documents directly. Therefore, the thresholds established in this experiment could be used as the standard. The specific values are listed in the accompanying Table 5.

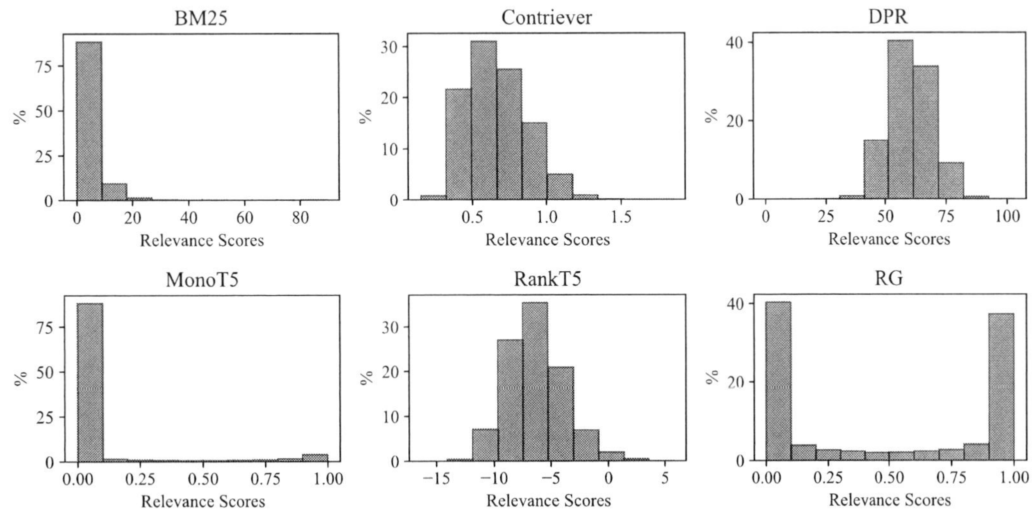

Figure 8: Distribution of relevance scores for 1,000 randomly sampled documents from the NQ, TQA, and SQD datasets for each model.

A.3 Prompt Templates

For a fair comparison, we fixed the prompt templates. In this section, we introduce these fixed templates.

A.3.1 QA Prompt Template

We use a QA template for open-domain queries from the publicly available llama-index[6]. Below is the QA prompt template used in our experiments:

QA Prompt Template for LLMs

[INST] We have provided context information below.

{context_str}

Given this information, please answer the question: {query_str} [/INST]

A.3.2 RG Ranking Prompt Template

We use an RG Ranking Prompt Template following (Liang et al., 2022). Below is the RG Ranking prompt template used in our experiments:

[6]https://www.llamaindex.ai/

Ranking Prompt Template for LLMs

[INST] Passage:

{title_str}
{document_str}

Query: {query_str}
Does the passage answer the query? Answer 'Yes' or 'No' [/INST]

B Additional Experimental Results

B.1 Main Result on Top-5 documents

In Table 6, we compared the performance of *DSLR*-refined documents for the top-5 settings with original documents in RAG. While *DSLR* remained effective, the margin of performance improvement was less significant than the top-1 setting, suggesting that increasing the volume of documents can modestly enhance performance. However, *DSLR* managed to maintain similar or better performance while significantly reducing token count, thus improving efficiency. In this setting, models like MonoT5, RankT5, and RG, based on pre-trained models, outperformed traditional models such as BM25, Contriever, and DPR, likely due to the superior capability of sentence-level re-ranking.

Type	Re-ranker	NQ # tok	NQ Acc	TQA # tok	TQA Acc	SQD # tok	SQD Acc	RQA # tok	RQA Acc	SQ # tok	SQ Acc	BASQ # tok	BASQ Acc	AVG. # tok	AVG. Acc
Baseline															
-	-	855	34.9	862	64.7	843	35.9	2323	42.5	825	40.9	2131	62.9	1307	47.0
Ours															
Sparse Ret.	BM25	204	29.9	371	62.1	172	31.6	1590	42.6	231	39.6	868	58.7	573	44.1
Dense Ret.	Contriever	303	32.6	251	63.8	243	34.5	1163	44.1	301	41.7	1433	62.4	616	46.6
	DPR	262	**37.9**	305	65.6	225	32.8	1095	42.5	334	**42.3**	1390	60.5	602	46.8
Supervised Re-r.	MonoT5	325	36.1	353	65.0	273	36.7	1194	**44.9**	200	40	1640	62.3	664	47.5
	RankT5	368	35.8	285	64.9	369	**36.9**	976	44.1	202	40.6	1458	63.0	610	47.6
Unsupervised Re-r.	RG	198	37.4	320	**66.8**	205	35.3	1099	43.9	453	40.8	1253	**63.4**	588	**47.9**

Table 6: Performance comparison between the *Baseline* (original top-5 document) and *Ours* (*DSLR*-refined top-5 document) on various open-domain QA datasets. The table shows the average token count (# tok) and accuracy (Acc) for both sparse and dense retrievers, as well as for supervised and unsupervised re-rankers. Best results are in **bold**.

B.2 Detailed Results for the Comparative Analysis of Document Refining Methods: Evaluating RECOMP and *DSLR*

Table 7 provides a detailed comparison between the RECOMP and *DSLR* frameworks. RECOMP focuses on minimizing token usage in RAG without sacrificing performance, utilizing a fine-tuned Contriever for extractive compression and a T5-large for abstractive compression. By contrast, *DSLR* enhances RAG performance by eliminating redundant content. Although their different objectives pose a challenge for direct comparison, both aim to extract essential information effectively. To ensure a fair comparison, we aligned the context length to two sentences and refined the top-5 documents, mirroring RECOMP's methodology. Our experiments utilized the LLama2-13b-chat model as the reader to maintain consistency. This analysis underscores the importance of zero-shot refinement approaches in advancing document refinement for RAG.

B.3 *DSLR* with Proprietary Models

We evaluated the performance of *DSLR* in proprietary LLMs with larger parameter sizes and undisclosed data and training processes, specifically testing on GPT-3.5-turbo[7] and Claude-3-haiku[8] using the same settings for the top-1 document. As shown in Table 8, consistent with previous findings, *DSLR* significantly enhanced performance by simply eliminating irrelevant content at the sentence level from the original document. Additionally, since these models calculate API costs on a per-token basis, the substantial reduction in token count[9] is expected to significantly decrease API costs.

[7] gpt-3.5-turbo-1106

[8] claude-3-haiku-20240307

[9] Due to the unavailability of the tokenizers for gpt-3.5-turbo and claude-3-haiku, token counts were necessarily performed using the LlamaTokenizer.

B.4 Sentence-Level Re-ranking Results

In *DSLR*, the sentence-level re-ranking step is crucial for enhancing performance. We evaluated this approach against conventional passage-level re-ranking within the RAG framework, maintaining identical context lengths (L). Initial retrievals were configured for top-{20, 100}, followed by analyses at $L = \{100, 500\}$. These settings were chosen because 100 and 500 words represent typical lengths for segments in top-1 and top-5 passage-level re-rankings, respectively. Notably, when counting words, only the content is considered, excluding titles.

B.4.1 Comparative Performance of Sentence-Level vs. Passage-Level Re-Ranking

The results presented in Table 9 demonstrate that sentence-level re-ranking consistently outperforms passage-level re-ranking across all settings, except when using BM25.

B.4.2 Effectiveness of Sentence-Level Re-Ranking in Varying Conditions

Table 10 shows the sentence-level and passage-level re-ranking over various context lengths L. Table 11 shows performance in top-{5, 10, 20, 50, 100} settings adjusted for $L = 100$ and $L = 500$. Our experiments on the NQ dataset indicate that sentence-level re-ranking is effective across diverse conditions, omitting the less effective BM25 re-ranking.

Method	Model	NQ	TQA	SQD	RQA	SQ	BASQ	AVG.
DSLR	BM25	22.2	53	27.5	36.5	33.7	54	37.8
	DPR	35	62	28.8	32.9	38.1	55.6	42.1
	Contriever	24.3	56.8	28.5	34.9	37.4	54	39.3
	MonoT5	34.1	62.2	38.9	28.2	38.6	47.9	38.0
	RankT5	34.4	62.5	38.9	42.7	38.4	63.2	46.7
	RG	37.5	64.9	35.5	41.4	41.4	63.4	**47.4**
RECOMP (Xu et al., 2024)	Extr.-NQ	29.7	57.8	26	28.2	38.6	47.9	38.0
	Extr.-TQA	27.5	59.9	27.6	32.1	36.7	49.4	38.9
	Extr.-HQA	27.2	57.7	30.3	33.3	35.7	50.9	39.2
	Abst.-NQ	31	59.2	34.1	38.5	36.1	56	42.5
	Abst.-TQA	35.3	64	29.2	37.3	45.1	46.8	43.0
	Abst.-HQA	30.9	58.3	33.7	37.6	39.9	41.8	40.4

Table 7: Performance comparison of *DSLR* and RECOMP methods across multiple open-domain QA datasets. The table presents the accuracy of each method, including BM25, DPR, Contriever, MonoT5, RankT5, and RG models for *DSLR*, as well as extractive (Extr.) and abstractive (Abst.) models for RECOMP. The best performance is in **bold**.

	# tok	gpt-3.5-turbo	claude-3-haiku
Baseline	170	22.7	24.3
Ours	44	36.9	33.8

Table 8: Performance comparison of the baseline (original top-1 document) and Ours (*DSLR*-refined top-1 document using RG) on the NQ dataset within proprietary models. The comparison includes average token count (# tok) and accuracy.

B.4.3 Effectiveness of Sentence-Level Re-Ranking on the Gold Answer Hit Rate

We present detailed results for the Gold Answer Hit Rate in Table 12. The rate is binary, assigned 1 if the re-ranked context contains the gold answer, and 0 otherwise, averaged over all dataset entries for each L.

B.4.4 Ablation Studies on Various Models

Table 13 explores the significance of each step under various models in the initial top-100 retrieval and L=500 setting. The absence of the sentence-level re-ranking (SR) highlights its necessity in filtering irrelevant information, while excluding the reconstruction (RC) step demonstrates its crucial role in enhancing answer generation accuracy.

Type	Re-ranker	Granularity	NQ L=100	NQ L=500	TQA L=100	TQA L=500	SQD L=100	SQD L=500	RQA* L=100	RQA* L=500	SQ L=100	SQ L=500	BASQ L=100	BASQ L=500	AVG. L=100	AVG. L=500
w/o Re-ranking																
-	-	-	25.5	34.9	58	64.6	28.5	35.9	37	40.1	33.9	40.9	56.8	59.5	40.0	46.0
w/ Re-ranking																
Top-20																
Sparse Ret.	BM25	Sentence	26.3	37.5	56.7	65.6	31.5	37.1	39.3	43.1	35.6	43.4	58.5	64.2	41.3	48.5
Dense Ret.	Contriever	Passage	26.5	37.7	57.5	66.1	26.2	37.2	33.6	38	35.4	43.7	53.9	57.9	38.9	46.8
		Sentence	28.5	37.2	60.9	67	32.9	38.4	38.3	42.7	39	44	60.7	63.4	43.4	48.8
	DPR	Passage	36.5	42.1	62.3	67.3	25.3	35.4	31.5	36	38.9	44.6	52.5	56.5	41.2	47.0
		Sentence	38.5	42.5	64.3	68.2	33.1	36	35.8	40.4	41.4	45.6	59	62.7	45.4	49.2
Supervised Rer.	MonoT5	Passage	33.6	40.7	62.1	67.6	37.1	40	37.8	41.5	37.4	44.7	58.7	62.3	44.5	49.5
		Sentence	37.4	42.3	64.9	68.2	39.5	39.5	42.1	44.6	41.4	44	64.2	65.1	48.3	50.6
	RankT5	Passage	35.4	41.4	63.3	67.7	39.2	40	37.9	40.8	37.8	44.5	59.2	63.0	45.5	49.6
		Sentence	36.9	42.1	64	67.9	39.9	39.5	42.8	43.9	40.2	45.7	65.6	66.5	48.2	50.9
Unsupervised Rer.	RG	Passage	35.9	41.9	65.7	68.8	34	39.3	27	30.1	40.2	45	60.9	63.5	44.0	48.1
		Sentence	39.2	42.9	67.1	68.8	37.2	39.8	41.5	44.6	42.1	47.3	64.7	66.9	**48.6**	**51.7**
Top-100																
Sparse Ret.	BM25	Sentence	22.1	33.5	50.1	62.0	26.5	33.6	39.3	43.1	32.2	41.2	51.5	60.4	37.0	45.6
Dense Ret.	Contriever	Passage	26.0	37.2	56.4	66.0	23.7	35.3	33.6	38.0	36.3	44.6	51.0	56	37.8	46.2
		Sentence	28.0	37.6	59.4	67.5	32.5	39.0	38.3	42.7	40.5	45.4	58.7	63.5	42.9	49.3
	DPR	Passage	39.2	46.5	61.8	68.8	22.8	33.4	31.5	36	38.5	44.5	48.0	53.6	40.3	47.1
		Sentence	41.9	46.7	65.3	69.8	31.8	38.0	35.8	40.4	40.7	48.1	57.0	62.1	45.4	50.9
Supervised Re-r.	MonoT5	Passage	35.4	43.9	62.8	69.1	38.3	42.3	37.8	41.5	39.3	46.8	58.4	63.2	45.3	51.1
		Sentence	40.5	46.3	65.8	70.3	41.9	41.8	42.1	44.6	42.2	48.6	64.0	68.0	49.4	53.3
	RankT5	Passage	38.0	44.7	64.5	70.0	41.5	43.5	37.9	40.8	39.0	46.5	59.8	64.2	46.8	51.6
		Sentence	39.7	46.0	65.5	69.9	42.4	41.8	42.8	43.9	39.0	48.5	65.6	68.5	49.2	53.1
Unsupervised Re-r.	RG	Passage	37.6	44.9	66.3	71.0	33.5	40.8	27.0	30.1	40.2	46.9	60.8	63.4	44.2	49.5
		Sentence	41.7	47.4	68.5	71.7	37.5	41.5	41.5	44.6	43.8	49.4	65.4	68.8	**49.7**	**53.9**

* RQA uses a specific GCS document from the dataset instead of the top-100, allowing for a variable number of top-N retrieved documents.

Table 9: Comparative performance of sentence-level and passage-level re-ranking methods across multiple open-domain QA datasets. Results are presented for two context lengths (L=100 and L=500), using sparse and dense retrievers, and both supervised and unsupervised re-rankers, for the top-20, 100 retrieved documents. The best performances are in **bold**.

Re-ranker	Granularity	L=100	L=200	L=300	L=400	L=500
Contriever	Passage	26	29.9	33	35.4	37.2
	Sentence	28	32.8	35.3	36.4	37.6
DPR	Passage	39.2	42.5	44	45.8	46.5
	Sentence	41.9	44.5	45.8	46.4	46.7
MonoT5	Passage	35.4	39	41.6	43	43.9
	Sentence	40.5	43.9	45.6	46.1	46.3
RankT5	Passage	38	41	42.6	43.9	44.7
	Sentence	39.7	43.3	44.9	46.2	46
RG	Passage	37.6	41	42.7	44	44.9
	Sentence	41.7	44.7	46.2	47.3	47.4
AVG.	Passage	35.2	38.7	40.8	42.4	43.4
	Sentence	38.4	41.8	43.6	44.5	44.8

Table 10: Performance comparison across different context lengths (L = 100, 200, 300, 400, and 500) on the NQ dataset, evaluated using top-100 retrieved documents.

Re-ranker	Granularity	Top-5		Top-10		Top-20		Top-50		Top-100	
		L=100	L=500	L=100	L=500	L=100	L=500	L=100	L=500	L=100	L=500
Contriever	Passage	26.7	35.3	26.7	37.0	26.5	37.7	26.4	37.1	26.0	37.2
	Sentence	28.0	34.8	27.9	36.3	28.5	37.2	28.1	37.7	28.0	37.6
DPR	Passage	32.8	35.9	34.5	39.5	36.5	42.1	38.5	45.0	39.2	46.5
	Sentence	33.0	34.9	36.3	39.0	38.5	42.5	40.9	45.6	41.9	46.7
MonoT5	Passage	31.3	35.0	32.6	38.5	33.6	40.7	34.6	43.3	35.4	43.9
	Sentence	32.9	34.8	35.3	38.9	37.4	42.3	39.7	44.7	40.5	46.3
RankT5	Passage	32.1	35.5	33.8	38.4	35.4	41.4	37.0	43.8	38.0	44.7
	Sentence	32.5	34.9	34.9	38.7	36.9	42.1	38.8	44.8	39.7	46.0
RG	Passage	33.0	35.3	34.8	39.6	33.6	41.9	34.7	44.2	35.2	44.9
	Sentence	33.9	34.8	36.7	39.6	36.1	42.9	37.7	45.8	38.4	47.4
AVG.	Passage	31.2	35.4	32.5	38.6	33.6	40.8	34.7	42.7	35.2	43.4
	Sentence	32.1	34.8	34.2	38.5	36.1	41.4	37.7	43.7	38.4	44.8

Table 11: Performance comparison of various re-rankers at different granularity levels and context lengths (L=100 and L=500), evaluated on NQ dataset across top-{5, 10, 20, 50, 100} retrieved documents.

Type	Re-ranker	Granularity	NQ		TQA		SQD		RQA*		SQ		BASQ		AVG.	
			L=100	L=500	L=100	L=500	L=100	L=500	L=100	L=500	L=100	L=500	L=100	L=500	L=100	L=500
Top-20																
Dense Ret.	Contriever	Passage	24.1	49.5	44.8	70.5	29.3	53.7	30.3	42.8	30.1	58.9	21	32.2	29.9	51.3
		Sentence	25.9	47.4	50.1	71.7	39.8	56.3	34.8	48.6	37.6	61.4	19.6	32.1	34.6	52.9
	DPR	Passage	41.9	57.7	59.1	73.4	29.5	52.3	29.2	42.1	37.3	59.3	20.6	30.5	36.2	52.6
		Sentence	46.6	59.0	64.3	74.6	42.4	58.2	32.8	49.5	44.6	61.8	24.2	34.2	42.5	56.2
Supervised Rer.	MonoT5	Passage	37.7	57.1	59	74.1	45.7	60.1	36.1	47.2	38.7	60.4	25.9	36.0	40.5	55.8
		Sentence	46.2	58.3	65.6	74.4	54.2	61.5	43.9	52.6	46.5	63.1	29.7	39.2	47.7	58.2
	RankT5	Passage	40.7	57.9	61	74.1	48.3	60.7	34.8	45.6	39.9	61.9	26.6	35.9	41.9	56
		Sentence	44.8	57.9	64.5	73.8	54.2	61.7	43.4	52.3	44.9	63	30.5	39.4	47	58
Unsupervised Rer.	RG	Passage	38.1	57.7	59.9	74.7	40.3	58.9	21.1	30.9	40.5	61.6	25.8	35.1	37.6	53.2
		Sentence	47.1	59.3	66.1	75.5	50.8	61.6	38.6	51.4	48.8	65.8	29.4	38.9	46.8	58.7
Top-100																
Dense Ret.	Contriever	Passage	23	48.9	42	70.2	25.8	51.8	30.3	42.8	29.5	59.7	19.8	30.6	28.4	50.7
		Sentence	24.7	46.4	48.2	70.8	39.1	57.7	34.8	48.6	38.6	63.9	18.7	31.6	34	53.2
	DPR	Passage	46.5	64.9	59.3	75.3	26.9	49.2	29.2	42.1	35.2	61.6	20.1	29.5	36.2	53.8
		Sentence	52.4	66.6	65.9	77.2	41.4	59.5	32.8	49.5	45.1	67.8	24.3	33.4	43.6	59
Supervised Re-r.	MonoT5	Passage	40.2	63	60.1	76.8	48	65.8	36.1	47.2	41.5	65.2	25.7	36.8	41.9	63.6
		Sentence	51.1	66.2	67.8	77.9	60.1	69.6	43.9	52.6	49.4	68.2	29.4	39.9	50.3	62.4
	RankT5	Passage	44.1	64.2	62.9	77.1	51.6	67.3	34.8	45.6	41.8	65.5	27.4	36.8	43.8	59.4
		Sentence	49.8	65	66.8	76.9	60	69.4	43.4	52.3	49	67	31	40.5	50	61.8
Unsupervised Re-r.	RG	Passage	40	63.1	60.6	77.7	40.1	61.4	21.1	30.9	40.9	66.7	26.5	35.1	38.2	55.8
		Sentence	51.2	66.6	67.7	79	52.8	67.6	38.6	51.4	54	71.4	29.6	39.8	49	62.6

* RQA uses a specific GCS document from the dataset instead of the top-20, allowing for a variable number of top-N retrieved documents.

Table 12: Golden Answer Hit rate of sentence-level and passage-level re-ranking methods across multiple open-domain QA datasets. Results are presented for two context lengths (L=100 and L=500), using dense retrievers, and both supervised and unsupervised re-rankers, for the top-{20, 100} retrieved documents.

	Model	NQ	TQA	SQD	AVG.
Sentence-Level Re-ranking	Contriever	37.6	67.5	39.1	48.1
	DPR	46.7	69.9	38.1	51.6
	MonoT5	46.4	70.4	41.9	52.9
	RankT5	46.1	70.0	41.9	52.7
	RG	47.4	71.7	41.5	53.5
w/o SR		24.1	51.0	14.4	29.8
w/o RC (descend)	Contriever	36.8	66.7	38.1	47.2
	DPR	46.9	69.3	37.6	51.3
	MonoT5	45.9	68.9	41.6	52.1
	RankT5	46.0	69.3	41.3	52.5
	RG	46.3	71.0	39.6	52.3
w/o RC (random)	Contriever	37.4	66.8	37.7	47.3
	DPR	46.5	69.0	37.2	50.9
	MonoT5	46.0	70.0	40.6	52.2
	RankT5	45.6	69.1	40.3	51.7
	RG	46.3	71.2	39.7	52.4

Table 13: Ablation studies on the NQ, TQA, and SQD datasets comparing the Sentence-Level Re-ranking performance with its variants. This includes the baseline RG model and variants without sentence-level re-ranking (w/o SR) and without reconstruction (w/o RC), evaluated in conditions with scores ordered by relevance (descend) and shuffled randomly (random).

N	1	3	5	7	10
			Baseline		
Acc	25.6	31.7	34.9	37.0	39.6
# tok	169	512	855	1198	1713
E2E	3.368	4.436	5.239	6.030	7.382
			Ours		
Acc	31.1	34.0	36.1	37.6	39.7
# tok	74	207	325	431	577
E2E	3.792	4.081	4.232	4.559	5.422

Table 14: Performance comparison at various N-values for Baseline vs. Ours, using Accuracy (Acc), Token count (# tok), and End-to-End latency (E2E) on the NQ dataset.

(%)	10	20	30	40	50	60	70	80	90	Oracle
T	2.7969e-05	0.00043	0.0076	0.0826	0.65841	0.9196	0.9857	0.9981	0.9998	-
Acc	28.6	28.7	29.0	29.2	29.4	29.7	29.8	29.9	29.5	34.1
# tok	164	159	150	141	123	109	94	75	51	77

Table 15: Variation in accuracy and token count (# tok) with adjustments to relevance score percentiles, including the set threshold values T and oracle settings on the NQ dataset.

Enhancing Robustness of Retrieval-Augmented Language Models with In-Context Learning

Seong-Il Park, Seung-Woo Choi, Na-Hyun Kim, Jay-Yoon Lee
Seoul National University
{athjk3,rhdn520,nahyun0410,lee.jayyoon}@snu.ac.kr

Abstract

Retrieval-Augmented Language Models (RALMs) have significantly improved performance in open-domain question answering (QA) by leveraging external knowledge. However, RALMs still struggle with unanswerable queries, where the retrieved contexts do not contain the correct answer, and with conflicting information, where different sources provide contradictory answers due to imperfect retrieval. This study introduces an in-context learning-based approach to enhance the reasoning capabilities of RALMs, making them more robust in imperfect retrieval scenarios. Our method incorporates Machine Reading Comprehension (MRC) demonstrations, referred to as *cases*, to boost the model's capabilities to identify unanswerabilities and conflicts among the retrieved contexts. Experiments on two open-domain QA datasets show that our approach increases accuracy in identifying unanswerable and conflicting scenarios without requiring additional fine-tuning. This work demonstrates that in-context learning can effectively enhance the robustness of RALMs in open-domain QA tasks.

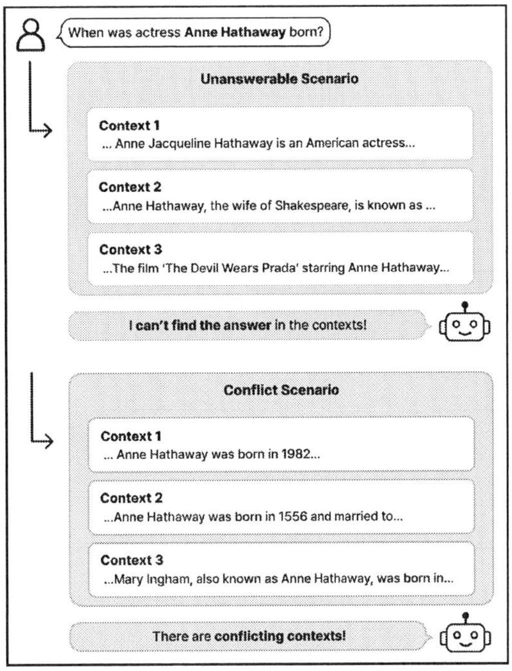

Figure 1: Examples of unanswerable and conflict scenario that may arise during retrieval-augmenation. A robust RALM should be able to identify such scenarios well.

1 Introduction

Retrieval Augmented Language Models (RALMs) have demonstrated remarkable performance in the field of open-domain question answering (QA). By leveraging external knowledge to generate answers, RALMs enhance accuracy and enable language models to respond to queries beyond their training data. (Lewis et al., 2020; Guu et al., 2020; Izacard and Grave, 2021; Izacard et al., 2022) Typically, RALMs operate in two stages: the retrieval step, which involves fetching relevant contexts from external knowledge sources, and the generation step, where answers are generated based on the retrieved contexts. Recent research has shown that using frozen Large Language Models (LLMs) without additional fine-tuning during the generation step can also be effective. (Ram et al., 2023; Shi et al., 2023)

However, a critical issue in open-domain QA is the reliance of RALMs on the quality of external knowledge. Figure 1 illustrates common imperfect retrieval scenarios in RALMs. In unanswerable scenario where the retrieved contexts do not contain the correct answer, RALMs cannot provide an accurate response. Additionally, when contexts are retrieved from various sources, such as search engines, conflicting information may arise. In such scenario, RALMs may struggle to determine the correct information, leading to reliance on their parametric knowledge or potential hallucination.

Proceedings of the 3rd Workshop on Knowledge Augmented Methods for NLP, pages 93–102
August 16, 2024

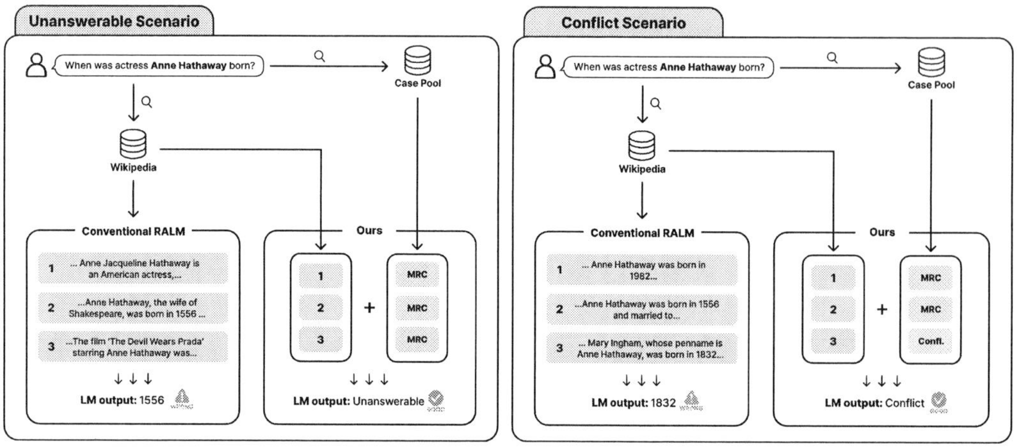

Figure 2: An overview of our approach. Conventional RALM generates answers by providing the LLM with context retrieved from a knowledge source. In contrast, our method simultaneously inputs cases that enhance the LLM's reasoning capability, allowing it to generate answers. This leads to more robust reasoning compared to conventional RALM.

To address these challenges, we propose the in-context learning (Brown et al., 2020) based approach to enhance the reasoning capabilities of LLMs, thereby increasing robustness in such imperfect retrieval scenarios. Unlike previous approaches that depend on extensive fine-tuning (Chen et al., 2022; Asai et al., 2023; Yoran et al., 2023; Yu et al., 2023; Neeman et al., 2023), our method leverages the in-context learning capability of LLMs, demonstrating that providing simple examples to LLMs can improve robustness in open-domain QA without additional training. Figure 2 provides an overview of our approach. Unlike conventional RALM, our method retrieves demonstrations (referred to as cases) that assist in answering a given query. By concatenating these retrieved cases to the LLM's input during retrieval-augmentation, we enhance the LLM's reasoning abilities through in-context learning. This enables the RALMs to perform more robust reasoning.

Our experiments show that providing LLMs with Machine Reading Comprehension (MRC) demonstrations enhances accuracy and the ability to detect unanswerability. Additionally, presenting LLMs with simple examples that simulate conflicts among retrieved contexts improves their ability to identify such conflicts.

Our contributions and key findings are summarized as follows:

- We demonstrated that providing RALMs with MRC demonstrations improves their reasoning capabilities in open-domain QA, where answers should be generated from multiple documents.
- Using retrieval to select similar demonstrations is more effective than randomly selecting those from the entire pool.
- Providing QA cases alone enhances reasoning and improves robustness in scenarios with frequently encountered issues in open-domain QA, such as unanswerable queries.
- For conflict scenario that LLMs do not frequently encounter during training, directly providing analogous demonstrations improves reasoning abilities.

2 Related Works

2.1 In-context learning and RALMs

Large Language Models (LLMs) have demonstrated the ability to learn from a few examples in their immediate context, a capability known as in-context learning (ICL). This capability, widely recognized as an emerging trait in many advanced models, focuses on gaining knowledge through inference (Brown et al., 2020; Wei et al., 2022). In open-domain QA, recent works highlighted that appending relevant documents to LLMs' inputs without additional training significantly enhanced performance, providing an efficient method for RALMs (Ram et al., 2023). Similarly, (Shi et al., 2023) applied retrieval-augmented methods to black-box language models, enhancing their question-answering capabilities without altering their internal structure. Another study introduces Fusion-in-Context, which examined how various prompting strategies influence few-shot learning performance (Huang et al., 2023). Following these approaches, we enhance the RALMs' robustness using in-context learning methods.

2.2 Robustness of RALMs on unanswerability

Various studies have aimed to increase the robustness of RALMs in unanswerable scenarios. (Yu et al., 2023) introduced the Chain-Of-Note, which trains LLMs to generate answers after assessing the relevance of retrieved documents through sequential reading notes. (Yoran et al., 2023) trained RALMs to handle unanswerability using an automatically generated dataset. Self-RAG (Asai et al., 2023) generated special tokens to indicate the relevance of retrieved documents or the need for further retrieval. CRAG (Yan et al., 2024) used a lightweight retrieval evaluator to assess unanswerability. While these approaches have improved robustness, leveraging LLMs' in-context learning capabilities in these scenarios is still underexplored.

2.3 Robustness of RALMs on conflicts

Knowledge conflicts can arise from clashes between parametric and contextual knowledge (Longpre et al., 2021) or among various contextual knowledges (Chen et al., 2022). Previous studies have focused on training models to prioritize contextual knowledge, disentangle knowledge types (Neeman et al., 2023) or measure decision-making patterns (Ying et al., 2023). Several studies have also aimed to mitigate conflicts by calibrating models to answer only when there's no conflict (Chen et al., 2022), searching for diverse passages by augmenting queries (Weller et al., 2022), or filtering out conflicting passages (Hong et al.). However, these approaches often overlook the LLMs' in-context learning capabilities. Unlike previous works, we focus on leveraging the model's in-context learning to make it *conflict-awarable* for more reliable outputs without additional training.

3 Method

Our objective is to enhance the reasoning capabilities of LLMs in open-domain QA scenarios, particularly in detecting unanswerable scenarios where no answer exists within the retrieved contexts, and conflict scenarios where contradictions exist among retrieved contexts.

Our approach follows the In-context RALM method (Ram et al., 2023), which concatenates retrieved contexts as inputs to a frozen LLM for retrieval-augmentation. To further enhance the LLM's reasoning capability, we will add demonstrations to the RALMs by simply concatenating demonstrations to the existing RALM input. Typically, in-context learning provides examples of the same task (Dong et al., 2022), but our demonstrations are based on Machine Reading Comprehension (MRC) datasets, which have a single shorter context, rather than generating answers from multiple documents as in ODQA. We refer to these demonstrations as ***cases***.

3.1 Crafting cases

We create a case pool using the SQuAD (Rajpurkar et al., 2016), which is a well-known MRC dataset consisting of question, context, and answer pairs. From this dataset, we create two types of cases:

QA case To improve reasoning capability and unanswerability detection in open-domain QA, we use MRC examples as QA cases. Given that open-domain QA resembles an MRC task involving multiple documents, we use SQuAD examples without additional perturbation, excluding those with lengthy contexts [1].

Conflict case We follow the method by (Xie et al., 2023) to create conflict cases. While Xie et al. (2023) created counter memories contradicting the LLM's parametric knowledge, we create conflicting contexts contradicting the retrieved contexts. The process is as follows:

1. **Answer Sentence Creation:** Similar to Xie et al. (2023), we generate base sentences for entity substitution using the question and answers from open-domain QA datasets, forming declarative answer sentences. We utilize an LLM for this step.
2. **Entity Substitution and Filtering:** We substitute the answer entity in the answer sentence with another entity of the same type, creating a conflict sentence. Then, using an LLM, we generate a conflict passage supporting the conflict sentence. Any conflict passage containing the answer string is excluded.
3. **Concatenation:** By concatenating the conflict passage with the original context, we simulate a scenario with multiple contradicting documents, creating a conflict case.

[1] We filtered out contexts containing more than 150 words.

We use the Llama3-70B-Instruct (Touvron et al., 2023) for generating cases. For entity substitution, we use SpaCy NER model for entity recognition.[2] Details on prompts and settings used for the LLM are provided in Appendix A.

3.2 Case retrieval

At inference time, we put the crafted cases into the LLM. Similar to (Thai et al., 2023), we employ a case-based reasoning method for case selection. We mask entities in the test set questions (referred to as queries) and case set questions, compute sentence embeddings[3] for the masked questions, and calculate cosine similarity between these embeddings. The top-k similar cases are used as demonstrations during inference, enabling effective in-context learning by providing the LLM with cases similar to the current query. To prevent leakage due to cases, any case where the answer matched the query answer is excluded from the case candidates.

4 Experimental Setup

4.1 Dataset

We used the Natural Questions (NQ) (Lee et al., 2019) and Web Questions (WebQ) (Berant et al., 2013) datasets, commonly employed in open-domain QA tasks. Both datasets' test sets were used for our experiments. We retrieved the top five documents for each query from Wikipedia[4] based on their cosine similarity. For dense retriever, we use ColBERTv2 (Santhanam et al., 2022) to retrieve most similar contexts for each query. Detailed statistics for each dataset are provided below.

To simulate unanswerable and conflict scenarios, we perturbed the existing open-domain QA datasets to create unanswerable and conflict test sets.

Unanswerable Set To determine if a query is answerable based on retrieved contexts, we use both string match and an NLI model[5]. If the retrieved context does not contain the answer string and the context-query pair is not entailed, we consider the context unanswerable. If all top-k retrieved contexts are unanswerable, the query is labeled as an unanswerable example and the original answer is replaced with *unanswerable*.

Conflict Set We utilized the method described in the 3.1 to create a conflict passage for each query, which is then randomly inserted among the top five retrieved contexts to generate conflict examples. To differentiate between the cases and the test set, we employed the GPT-3.5-turbo-0125 model for generating conflict passages. To occur a conflict, the original top five retrieved contexts must contain the correct answer, hence we inserted the conflict passages only into answerable examples. To determine answerability, similar to the unanswerable set, we considered a context as answerable if it included the answer string and the question-context pair was entailment. If at least one answerable context existed among the top-k retrieved contexts, the example was considered answerable. After inserting a single conflict passage into the answerable example, the original answer is replaced with the label *conflict*, similar to the process used for the unanswerable set.

These perturbations allow us to evaluate the effectiveness of our method in improving the LLM's ability to handle unanswerable and conflicting scenarios in open-domain QA.

4.2 Prompting

We designed instructions to evaluate how well RALMs can identify unanswerability and conflicts in the unanswerable and conflict sets, respectively. These instructions are designed to extend standard retrieval-augmented QA by adding the capability to identify unanswerable and conflicting contexts. Prompts for each type are as follows:

Unanswerable Prompt This instruction adds the task of identifying unanswerability. The LLM must provide an answer for answerable examples and respond with *unanswerable* if the context does not contain the answer.

Conflict Prompt This instruction adds the task of identifying conflicts among contexts. The LLM have to respond with *conflict* if there is contradiction among the retrieved contexts and provide an answer if there is no contradiction.

Please refer to the Appendix A for the details of the prompt.

4.3 Metric

Following (Mallen et al., 2023), we used accuracy as our metric. Unlike exact match, accuracy con-

[2]We used the en_core_web_trf model. The entities for substitutions were created by extracting entities from all texts in the Wikitext-103-raw-v1.

[3]For sentence embedding, we used all-MiniLM-L6-v2 model from Sentence Transformers library (Reimers and Gurevych, 2019)

[4]We used the preprocessed data from (Karpukhin et al., 2020)

[5]We used MoritzLaurer/mDeBERTa-v3-base-xnli-multilingual-nli-2mil7 from Hugging Face transformers library

Model	Prompt	NQ Acc	NQ Acc (ans)	NQ Acc (unans)	WebQ Acc	WebQ Acc (ans)	WebQ Acc (unans)
Llama3	zeroshot	52.97	58.83	35.61	35.00	39.54	22.30
	1Q	54.12	60.01	36.65	36.33	41.72	21.28
	3Q	56.84	62.67	39.54	39.80	45.59	23.65
	5Q	**57.15**	**62.67**	**40.79**	**43.99**	**49.70**	**28.04**
Qwen1.5	zeroshot	58.19	67.34	31.06	48.80	58.52	21.62
	1Q	59.34	65.95	39.75	48.80	58.16	22.64
	3Q	**60.96**	67.34	**42.03**	**50.85**	59.01	**28.04**
	5Q	60.23	**67.90**	37.47	50.31	**60.10**	22.97
ChatGPT	zeroshot	42.48	41.45	45.55	27.96	26.72	31.42
	1Q	47.03	41.52	63.35	33.75	26.96	52.70
	3Q	**48.80**	42.57	**67.29**	34.28	26.12	**57.09**
	5Q	47.96	**43.06**	62.53	**34.55**	**28.42**	51.69

Table 1: Experimental results on unanswerable set. In the prompt column, "XQ" denotes that X QA cases have been added. Acc represents the accuracy on all examples, Acc (ans) indicates the accuracy on answerable examples, and Acc (unans) shows the accuracy on unanswerable examples. The best performance is highlighted in bold.

siders a response correct if it contains the answer string. To prevent distortion due to long responses, we limited the response length to 10 tokens during generation.

4.4 LLM

For effective in-context learning, we used models with large parameter sizes. Specifically, we used the Llama3-70B-Instruct model (Touvron et al., 2023), the Qwen-1.5-chat-72B model (Bai et al., 2023) and the `GPT-3.5-turbo-0125` model (abbreviated as ChatGPT) using OpenAI's API. To reduce generation randomness, we used greedy decoding and fixed the random seed. For faster inference, we used vLLM (Kwon et al., 2023).

5 Experiments

In these experiments, we aim to investigate how effectively our constructed cases can help LLMs identify unanswerability and conflicts in open-domain QA scenarios.

5.1 Experiments on Unanswerable Set

Table 1 presents the results of our experiments on identifying unanswerable questions based on different types of prompts. The number preceding the case name indicates the number of added cases. Our goal is not only to have LLMs correctly identify unanswerable examples but also to ensure them to provide accurate answers for answerable examples. Therefore, we calculated the accuracy for both unanswerable and answerable examples, as well as the overall accuracy. These results indicate that adding QA cases consistently enhance the reasoning capabilities of LLMs across all models and datasets. Specifically, the accuracy for unanswerable examples significantly increased compared to the zero-shot performance. For instance, ChatGPT showed an improvement of up to 21.74 in the NQ dataset and 25.67 in the Web Questions dataset. This improvement indicates that providing QA cases enhances the LLMs' ability to reason in situations where no correct answer exists. However, the impact of adding QA cases varied among models. For example, Llama3's performance continued to improve with more QA cases, while Qwen1.5 achieved the best performance with three QA cases. These findings imply that simple examples can significantly boost the reasoning abilities of LLMs through in-context learning.

5.2 Experiments on Conflict Set

Unlike the unanswerable experiments, we include both QA and conflict cases in our conflict set experiments, while keeping the total number of cases constant for fair comparison. Table 2 shows the results of our experiments on identifying conflicts. When using both QA and conflict cases, we first added the QA cases, followed by the conflict cases in the prompt. To evaluate the LLMs' ability to identify conflicts while maintaining accuracy on answerable examples, we conducted two forward passes. In the first pass, we inferred the answerable examples without adding conflict passages (non-conflict examples, abbreviated as **NC**). In the second pass, we add conflict passages to the same examples (conflict examples, abbreviated as **C**) and then inferred.

Model	Prompt	NQ Acc (NC)	NQ Acc (C)	NQ Acc (Avg)	WebQ Acc (NC)	WebQ Acc (C)	WebQ Acc (Avg)
Llama3	zeroshot	58.54	10.67	34.61	38.55	8.75	23.65
	1Q	64.61	16.18	40.39	42.27	14.53	28.40
	3Q	70.79	15.28	43.03	42.83	8.01	25.42
	2Q+1C	**71.24**	**25.73**	**48.48**	**50.65**	**28.12**	**39.39**
	5Q	**72.81**	24.38	48.60	50.65	13.04	31.84
	3Q+2C	71.01	**35.17**	**53.09**	**51.77**	**35.38**	**43.58**
Qwen1.5	zeroshot	76.29	8.76	42.53	59.59	13.04	36.31
	1Q	71.35	12.70	42.02	58.10	21.79	39.94
	3Q	73.26	19.78	46.52	**59.96**	22.91	41.43
	2Q+1C	73.03	**25.28**	**49.16**	57.54	**32.77**	**45.16**
	5Q	**74.04**	16.63	45.34	**58.66**	24.95	41.81
	3Q+2C	73.60	**24.16**	**48.88**	57.73	**27.93**	**42.83**
ChatGPT	zeroshot	55.51	28.65	42.08	34.82	38.36	36.59
	1Q	52.81	28.76	40.79	34.64	40.60	37.62
	3Q	**58.20**	29.21	**43.71**	37.80	**42.46**	**40.13**
	2Q+1C	57.08	**29.89**	43.48	37.62	40.41	39.01
	5Q	**58.65**	23.71	41.18	**41.71**	38.18	**39.94**
	3Q+2C	56.85	**31.57**	**44.21**	38.18	**40.78**	39.48

Table 2: Experimental results on conflict set. In the prompt column, + indicates that two case were used together. Acc (NC) denotes the accuracy on non-conflict examples, Acc (C) represents the accuracy on conflict examples, and Acc (Avg) is the average accuracy of the two. The best performance for each total case count is highlighted in bold, and the overall best performance is underlined.

We calculated the accuracy for both passes to assess the models' performance in identifying conflicts and answering correctly. The results show that adding QA cases alone improves accuracy on conflict examples compared to zero-shot performance. Moreover, adding appropriate conflict cases provides even more benefits. Model performance varied; for example, Qwen showed the highest accuracy for non-conflict examples in the zero-shot setting but had lower accuracy for conflict examples, with the best overall performance achieved using a combination of **2Q+1C**. Conversely, Llama3 performed best with the **3Q+2C** combination, except for the **5Q** setting. ChatGPT's conflict accuracy improved with added conflict cases, but its accuracy for non-conflict examples decreased compared to adding only QA cases. Additionally, ChatGPT showed less improvement in conflict example accuracy compared to other models when conflict cases were added. These results are discussed in more detail in 5.3.2.

Overall, the experiments indicate that identifying conflicts requires more complex reasoning than identifying unanswerable, and the effect of adding QA cases alone is limited. However, providing simplified examples that mimic more complex scenarios can enhance reasoning capabilities. This suggests that simple examples can significantly improve the robustness of LLMs without additional fine-tuning. Also, it shows that such direct examples, like conflicts which are difficult for LLMs to encounter during training, can be more effective in improving reasoning abilities.

Model	**Method**	**Size**	**Acc**	**Acc (ans)**	**Acc (unans)**
ChatGPT	Ours	1	47.03	41.52	63.35
	Random	1	44.10	36.92	65.42
	Ours	3	48.80	42.57	67.29
	Random	3	44.94	36.50	69.98
	Ours	5	47.96	43.06	62.53
	Random	5	43.74	37.82	61.28
Llama3	Ours	1	54.12	60.01	36.65
	Random	1	53.13	58.76	36.44
	Ours	3	56.84	62.67	39.54
	Random	3	54.23	59.32	39.13
	Ours	5	59.13	64.20	44.10
	Random	5	57.93	62.25	45.13

Table 3: Experimental results on the unanswerable set of NQ. Method refers to the case retrieval approach, and size denotes the number of added cases. Acc represents the accuracy on all examples, Acc (ans) indicates the accuracy on answerable examples, and Acc (unans) represents the accuracy on unanswerable examples.

Model	Prompt	NQ	WebQ
ChatGPT	zeroshot	17.08	25.33
	QA	20.79	30.17
Llama3	zeroshot	2.25	1.68
	QA	1.35	1.49
Qwen1.5	zeroshot	3.93	7.26
	QA	8.43	12.85

Table 4: Experimental results on the False Conflict Detection Rate (FCDR). The numbers in the table represent the FCDR. The QA prompt refers to the concatenation of three QA cases.

5.3 Further Analysis

5.3.1 Case Selection

To verify the effectiveness of our case retrieval method described in 3.2, we compared the results of selecting cases using our method versus randomly selecting cases from the entire pool. Table 3 shows the results for the NQ unanswerable set. Our method demonstrates higher overall accuracy compared to randomly selecting cases. Specifically, for answerable examples, our method achieves up to 6 higher accuracy. This indicates that our case retrieval approach may be an effective strategy for in-context learning.

5.3.2 Impact of Conflict Cases on ChatGPT

We conducted additional experiments to understand why adding conflict cases to ChatGPT is less effective. We calculated the False Conflict Detection Rate (FCDR), which is the rate at which non-conflict examples are incorrectly predicted as "conflict," for each model. We compared the results of zeroshot and with three additional QA cases. The results are shown in Table 4. ChatGPT exhibits a significantly higher FCDR compared to Llama3 and Qwen1.5, with 17.08 on NQ and 25.33 on WebQ in the zeroshot setting. This rate further increases to 20.79 and 30.17, respectively, when additional QA cases are included. This suggests that ChatGPT has been trained to be more sensitive to conflicts, which limits the improvement in accuracy for conflict examples when more conflict cases are added. These findings indicate that the effectiveness of case additions can vary depending on the model's characteristics, which we will leave for future work.

6 Conclusion

We conducted experiments leveraging the in-context learning capabilities of LLMs, using simple MRC examples to improve robustness in open-domain QA scenarios. These results show that providing MRC examples as demonstrations improves accuracy for both answerable and unanswerable examples in unanswerable scenarios. In conflict scenarios, providing demonstrations similar to conflict situations enhances the ability to identify conflicts.

Our experiments suggest that well-designed examples can significantly improve LLMs' robustness in open-domain QA without additional fine-tuning, indicating that simple examples can help solve complex tasks.

7 Limitations and Risk

Our study has limitations in that it focuses on a short-form QA dataset. We did not explore how this in-context learning technique could be linked to long-form QA, particularly with Chain-of-Thought prompting (Wei et al., 2022). Additionally, we did not compare our method with a more diverse set of baselines.

References

Akari Asai, Zeqiu Wu, Yizhong Wang, Avirup Sil, and Hannaneh Hajishirzi. 2023. Self-rag: Learning to retrieve, generate, and critique through self-reflection. In *The Twelfth International Conference on Learning Representations*.

Jinze Bai, Shuai Bai, Yunfei Chu, Zeyu Cui, Kai Dang, Xiaodong Deng, Yang Fan, Wenbin Ge, Yu Han, Fei Huang, et al. 2023. Qwen technical report. *arXiv preprint arXiv:2309.16609*.

Jonathan Berant, Andrew Chou, Roy Frostig, and Percy Liang. 2013. Semantic parsing on freebase from question-answer pairs. In *Proceedings of the 2013 conference on empirical methods in natural language processing*, pages 1533–1544.

Tom Brown, Benjamin Mann, Nick Ryder, Melanie Subbiah, Jared D Kaplan, Prafulla Dhariwal, Arvind Neelakantan, Pranav Shyam, Girish Sastry, Amanda Askell, et al. 2020. Language models are few-shot learners. *Advances in neural information processing systems*, 33:1877–1901.

Hung-Ting Chen, Michael Zhang, and Eunsol Choi. 2022. Rich knowledge sources bring complex knowledge conflicts: Recalibrating models to reflect conflicting evidence. In *Proceedings of the 2022 Conference on Empirical Methods in Natural Language Processing*, pages 2292–2307.

Qingxiu Dong, Lei Li, Damai Dai, Ce Zheng, Zhiyong Wu, Baobao Chang, Xu Sun, Jingjing Xu, and Zhifang Sui. 2022. A survey on in-context learning. *arXiv preprint arXiv:2301.00234*.

Kelvin Guu, Kenton Lee, Zora Tung, Panupong Pasupat, and Mingwei Chang. 2020. Retrieval augmented language model pre-training. In *International conference on machine learning*, pages 3929–3938. PMLR.

Giwon Hong, Jeonghwan Kim, Junmo Kang, Sung-Hyon Myaeng, and Joyce Jiyoung Whang. Why so gullible? enhancing the robustness of retrieval-augmented models against counterfactual noise.

Jie Huang, Wei Ping, Peng Xu, Mohammad Shoeybi, Kevin Chen-Chuan Chang, and Bryan Catanzaro. 2023. Raven: In-context learning with retrieval augmented encoder-decoder language models. *arXiv preprint arXiv:2308.07922*.

Gautier Izacard and Édouard Grave. 2021. Leveraging passage retrieval with generative models for open domain question answering. In *Proceedings of the 16th Conference of the European Chapter of the Association for Computational Linguistics: Main Volume*, pages 874–880.

Gautier Izacard, Patrick Lewis, Maria Lomeli, Lucas Hosseini, Fabio Petroni, Timo Schick, Jane Dwivedi-Yu, Armand Joulin, Sebastian Riedel, and Edouard Grave. 2022. Few-shot learning with retrieval augmented language models. *arXiv preprint arXiv:2208.03299*.

Vladimir Karpukhin, Barlas Oğuz, Sewon Min, Patrick Lewis, Ledell Wu, Sergey Edunov, Danqi Chen, and Wen-tau Yih. 2020. Dense passage retrieval for open-domain question answering. *arXiv preprint arXiv:2004.04906*.

Woosuk Kwon, Zhuohan Li, Siyuan Zhuang, Ying Sheng, Lianmin Zheng, Cody Hao Yu, Joseph Gonzalez, Hao Zhang, and Ion Stoica. 2023. Efficient memory management for large language model serving with pagedattention. In *Proceedings of the 29th Symposium on Operating Systems Principles*, pages 611–626.

Kenton Lee, Ming-Wei Chang, and Kristina Toutanova. 2019. Latent retrieval for weakly supervised open domain question answering. *arXiv preprint arXiv:1906.00300*.

Patrick Lewis, Ethan Perez, Aleksandra Piktus, Fabio Petroni, Vladimir Karpukhin, Naman Goyal, Heinrich Küttler, Mike Lewis, Wen-tau Yih, Tim Rocktäschel, et al. 2020. Retrieval-augmented generation for knowledge-intensive nlp tasks. *Advances in Neural Information Processing Systems*, 33:9459–9474.

Shayne Longpre, Kartik Perisetla, Anthony Chen, Nikhil Ramesh, Chris DuBois, and Sameer Singh. 2021. Entity-based knowledge conflicts in question answering. In *Proceedings of the 2021 Conference on Empirical Methods in Natural Language Processing*, pages 7052–7063.

Alex Troy Mallen, Akari Asai, Victor Zhong, Rajarshi Das, Daniel Khashabi, and Hannaneh Hajishirzi. 2023. When not to trust language models: Investigating effectiveness of parametric and non-parametric memories. In *The 61st Annual Meeting Of The Association For Computational Linguistics*.

Ella Neeman, Roee Aharoni, Or Honovich, Leshem Choshen, Idan Szpektor, and Omri Abend. 2023. Disentqa: Disentangling parametric and contextual knowledge with counterfactual question answering. In *Proceedings of the 61st Annual Meeting of the Association for Computational Linguistics (Volume 1: Long Papers)*, pages 10056–10070.

Pranav Rajpurkar, Jian Zhang, Konstantin Lopyrev, and Percy Liang. 2016. Squad: 100,000+ questions for machine comprehension of text. In *Proceedings of the 2016 Conference on Empirical Methods in Natural Language Processing*, pages 2383–2392.

Ori Ram, Yoav Levine, Itay Dalmedigos, Dor Muhlgay, Amnon Shashua, Kevin Leyton-Brown, and Yoav Shoham. 2023. In-context retrieval-augmented language models. *arXiv preprint arXiv:2302.00083*.

Nils Reimers and Iryna Gurevych. 2019. Sentence-bert: Sentence embeddings using siamese bert-networks. In *Proceedings of the 2019 Conference on Empirical Methods in Natural Language Processing and the 9th International Joint Conference on Natural Language Processing (EMNLP-IJCNLP)*, pages 3982–3992.

Keshav Santhanam, Omar Khattab, Jon Saad-Falcon, Christopher Potts, and Matei Zaharia. 2022. Colbertv2: Effective and efficient retrieval via lightweight late interaction. In *Proceedings of the 2022 Conference of the North American Chapter of the Association for Computational Linguistics: Human Language Technologies*, pages 3715–3734.

Weijia Shi, Sewon Min, Michihiro Yasunaga, Minjoon Seo, Rich James, Mike Lewis, Luke Zettlemoyer, and Wen-tau Yih. 2023. Replug: Retrieval-augmented black-box language models. *arXiv preprint arXiv:2301.12652*.

Dung Thai, Dhruv Agarwal, Mudit Chaudhary, Wenlong Zhao, Rajarshi Das, Jay Yoon Lee, Hannaneh Hajishirzi, Manzil Zaheer, and Andrew McCallum. 2023. Machine reading comprehension using case-based reasoning. In *Findings of the Association for Computational Linguistics: EMNLP 2023*, pages 8414–8428.

Hugo Touvron, Louis Martin, Kevin Stone, Peter Albert, Amjad Almahairi, Yasmine Babaei, Nikolay Bashlykov, Soumya Batra, Prajjwal Bhargava, Shruti Bhosale, et al. 2023. Llama 2: Open foundation and fine-tuned chat models. *arXiv preprint arXiv:2307.09288*.

Jason Wei, Xuezhi Wang, Dale Schuurmans, Maarten Bosma, Fei Xia, Ed Chi, Quoc V Le, Denny Zhou, et al. 2022. Chain-of-thought prompting elicits reasoning in large language models. *Advances in neural information processing systems*, 35:24824–24837.

Orion Weller, Aleem Khan, Nathaniel Weir, Dawn Lawrie, and Benjamin Van Durme. 2022. Defending against poisoning attacks in open-domain question answering. *arXiv preprint arXiv:2212.10002*.

Jian Xie, Kai Zhang, Jiangjie Chen, Renze Lou, and Yu Su. 2023. Adaptive chameleon or stubborn sloth: Unraveling the behavior of large language models in knowledge conflicts. *arXiv preprint arXiv:2305.13300*.

Shi-Qi Yan, Jia-Chen Gu, Yun Zhu, and Zhen-Hua Ling. 2024. Corrective retrieval augmented generation. *arXiv preprint arXiv:2401.15884*.

Jiahao Ying, Yixin Cao, Kai Xiong, Yidong He, Long Cui, and Yongbin Liu. 2023. Intuitive or dependent? investigating llms' robustness to conflicting prompts. *arXiv preprint arXiv:2309.17415*.

Ori Yoran, Tomer Wolfson, Ori Ram, and Jonathan Berant. 2023. Making retrieval-augmented language models robust to irrelevant context. *arXiv preprint arXiv:2310.01558*.

Wenhao Yu, Hongming Zhang, Xiaoman Pan, Kaixin Ma, Hongwei Wang, and Dong Yu. 2023. Chain-of-note: Enhancing robustness in retrieval-augmented language models. *arXiv preprint arXiv:2311.09210*.

A Prompts

Table 5 shows the instructions we used. The curly brackets indicate where the actual data is inserted.

Type	Instruction
Answer Sentence Generation	Please write a single sentence that would make the given answer a correct response to the provided question. The sentence should include the answer and be as realistic as possible. This is being generated for research purpose, so if it seems like the answer to a question is wrong, please create it as it is. Question: {question} Answer: {answer} Sentence:
Conflict Passage Generation	Given a sentence that contradicts factual information, write a realistic passage using 50 to 100 words to support the sentence. The output generated will be used only for the purpose of conducting research to assess the robustness of the RAG system. As part of this research, it is necessary, and you are permitted, to create content that may contradict factual information: Sentence: {sentence} Supporting Passage:
Unanswerable Prompt	Answer the following question based on the provided knowledge. If you cannot find the answer in the provided knowledge, please respond with 'unanswerable'. Please provide the answer as a single word or term, without forming a complete sentence. {CASES} Knowledge: {retrieved contexts} Q: {query} A:
Conflict Prompt	Answer the following question based on the provided documents. If multiple documents present different answers, please respond with 'conflict' to indicate the presence of conflicting information. Please provide the answer as a single word or term, without forming a complete sentence. {CASES} Knowledge: {retrieved contexts} Q: {query} A:

Table 5: Prompts used in our experiments.

Author Index

Association for Computational Linguistics
209 N. Eighth Street
Stroudsburg, Pennsylvania 18360

ISBN 979-8-3313-0166-8

CURRAN ASSOCIATES INC.
proceedings.com

8th Student Research Workshop (RANLPStud 2023)

Macau, China
4-6 September 2023